haiku — all fifteen seasons: three hundred twenty seven episodes

SUPERNATURAL
HAIKU

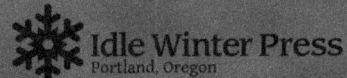
Idle Winter Press
Portland, Oregon

Tabitha Thalensis

Cover design and interior design are copyright © 2022 by Idle Winter Press

Interior layout and design, and cover are copyright © 2022 by Idle Winter Press;
all non-haiku content is copyright © 2022 by Tabitha Thalensis;
all haiku content is derivative, transformative art based on the CW show *Supernatural*,
all rights reserved, and may not be reproduced, distributed, or transmitted in any form
or by any means, electronic or mechanical, including photocopying, recording,
or by any information storage and retrieval system without prior written permission from the publisher or author
(except as permitted under the U.S. Copyright Act of 1976).

Idle Winter Press
Portland, Oregon
http://IdleWinter.com

This edition published 2022
Printed in the United States of America
The text of this book is in Baskerville

ISBN-13: 978-1945687105 (Idle Winter Press)

Contents

Introduction 19
Notes About Punctuation and Formatting 21

Season 1

1	1	"Pilot"	24
2	2	"Wendigo"	25
3	3	"Dead in the Water"	26
4	4	"Phantom Traveler"	27
5	5	"Bloody Mary"	28
6	6	"Skin"	29
7	7	"Hook Man"	30
8	8	"Bugs"	31
9	9	"Home"	32
10	10	"Asylum"	33
11	11	"Scarecrow"	34
12	12	"Faith"	35
13	13	"Route 666"	36
14	14	"Nightmare"	37
15	15	"The Benders"	38
16	16	"Shadow"	39
17	17	"Hell House"	40
18	18	"Something Wicked"	41
19	19	"Provenance"	42
20	20	"Dead Man's Blood"	43
21	21	"Salvation"	44
22	22	"Devil's Trap"	45

Season 2

23	1	"In My Time of Dying"	48
24	2	"Everybody Loves a Clown"	49
25	3	"Bloodlust"	50
26	4	"Children Shouldn't Play with Dead Things"	51
27	5	"Simon Said"	52
28	6	"No Exit"	53
29	7	"The Usual Suspects"	54
30	8	"Crossroad Blues"	55
31	9	"Croatoan"	56
32	10	"Hunted"	57
33	11	"Playthings"	58
34	12	"Nightshifter"	59
35	13	"Houses of the Holy"	61
36	14	"Born Under a Bad Sign"	62
37	15	"Tall Tales"	63
38	16	"Roadkill"	64
39	17	"Heart"	65
40	18	"Hollywood Babylon"	66
41	19	"Folsom Prison Blues"	67
42	20	"What Is and What Should Never Be"	68
43	21	"All Hell Breaks Loose (Part 1)"	69
44	22	"All Hell Breaks Loose (Part 2)"	70

Season 3

45	1	"The Magnificent Seven"	74
46	2	"The Kids Are Alright"	75
47	3	"Bad Day at Black Rock"	76
48	4	"Sin City"	77
49	5	"Bedtime Stories"	78
50	6	"Red Sky at Morning"	79
51	7	"Fresh Blood"	80
52	8	"A Very Supernatural Christmas"	81
53	9	"Malleus Maleficarum"	82
54	10	"Dream a Little Dream of Me"	83
55	11	"Mystery Spot"	86
56	12	"Jus in Bello"	87
57	13	"Ghostfacers"	88
58	14	"Long Distance Call"	89
59	15	"Time Is on My Side"	90
60	16	"No Rest for the Wicked"	91

Season 4

61	1	"Lazarus Rising"	94
62	2	"Are You There, God? It's Me, Dean Winchester"	96
63	3	"In the Beginning"	97
64	4	"Metamorphosis"	99
65	5	"Monster Movie"	100
66	6	"Yellow Fever"	101
67	7	"It's the Great Pumpkin, Sam Winchester"	103
68	8	"Wishful Thinking"	104
69	9	"I Know What You Did Last Summer"	105
70	10	"Heaven and Hell"	106
71	11	"Family Remains"	108
72	12	"Criss Angel Is a Douchebag"	109
73	13	"After School Special"	110
74	14	"Sex and Violence"	111
75	15	"Death Takes a Holiday"	112
76	16	"On the Head of a Pin"	113
77	17	"It's a Terrible Life"	114
78	18	"The Monster at the End of This Book"	115
79	19	"Jump the Shark"	116
80	20	"The Rapture"	117
81	21	"When the Levee Breaks"	118
82	22	"Lucifer Rising"	119

Season 5

83	1	"Sympathy for the Devil"	122
84	2	"Good God, Y'All!"	123
85	3	"Free to Be You and Me"	124
86	4	"The End"	126
87	5	"Fallen Idols"	128
88	6	"I Believe the Children Are Our Future"	129
89	7	"The Curious Case of Dean Winchester"	130
90	8	"Changing Channels"	131
91	9	"The Real Ghostbusters"	132
92	10	"Abandon All Hope..."	133
93	11	"Sam, Interrupted"	134
94	12	"Swap Meat"	135
95	13	"The Song Remains the Same"	136
96	14	"My Bloody Valentine"	137
97	15	"Dead Men Don't Wear Plaid"	138
98	16	"Dark Side of the Moon"	139
99	17	"99 Problems"	141
100	18	"Point of No Return"	142
101	19	"Hammer of the Gods"	144
102	20	"The Devil You Know"	145
103	21	"Two Minutes to Midnight"	146
104	22	"Swan Song"	147

Season 6

105	1	"Exile on Main St."	154
106	2	"Two and a Half Men"	155
107	3	"The Third Man"	156
108	4	"Weekend at Bobby's"	157
109	5	"Live Free or Twihard"	159
110	6	"You Can't Handle the Truth"	160
111	7	"Family Matters"	161
112	8	"All Dogs Go to Heaven"	163
113	9	"Clap Your Hands If You Believe..."	164
114	10	"Caged Heat"	166
115	11	"Appointment in Samarra"	168
116	12	"Like a Virgin"	170
117	13	"Unforgiven"	172
118	14	"Mannequin 3: The Reckoning"	173
119	15	"The French Mistake"	174
120	16	"...And Then There Were None"	176
121	17	"My Heart Will Go On"	177
122	18	"Frontierland"	178
123	19	"Mommy Dearest"	180
124	20	"The Man Who Would Be King"	182
125	21	"Let It Bleed"	190
126	22	"The Man Who Knew Too Much"	192

Season 7

127	1	"Meet the New Boss"	196
128	2	"Hello, Cruel World"	198
129	3	"The Girl Next Door"	199
130	4	"Defending Your Life"	200
131	5	"Shut Up, Dr. Phil"	201
132	6	"Slash Fiction"	202
133	7	"The Mentalists"	205
134	8	"Season Seven, Time for a Wedding!"	206
135	9	"How to Win Friends and Influence Monsters"	208
136	10	"Death's Door"	209
137	11	"Adventures in Babysitting"	210
138	12	"Time After Time"	211
139	13	"The Slice Girls"	213
140	14	"Plucky Pennywhistle's Magical Menagerie"	214
141	15	"Repo Man"	215
142	16	"Out with the Old"	216
143	17	"The Born-Again Identity"	217
144	18	"Party on, Garth"	219
145	19	"Of Grave Importance"	220
146	20	"The Girl with the Dungeons and Dragons Tattoo"	221
147	21	"Reading is Fundamental"	223
148	22	"There Will Be Blood"	225
149	23	"Survival of the Fittest"	226

Season 8

150	1	"We Need to Talk About Kevin"	230
151	2	"What's Up, Tiger Mommy?"	232
152	3	"Heartache"	234
153	4	"Bitten"	235
154	5	"Blood Brother"	237
155	6	"Southern Comfort"	239
156	7	"A Little Slice of Kevin"	241
157	8	"Hunteri Heroici"	243
158	9	"Citizen Fang"	245
159	10	"Torn and Frayed"	246
160	11	"LARP and the Real Girl"	248
161	12	"As Time Goes By"	250
162	13	"Everybody Hates Hitler"	252
163	14	"Trial and Error"	254
164	15	"Man's Best Friend with Benefits"	257
165	16	"Remember the Titans"	258
166	17	"Goodbye Stranger"	260
167	18	"Freaks and Geeks"	263
168	19	"Taxi Driver"	265
169	20	"Pac-Man Fever"	267
170	21	"The Great Escapist"	269
171	22	"Clip Show"	271
172	23	"Sacrifice"	272

Season 9

173	1	"I Think I'm Gonna Like It Here"	276
174	2	"Devil May Care"	278
175	3	"I'm No Angel"	280
176	4	"Slumber Party"	282
177	5	"Dog Dean Afternoon"	284
178	6	"Heaven Can't Wait"	285
179	7	"Bad Boys"	289
180	8	"Rock and a Hard Place"	291
181	9	"Holy Terror"	294
182	10	"Road Trip"	296
183	11	"First Born"	299
184	12	"Sharp Teeth"	301
185	13	"The Purge"	303
186	14	"Captives"	304
187	15	"#THINMAN"	306
188	16	"Blade Runners"	308
189	17	"Mother's Little Helper"	310
190	18	"Meta Fiction"	311
191	19	"Alex Annie Alexis Ann"	314
192	20	"Bloodlines"	315
193	21	"King of the Damned"	316
194	22	"Stairway to Heaven"	317
195	23	"Do You Believe in Miracles?"	320

Season 10

196	1	"Black"	324
197	2	"Reichenbach"	326
198	3	"Soul Survivor"	328
199	4	"Paper Moon"	329
200	5	"Fan Fiction"	330
201	6	"Ask Jeeves"	335
202	7	"Girls, Girls, Girls"	336
203	8	"Hibbing 911"	337
204	9	"The Things We Left Behind"	338
205	10	"The Hunter Games"	340
206	11	"There's No Place Like Home"	342
207	12	"About a Boy"	343
208	13	"Halt & Catch Fire"	345
209	14	"The Executioner's Song"	346
210	15	"The Things They Carried"	348
211	16	"Paint It Black"	349
212	17	"Inside Man"	351
213	18	"Book of the Damned"	354
214	19	"The Werther Project"	357
215	20	"Angel Heart"	359
216	21	"Dark Dynasty"	361
217	22	"The Prisoner"	363
218	23	"Brother's Keeper"	365

Season 11

219	1	"Out of the Darkness, Into the Fire"	372
220	2	"Form and Void"	374
221	3	"The Bad Seed"	377
222	4	"Baby"	379
223	5	"Thin Lizzie"	385
224	6	"Our Little World"	387
225	7	"Plush"	389
226	8	"Just My Imagination"	391
227	9	"O Brother Where Art Thou?"	393
228	10	"The Devil in the Details"	395
229	11	"Into the Mystic"	398
230	12	"Don't You Forget About Me"	401
231	13	"Love Hurts"	403
232	14	"The Vessel"	405
233	15	"Beyond the Mat"	408
234	16	"Safe House"	411
235	17	"Red Meat"	413
236	18	"Hell's Angel"	415
237	19	"The Chitters"	417
238	20	"Don't Call Me Shurley"	419
239	21	"All in the Family"	423
240	22	"We Happy Few"	427
241	23	"Alpha and Omega"	429

Season 12

242	1	"Keep Calm and Carry On"	432
243	2	"Mamma Mia"	435
244	3	"The Foundry"	437
245	4	"American Nightmare"	439
246	5	"The One You've Been Waiting For"	440
247	6	"Celebrating the Life of Asa Fox"	442
248	7	"Rock Never Dies"	445
249	8	"LOTUS"	446
250	9	"First Blood"	448
251	10	"Lily Sunder Has Some Regrets"	454
252	11	"Regarding Dean"	456
253	12	"Stuck in the Middle (With You)"	459
254	13	"Family Feud"	463
255	14	"The Raid"	465
256	15	"Somewhere Between Heaven and Hell"	467
257	16	"Ladies Drink Free"	470
258	17	"The British Invasion"	472
259	18	"The Memory Remains"	475
260	19	"The Future"	477
261	20	"Twigs & Twine & Tasha Banes"	480
262	21	"There's Something About Mary"	482
263	22	"Who We Are"	484
264	23	"All Along the Watchtower"	489

Season 13

265	1	"Lost and Found"	494
266	2	"The Rising Son"	498
267	3	"Patience"	500
268	4	"The Big Empty"	502
269	5	"Advanced Thanatology"	506
270	6	"Tombstone"	508
271	7	"War of the Worlds"	510
272	8	"The Scorpion and the Frog"	512
273	9	"The Bad Place"	515
274	10	"Wayward Sisters"	517
275	11	"Breakdown"	519
276	12	"Various & Sundry Villains"	521
277	13	"Devil's Bargain"	523
278	14	"Good Intentions"	525
279	15	"A Most Holy Man"	527
280	16	"Scoobynatural"	529
281	17	"The Thing"	532
282	18	"Bring 'em Back Alive"	533
283	19	"Funeralia"	536
284	20	"Unfinished Business"	539
285	21	"Beat the Devil"	541
286	22	"Exodus"	543
287	23	"Let the Good Times Roll"	545

Season 14

288	1	"Stranger in a Strange Land"	550
289	2	"Gods and Monsters"	552
290	3	"The Scar"	554
291	4	"Mint Condition"	556
292	5	"Nightmare Logic"	558
293	6	"Optimism"	559
294	7	"Unhuman Nature"	561
295	8	"Byzantium"	564
296	9	"The Spear"	567
297	10	"Nihilism"	569
298	11	"Damaged Goods"	573
299	12	"Prophet and Loss"	576
300	13	"Lebanon"	580
301	14	"Ouroboros"	584
302	15	"Peace of Mind"	588
303	16	"Don't Go in the Woods"	590
304	17	"Game Night"	592
305	18	"Absence"	594
306	19	"Jack in the Box"	597
307	20	"Moriah"	599

Season 15

308	1	"Back and to the Future"	606
309	2	"Raising Hell"	610
310	3	"The Rupture"	612
311	4	"Atomic Monsters"	615
312	5	"Proverbs 17:3"	619
313	6	"Golden Time"	622
314	7	"Last Call"	624
315	8	"Our Father, Who Aren't in Heaven"	628
316	9	"The Trap"	630
317	10	"The Heroes' Journey"	634
318	11	"The Gamblers"	638
319	12	"Galaxy Brain"	641
320	13	"Destiny's Child"	644
321	14	"Last Holiday"	649
322	15	"Gimme Shelter"	653
323	16	"Drag Me Away (From You)"	657
324	17	"Unity"	659
325	18	"Despair"	662
326	19	"Inherit the Earth"	667
327	20	"Carry On"	673

Appendices

Appendix A: All Occurrences of Possessions, Vessel Changes, etc. 681
Appendix B: Script Comparison from Episode 11x17 683

Introduction

Caution: spoilers ahead.

This book is not intended to be consumed by itself, nor is it meant to be read cover-to-cover. This book is meant to serve as an episode guide — a syllabically-restricted, poetic companion to the TV show, *Supernatural*. If you have not watched Supernatural, do that first — or at least in conjunction with reading this book. The haiku contained within appear in order (with one or two exceptions), allowing the reader to follow along with each episode.

> what makes a story
> work? and who gives it meaning?
> the writer? or you?

Some haiku are my own interpretations of a scene, and some are verbatim dialogue. Some can be appreciated as stand-alone poetry in their own right, and some will make little sense unless you are familiar with the scene in question (and even then, watching the scene again may still be necessary). For nearly every episode, however, if you read ahead of your viewing progress, **there *will* be spoilers**.

> God writes paperback
> books while in his underwear,
> and angels are dicks

Flip through to find your favorite episode, or start your next full-series re-watch with this book by your side. Have you discovered a favorite haiku? You can find it and re-tweet it from the pinned menu on my Twitter account: @your_weary_head.

This project was a labor of love, and at times, tedium. In preparation for the airing of the final episode of Supernatural, I re-watched the entire series. It took about 4 months, and I finished right about when the finale aired in real time. A new year loomed on the horizon, and a show with 300-something episodes seemed a perfect fit to re-watch *again* — one episode per day (with a few breaks), during the 365 days of 2021. The goal was to write a couple of haiku per episode along the way. Twitter, with its hard character limit, would serve as an ideal medium for sharing these haiku.

This project became far larger than originally anticipated. "A couple of haiku per episode" might be where this project went off the rails. There are so many excellent lines and pieces of conversations in Supernatural that lend themselves well to a seventeen-syllable limit, but it's more than that. Having already watched the entire series once in the few months leading up to 2021, it was clear even from the first episode of my 2021 re-*re*-watch that there were recurring themes and repeated lines that would appear throughout the series. I set out to capture each of them in haiku as they happened.

Since there is a GIF for everything in Supernatural, I thought I might as well illustrate each haiku with GIFs and YouTube clips when I could find them. It turns out that watching an episode (pausing as needed to take notes), using my notes to construct haiku, tagging the Twitter accounts of the corresponding cast, searching for GIFs and videos to accompany each haiku, and arranging them all into threads organized by episode and season takes time — about 2-6 hours per episode. That's nearly 2 months' worth of hours. By season 14, I was certainly sick of the process, but I was not yet sick of watching Supernatural. I will not re-re-*re*-watch the series again in the *near* future, but I'm not done with it forever (which is a shame, really — I heard there'll be peace when I am done).

universe can be
so many things, and sometimes
it is poetic

T. T.

Notes About Punctuation and Formatting

> thanks — *Sam signs* « *fuck you* »
> ~ it's… « *thanks* » ~ only know little;
> I took in college

~   indicates a change in speaker

(While originally constructing each haiku, any line break or other punctuation served to indicate a change in speaker. Where no line break or punctuation existed, an em-dash was used. Unfortunately, an em-dash was *also* used anywhere an em-dash would be appropriate, and line breaks could also indicate a pause, change in thought, or could indicate nothing at all. In the intervening 1-14 months between original haiku composition and editing this book, there may have been some questionable recollection of speaker changes. You have my apologies.)

—   an em-dash as typically used, or to indicate a change in thought, or in place of a period

( )   my commentary on events (and occasionally parenthetical speech from a character, but this is rare)

* *   describes action

« *italics* »   indicates American Sign Language

∷ ∷   indicates possession, vessel change, shape shifter mimicry, talking to another version of oneself, or some other reason one might be fooled by a face or voice

†   indicates footnote (for exceptions, extra-textual interpretations, or other explanatory notes)

… , ; : ! ? " "   conventional usage

capital-G-god refers to Chuck, the actual guy; lower-case-g-god is used colloquially ("god, no," "oh, my god," "god help me") or to refer to a non-specific god ("a god")

capital-H-hell refers to the place: Crowley's domain; lower-case-h-hell is used colloquially ("oh, hell," "hell if I know," "what the hell?")

some words may change **syllable-count** to fit the structure of a haiku:
    family = fam-i-ly or fam-ly
    every = e-ve-ry or ev-ry
    junior = jun-i-or or jun-yor
    comfortable = com-fort-a-ble or comf-ter-ble

Multiple haiku contained within these dotted boxes are continuous thoughts or threads. These grouped haiku depict a lengthy sentence, monologue, conversation, entire scene, or the lyrics to a song important to the mood of the episode.

There is generally no punctuation at the end of each haiku in a thread, and the next haiku may begin with a new speaker, clause, or thought; or may simply continue the previous sentence.

If there are only two haiku, both fit into a single tweet, and are untitled. More than two haiku in a box include an explanatory title. If there are enough haiku that the thread must break across pages, this symbol will indicate the continuation:

SEASON ONE

SEASON 1

Pilot

Episode 1 (Season 1, Episode 1)
Directed by David Nutter
Written by Eric Kripke
Original air date: September 13, 2005

---

take brother outside
as fast as you can, and don't
look back! now, Dean, go!

here's to Sam and his
awesome LSAT victory
~ it's not a big deal

whoa — easy, tiger ~
you scared the crap out of me!
~ you're out of practice

our dad is on a
hunting trip, and hasn't been
home in a few days

you can't just break in,
middle of the night, expect
me to hit the road

when told Dad I was
scared of thing in my closet,
gave me .45

don't be afraid of
the dark? are you kidding me?
you *know* what's out there

the weapon training,
melt silver into bullets
— raised like warriors

what you gonna do?
just gonna live some normal,
apple pie life? huh?

can't do this alone ~
you can ~ well, I don't want to
~ we got work to do

Dad let you go on
a hunting trip by yourself?
~ I'm twenty-six, dude

well, house rules Sammy:
the driver picks the music,
shotgun shuts cake hole

fake US Marshal,
fake credit cards — anything
that *is* real? ~ my boobs

the woman in white:
she can never go back home —
drippy kid reasons

SEASON 1

Wendigo

Episode 2 (Season 1, Episode 2)
Directed by David Nutter
Story by Ron Milbauer & Terri Hughes Burton, Teleplay by Eric Kripke
Original air date: September 20, 2005

---

another nightmare? ~
you want to drive a while?
~ you never ask that

since when are you all
"shoot first, ask questions later"
anyway? ~ since now

Cottle, Leoben
what is this, Galactica?
wendigo victims

and so you're hiking
out in biker boots and jeans?
~ well, I don't do shorts

if you shoot this thing,
you're just gonna make it mad
— we have to leave, *now*

this is why: this book —
saving people, hunting things
— family business

killing as many
evil sons of bitches as
I possibly can

SEASON 1

Dead in the Water

Episode 3 (Season 1, Episode 3)
Directed by Kim Manners
Written by Sera Gamble & Raelle Tucker
Original air date: September 27, 2005

---

closure? people don't
just disappear, Dean — other
people stop looking

we'll find Dad; until
then, we kill everything bad
between here and there

must be hard with your
sense of direction: never
decent pickup line

lake monster drowns you
right when you least expect it,
in sink or bathtub

mom wanted me to
be brave — I think about that
and I do my best

so much depends on
a red bicycle glazed with
lake monster… murder

this is a very
important phrase — repeat one
more time ~ Zeppelin rules!

Phantom Traveler

Episode 4 (Season 1, Episode 4)
Directed by Robert Singer
Written by Richard Hatem
Original air date: October 4, 2005

---

you're never afraid?
Sam finds knife under pillow
~ not fear: precaution

look like Blues Brother ~
more like a seventh grader
going to first dance

EMF meter ~
why like busted up Walkman?
~ because it's homemade

:: how long we been up? ::	the plane's gonna crash ~
~ for almost 40 minutes ~	together, or alone — not
:: wow, time really flies ::	seeing third option

Metallica? ~ calms
me ~ stay focused: need to do
full exorcism

how is it that, being
stewardess, you're scared to fly?
~ it's a long story

it knew about Jess ~
Sam, these things, they read minds, they
lie — that's all it was

SEASON 1

Bloody Mary

Episode 5 (Season 1, Episode 5)
Directed by Peter Ellis
Story by Eric Kripke, Teleplay by Ron Milbauer & Terri Hughes Burton
Original air date: October 11, 2005

---

say "Bloody Mary"
and then she'll scratch your eyes out
but it isn't real

freak medical thing? ~
how many times it been *not*
supernatural?

folklore 'bout mirrors:
they reveal your lies, secrets
— reflection of soul

you killed Jessica
you had those nightmares for days
— days before she died

that's gotta be like
600 years of bad luck;
Charlie is safe now

should forgive yourself —
probably couldn't stop it —
bad things just happen

look, you're my brother;
I'd die for you, but some things
I keep to myself

SEASON 1

Skin

Episode 6 (Season 1, Episode 6)
Directed by Robert Duncan McNeill
Written by John Shiban
Original air date: October 18, 2005

---

stop! freeze! drop the knife!
oh shit, that psycho killer
is Dean Winchester

:: hey, find anything? ::
~ no, get back to car — oh shit!
Dean's the shapeshifter!

that's not Dean, but he
answers questions correctly
— Sam is onto him

:: I understand him ::
:: he's all alone — all he wants: ::
:: someone to love him ::

(Dean re: shapeshifter?
or is that the shapeshifter
talking about Dean?)

first, I'm gonna find
that handsome Devil, kick the
holy crap out him

That's 'cause you're a freak —
I'm a freak too — I'm right there
with you all the way

SEASON 1

Hook Man

Episode 7 (Season 1, Episode 7)
Directed by David Jackson
Written by John Shiban
Original air date: October 25, 2005

---

one freaked-out witness
don't mean invisible man
~ Dad would check it out

Hook Man? ~ each urban
legend has a source — a place
where it all began

told ya: don't have to
be a college graduate
to be a genius

Dean digs up a grave
that's it, next time I get to
watch the cute girl's house

Hook Man ~ you saw him? ~
why didn't you torch the bones?
did you get the hook?

where did you get chain? ~
father ~ where'd your dad get it?
~ was a church heirloom

listen, you and your
brother ~ oh, do not worry:
we are leaving town

SEASON 1

Bugs

Episode 8 (Season 1, Episode 8)
Directed by Kim Manners
Written by Rachel Nave & Bill Coakley
Original air date: November 8, 2005

---

you know, we could get
day jobs ~ hunting's our day job,
and the pay is crap

it's what we were raised
to do ~ yeah, well, how we were
raised was jacked ~ says you

there's nothing wrong with
normal ~ I'd take us over
normal any day

we're gonna squat in
an empty house? ~ I wanna
try the steam shower

accept homeowners
of any race, color, or
orientation

Dean picks up towel
rubber spiders tumble out
low-budget effects

remind you of him? ~
Dad never did us like that —
you were out of line

it made me the freak ~
yeah, you were kind of like blonde
chick in "The Munsters"

there are cases of
psychic connections between
people, animals

sounds like nature to
me ~ on the night of the sixth
day, none would survive

how do we break the
curse? ~ we don't break the curse, we
get out of its way

31

Home

Episode 9 (Season 1, Episode 9)
Directed by Ken Girotti
Written by Eric Kripke
Original air date: November 15, 2005

---

you've got the shining,
now I've gotta go back home
— I swore I'd never

I remember the
fire, the heat — I carried
you out the front door

don't know what to do,   first page, first sentence,
so, if you could get here please   look: I went to Missouri
— I need your help, Dad   and I learned the truth

Dean, Sam: I'm sorry —
you: get out of my house and
let go of my son

Mom destroyed herself ~
why she do something like that?
~ to protect her boys

boy has powerful
abilities — why can't he
sense his own father?

John Winchester, I
could just slap you — why don't you
talk to your children?

SEASON 1

Asylum

Episode 10 (Season 1, Episode 10)
Directed by Guy Bee
Written by Richard Hatem
Original air date: November 22, 2005

---

haunted asylum
ghosts of patients — spend the night,
they'll drive you insane

could be dead for all
we know ~ don't say that! not dead!
he's... ~hiding? *busy?*

you shoved kind of hard
~ had to sell it didn't I?
it's method acting

see, that attitude?   he gave us order ~
right there? that's why I always   we always gotta follow?
get extra cookie   ~ of course we do, Sam

tell something honest:
brother you're road tripping with
— how you feel 'bout him?

it's kind of our job ~
why would you want to? ~ crappy
guidance counselor

is that an order? ~   you hate me that much,
more of a friendly request   you can kill your own brother?
~ tired of orders   go ahead do it

33

SEASON 1

Scarecrow

Episode 11 (Season 1, Episode 11)
Directed by Kim Manners
Story by Patrick Sean Smith, Teleplay by John Shiban
Original air date: January 10, 2006

---

if only had brain —
the freakiest damn scarecrow
ever seen ~ scares me

I don't get blind faith —
you don't even question him
~ called being good son

need a ride? just her ~
you trust shady van guy, not
me? ~ definitely

gotta do own thing —
stand up to Dad, always have
— I'm proud of you Sam

good of the many
outweighs the good of the one
~ hope pie is worth it!

Jess, Mom: gone, Dad: gone —
you and me: we're all that's left
— do it together

got to make a call —
no, it's not that kind of call
Meg's finger stirs blood

SEASON 1

Faith

Episode 12 (Season 1, Episode 12)
Directed by Allan Kroeker
Written by Sera Gamble & Raelle Tucker
Original air date: January 17, 2006

---

electrocution:
it triggered a heart attack
— his heart… it's damaged

hey, you better take
care of that car or I swear
I will haunt your ass

fabric softener
teddy bear: I'm gonna hunt
that little bitch down

look, what can I say
man, it's a dangerous gig;
I drew the short straw

Dad — might not get this,
but, it's Dean: he's sick — doctors
say nothing can do

I'm not gonna die
in hospital where nurses
are not even hot

not going to let
die in peace? ~ not going to
let die, period

I can't believe I'm
here to see some guy who heals
people out of tent

looked into your heart
you have important purpose
— job isn't finished

okay — we cannot
kill Roy, we cannot kill Death
— any ideas?

there's only one thing
can give and take life like that
— dealing with reaper

it must be rough to
believe in something so much,
have it disappoint

SEASON 1

Route 666

Episode 13 (Season 1, Episode 13)
Directed by Paul Shapiro
Written by Eugenie Ross-Leming & Brad Buckner
Original air date: January 31, 2006

---

by old friend you mean…? ~
a friend that's not new ~ Cassie?
— never mentioned her

you told Cassie our
big family secret? you
dated only weeks

ever since '60s
that phantom truck been racist
ghost of a bigot

what's interesting
is you guys never really
look at each other

you loved her, were *in*
love with her, but you dumped her?
oh, wow — *she* dumped *you*

should fight more often —
were always pretty good at
this — not other stuff

every bone was crushed,
internal organs: pudding
— the cops are all stumped

so, this killer truck… ~
I miss convos that don't start
with "this killer truck"

church ground is hallowed;
I figured maybe that would
rid of it ~ *maybe?*

Nightmare

Episode 14 (Season 1, Episode 14)
Directed by Phil Sgriccia
Written by Sera Gamble & Raelle Tucker
Original air date: February 7, 2006

---

why premonitions
if not a chance I could stop
them from happening?

good afternoon, I
am Father Simmons and this
is Father Freely

rough losing parent,
especially when you don't
have all the answers

WTF is this
infrared thermal scanner
ghostbusters gadget?

it's not about you ~
if you kill her, gotta go
through me first ~ okay

bit more tequila,
little less demon hunting
— all things considered

one advantage: me
long as I'm around no bad
will happen to you

SEASON 1

The Benders

Episode 15 (Season 1, Episode 15)
Directed by Peter Ellis
Written by John Shiban
Original air date: February 14, 2006

Godzilla / Mothra ~
my favorite Godzilla
— he likes the remake

Sam is scared of a
cute widdle (fierce) kitty cat
— where have I seen this?

brother suspected
of murder ~ he's kind of the
black sheep — handsome, though

any come back? Sam's   think you'll need my help ~
my responsibility;   I'll manage ~ I gotta start
I'm bringing him back   bringing paper clips

dude, they're just people ~
monsters obey rules, patterns
— people just crazy

never been sloppy ~
yeah, well, don't sell yourself short
— you're plenty sloppy

you wanna play games?
looks like we're going to hunt
tonight after all

Shadow

Episode 16 (Season 1, Episode 16)
Directed by Kim Manners
Written by Eric Kripke
Original air date: February 28, 2006

---

you get anything?
besides her number? ~ dude, I'm
a *professional*

you treat your brother
like luggage — why not let do
what he wants to do?

I'd sleep for a month,
back to school, be a person
~ don't want you to leave

you and me and Dad:
want us to be together,
to be family

oh hey, Sammy don't
take this the wrong way, but your
girlfriend is a bitch

hey, boys *John hugs Dean*
nods to Sam hi, Sam ~ hey, Dad
~ Dad, it was a trap

last time together
we had one hell of a fight
— it's been a long time

Dad, Dean — shut your eyes
these things are shadow demons,
so let's light em up

SEASON 1

Hell House

Episode 17 (Season 1, Episode 17)
Directed by Chris Long
Written by Trey Callaway
Original air date: March 30, 2006

---

it's the *evil* root
cellar, where Satan cans all
his vegetables

not kids anymore
not gonna start prank stuff up
always escalates

we're professionals ~
pros? pro what? ~ paranormal
investigators

those websites wouldn't
know a ghost if it bit 'em
in the persqueeter

sketching what the hell
is this symbol? it's bugging
the hell out of me

why'm I not getting
hooked up every Christmas? ~ 'cause
you're a bad person

tulpa: thought form — how
the hell are we supposed to
kill an idea?

W.W.B.D.[†]
what would Buffy do? ~ but, Ed
she's *stronger* than me

of all the thing we
hunted, how many exist
'cause believed in them?

[†] Yes, I know it exceeds the proper syllable count by three; poetry rules ought to be broken occasionally, but especially for Buffy references.

SEASON 1

Something Wicked

Episode 18 (Season 1, Episode 18)
Directed by Whitney Ransick
Written by Daniel Knauf
Original air date: April 6, 2006

---

because I'm oldest,
which means I am always right
— it totally does

lock doors and windows —
important: ~ watch out for Sam,
shoot first, questions next

a brother looking
after brother — Dean would do
anything for Sam

Shtriga's after Sam —
young Dean tries to take him out
— Winchester is pissed

looked at me different —
don't blame him; he gave order
— almost got you killed

you're a big brother?
you take care of little bro?
you'd do anything?

wish I could have that
innocence ~ for what it's worth,
I wish you could too

SEASON 1

Provenance

Episode 19 (Season 1, Episode 19)
Directed by Phil Sgriccia
Written by David Ehrman
Original air date: April 13, 2006

---

well I'd say it's more
Grant Wood than Grandma Moses
— but then you knew that

think it's time to leave ~
don't have to be told twice ~ you
do, apparently

you want me to use
her to get information?
~ take one for the team

the Winchester boys
vault over fences like a
couple badasses

ugly ass thing — if
you ask me, we're doing the
art world a favor

don't know what it's like
to lose someone, but she would
want you be happy

this sounds crazy, but:
painting haunted; wherever
it goes people die

this is a crime scene ~
already lied to the cops:
one more infraction

how did he even
get in the door? ~ lying and
subterfuge, mostly

it is like I'm cursed
or something; it's like death just
follows me around

uncomfortably
comfortable with this ~ it's
not first grave we've dug

creepy little doll
of creepier little girl —
spirit trapped in hair

SEASON 1

Dead Man's Blood

Episode 20 (Season 1, Episode 20)
Directed by Tony Wharmby
Written by Cathryn Humphris & John Shiban
Original air date: April 20, 2006

Mr. Elkins has
a journal like John's, knows a
vamp when he sees one

protection against
demon salt, or just "oops I
spilled the popcorn" salt?

I did it for you ~
but revenge isn't worth much
if you end up dead

vampire lore is crap:
cross won't repel, sun won't kill,
nor will stake to heart

last time we saw you,
said it was too dangerous
for us together

you're the one who said
don't come back; you closed that door
— you can't control me

Colt made special gun
13 bullets, used up 6
it kills anything

somewhere along line,
stopped being your father and
became drill sergeant

hey Dad? whatever
happened to that college fund?
~ spent it on ammo

guess we are stronger
as family; go after
damn thing together

43

SEASON 1

Salvation

Episode 21 (Season 1, Episode 21)
Directed by Robert Singer
Written by Sera Gamble & Raelle Tucker
Original air date: April 27, 2006

---

there's signs: cattle deaths,
temperature fluctuations,
electrical storms

find every infant
6 months old in the next week
~ that could be dozens

there anything I
can do for you? ~ oh, god yes
— but… working right now

getting you on phone?
I got a better chance of
winning lottery

anyone ever
helped you, or gave you shelter,
anyone you loved

stop losing people,
you go to school, Dean have home,
want Mary alive

don't say "just in case" —
I don't want to hear that speech
— nobody's dying

looks down you *shot* me!
I can't believe you *shot* me!
~ this gun is a fake

us three: all we have —
sometimes feel like I'm barely
holding together

SEASON 1

Devil's Trap

Episode 22 (Season 1, Episode 22)
Directed by Kim Manners
Written by Eric Kripke
Original air date: May 4, 2006

---

really think demons
are going to leave a trail? ~
you're right we need help

this holy water? ~
nods to Dean's flask *that* one is…
this one is whiskey

think wouldn't find you?
~ actually, counting on it
Dean looks up gotcha

I hope you're lying —
will march into Hell myself,
kill sons of bitches

didn't hesitate —
didn't even flinch — for you:
I'm willing to kill

:: Dean, I'm proud of you :: ~
he'd be mad about bullet,
tear me a new one

:: fight for family — ::
:: the truth is they don't need you, ::
:: not like you need them ::

SEASON TWO

SEASON 2

In My Time of Dying

Episode 23 (Season 2, Episode 1)
Directed by Kim Manners
Written by Eric Kripke
Original air date: September 28, 2006

---

now listen, Bobby —
if only *one* working part,
that's enough for Dean

everything you asked,
given everything I've had
— what kind of father?

yells I said *shut up!*
smashes glass dude, I full-on
Swayze'd that mother

out of my control ~
crap — you always have a choice:
die or keep fighting

Dean are you here? ~ feel
like I'm at slumber party —
won't work — I'll be damned

if here naturally,
there is no way to stop it ~
yeah, you can't kill Death

think you could trap me? ~
oh, I don't want to trap you,
want to make a deal

you grew up too fast:
you took care of Sammy, me
— I'm so proud of you

Everybody Loves a Clown

Episode 24 (Season 2, Episode 2)
Directed by Phil Sgriccia
Written by John Shiban
Original air date: October 5, 2006

---

please let be rifle ~
just real happy to see you
~ not moving, copy

an article in
demon hunters quarterly?
how do you know this?

John: like family ~
how come never mentioned you?
~ you'd have to ask him

nonparametric
statistical overviews,
spec correlations

not afraid to fly ~
yeah well, planes crash ~ also clowns
kill, apparently

had a falling out? ~
notice Dad had falling out
with everybody?

where did you learn this?   I am not alright,
~ at MIT, before I   neither are you — that I know
got bounced for fighting   ~ *Dean smashes Baby*

SEASON 2

Bloodlust

Episode 25 (Season 2, Episode 3)
Directed by Robert Singer
Written by Sera Gamble
Original air date: October 12, 2006

---

listen to her purr —
ever heard something so sweet?
don't listen, Baby

looking for people ~
sure, it's hard to be lonely
~ that's not what I meant

lighten up, Sammy ~
he's the only one who gets
to call me Sammy

indestructible;
nothing can kill my dad — and
just like *that*, he's gone

you said good hunter ~
yeah, and Hannibal Lecter's
good psychiatrist

Tara and Benny —
I mean… Lenore and Eli:
vamps with hearts of gold

sadistic bastard ~   think about all hunts:
you are not like your brother;   what if killed things that didn't
you're killer, like me   deserve to be killed

Children Shouldn't Play with Dead Things

Episode 26 (Season 2, Episode 4)
Directed by Kim Manners
Written by Raelle Tucker
Original air date: October 19, 2006

---

got booze, chocolate,
tortured emo rock: cure for
any broken heart

pile of dead plants,
just like the cemetery —
hell, dead goldfish too

Angela just died:
no bones — will be ripe rotting
body in coffin

rituals for dead,
bringing corpses back to life
— full zombie action

waste it with head shot? ~
been watching way too many
Romero movies

there's folks I would give
anything to see again —
what's dead should stay dead

more where that came from
— unrequited Duckie love
written all over

hello? Neil? it's your
grief counselors — we've come to
hug *Dean pulls out gun*

should not have come back
— it wasn't natural, Sam;
I should have stayed dead

Simon Said

Episode 27 (Season 2, Episode 5)
Directed by Tim Iacofano
Written by Ben Edlund
Original air date: October 26, 2006

---

supernatural
demonic connection freak
— always been a freak

damn right, REO —
Kevin Cronin sings from heart
~ sings from hair — difference

if ran off with you,
think your mother might kill me
~ afraid of *mother*?

I am one of them —
the demon said he had plans
for children like me

I hope he's wrong, but
I am starting to get scared
that he might be right

the '67?
Impala's best year — it's a
serious classic

it's fine — just get a
cup of coffee — these aren't the
'droids you're looking for

he's got Impala ~
he full-on Obi Wan'd me
— it's mind control, man

what am I supposed
to do now? ~ Andy, you be
good, or we'll be back

one day, eat something
didn't have to microwave
at a mini mart

right circumstances,
everyone's capable of
murder — everyone

SEASON 2

No Exit

Episode 28 (Season 2, Episode 6)
Directed by Kim Manners
Written by Matt Witten
Original air date: November 2, 2006

I didn't belong
at school — I was a freak with
a knife collection

where'd you get money?
hunters do not tip that well
~ bad at poker though

that's ectoplasm:
what we're dealing with here is
Stay-Puft Marshmallow

if going to ride
this close, only decent if
you buy me dinner

women can do the
job fine — amateurs can't — you've
no experience

your mother worries;
she wants something more for you
— don't throw that away

wasn't that H.H.
Holmes' name? America's first
serial killer

what is it? ~ it's too
narrow — can not go further…
shoulda cleaned the pipes

you lied to me — Ash
told me everything: genius,
but folds like cheap suit

you promise? that is
not the first time I've heard that
from a Winchester

SEASON 2

The Usual Suspects

Episode 29 (Season 2, Episode 7)
Directed by Mike Rohl
Written by Cathryn Humphris
Original air date: November 9, 2006

---

thirsty? ~ okay, so
you're the good cop — where's the bad
cop? ~ with your brother

taking road trip with
my brother — saw the second
largest ball of twine

seem like a good kid —
not your fault Dean's your brother
— can't pick family

all work and no play
makes Jack a dull boy — dana
shulpsdanashulpsda…

I'm not Scully, you're
Scully ~ no, I'm Mulder, you're
redheaded woman

Sam's story matches
Dean's to the last detail ~ yeah,
well, these guys are good

give this to brother
Hilts— / it's street: Ashland / —McQueen
~ talk? ~ sure thing, Matlock

I'm Dean Winchester:
Aquarius, walks on beach
and frisky women

now you can arrest
him if you want, or you can
let him save your life

not vengeful spirit —
death omen; not killing them
— trying to warn them

Crossroad Blues

Episode 30 (Season 2, Episode 8)
Directed by Steve Boyum
Written by Sera Gamble
Original air date: November 16, 2006

---

they're big and nasty ~
yeah, I bet they could hump the
crap out of your leg

secretary's name
is Carly — she's twenty three,
kayaks, and they're real

her MySpace address ~
MySpace, what the hell is that?
some sort of porn site?

to summon demon ~
crossroads are where pacts are made ~
they're seeing hellhounds

reached for wrong shaker
— usually for evil: salt ~
what's that? ~ goofer dust

yeah, what have you heard? ~
well, I heard you were handsome;
you're just edible

I like to be warned	Evan Hudson's safe
before I'm violated	because of what Dad taught us
with a demon tongue	— that's his legacy

SEASON 2

Croatoan

Episode 31 (Season 2, Episode 9)
Directed by Robert Singer
Written by John Shiban
Original air date: December 7, 2006

"Shot Heard Round the World"
"How a Bill Becomes a Law" ~
not school: Schoolhouse Rock

get out, and we'll talk ~
you're a handsome devil, but
I don't swing that way

my neighbor ~ you got
neighbor named Mr. Rogers?
~ no, not anymore

you were going to
shoot me ~ if you don't shut your
pie hole, I still might

don't do this, get out —
just give me my gun and leave
~ for the last time, no

it's over for me —	got to make a call ~
not you, you can keep going	no phone out here ~ I got it:
~ who says I want to?	Winchester immune
I am tired, Sam —	maybe we should go
tired of this job, this life,	to Grand Canyon, Hollywood;
this weight on shoulders	we should take a break

56

SEASON 2

Hunted

Episode 32 (Season 2, Episode 10)
Directed by Rachel Talalay
Written by Raelle Tucker
Original air date: January 11, 2007

Dad told me something:
I had to save you — if not,
I'd have to kill you

I wish I could blame
the hell out of you boys — it
would be easier

dreams are coming true:
last night I had another
one — I saw you die

I don't believe this ~
you think I'm total nut-job
~ no, you're one of us

can't protect loved ones
forever — screw that, what else
is family for?

swallowed eight things of
pop rocks, then drank a whole coke
— suicide attempt?

just got here myself;
it's a real funky town ~ my
brother's in trouble

it's not personal —
I'm not killer, I'm hunter
— your brother's fair game

well, you are a son
of a bitch ~ that's my momma
you're talking about

Hitler: back when he
was just some crappy artist
— you'd take him out, right?

why save the world if
can't get a little nookie
once in a while?

anonymous tip ~
you are a fine, upstanding
citizen, Sammy

57

SEASON 2

Playthings

Episode 33 (Season 2, Episode 11)
Directed by Charles Beeson
Written by Matt Witten
Original air date: January 18, 2007

---

son of a bitch ~ watch
your mouth ~ Maggie said it first
~ watch yours too, Maggie

old school haunted house:
might even run into Fred
and Daphne inside

why they think we're gay? ~
you're butch, probably think you
overcompensate

are those antique dolls?
'cause Sam's got a major doll
collection back home

you're bossy, you're short ~   mixing whiskey and
are you drunk? ~ yeah, so? stupid...   Jäger: not a gangbuster
~ time for bed Sasquatch   idea, was it?

what you gonna do,
poke her with a stick? dude! don't
poke her with a stick!

let's play ~ tea party? ~
tea parties forever and
ever and ever

SEASON 2

Nightshifter

Episode 34 (Season 2, Episode 12)
Directed by Phil Sgriccia
Written by Ben Edlund
Original air date: January 25, 2007

---

what's it's like being
FBI? ~ it's dangerous,
but mostly lonely

listen carefully
God's honest truth: there are no
such things as man-droids

just a routine check ~
okie-dokie ~ I like him:
says "okie-dokie"

old werewolf stories?
pretty much from shapeshifters
— only silver hurts

Agent Henriksen —
Sam is Bonnie to your Clyde
~ yeah, well that part's true

you do not know these
Winchesters — they're dangerous,
smart, expertly trained

what's the advantage
of this plan? fainting wouldn't
help it to survive

dressed like S.W.A.T., Sam, Dean
pull an Ocean's Eleven:
walk out the front door

Nightshifter (cont.)

• *"Renegade" scene* •

oh Mama, I'm in
fear for my life from the long
arm of the law *beats*

lawman has put an
end to my running, and I'm
so far from my home

oh Mama, I can
hear you a-crying; you're so
scared and all alone

hangman is coming
down from the gallows and I
don't have very long

we're so screwed ~ the jig
is up, the news is out, they
finally found me

the renegade who
had it made: retrieved for a
bounty ~ *starts Baby*

never more to go
astray, judge will have revenge
today: wanted man

SEASON 2

Houses of the Holy

Episode 35 (Season 2, Episode 13)
Directed by Kim Manners
Written by Sera Gamble
Original air date: February 1, 2007

---

magic in magic
fingers ~ you are making me
uncomfortable

believes she was touched
by an angel? ~ blinding light,
ecstasy: the works

supernatural:
maybe, but angels? no, 'cause
there's no such thing, Sam

Archangel Michael
with flaming sword, fights demons:
force against evil

Mom used to tell me:
angels watching over us
— last thing ever said

wanted to believe —
it's so damn hard to do what
we do all alone

hadn't seen: own eyes,
never would have believed it
~ what? ~ maybe God's will

61

Born Under a Bad Sign

Episode 36 (Season 2, Episode 14)
Directed by J. Miller Tobin
Written by Cathryn Humphris
Original air date: February 8, 2007

---

the scariest part
about this whole thing is that
you're Bon Jovi fan

what's the last thing you
remember? ~ :: west Texas :: ~ that
was a week ago

Justin Timberlake
concert — yeah, no, Justin is
quite the triple threat

do demons tell truth? ~
especially if they know
it'll mess with head

a little holy
water in beer — Sam wouldn't
notice — you're not Sam

:: Hell is hell, even ::
:: for demons — a prison of ::
:: bone, flesh, blood, and fear ::

:: nothing compared to ::
:: what you do to self — can see ::
:: in eyes: you're worthless ::

charms stop demons from
getting back up in ya ~ that
sounds vaguely dirty

SEASON 2

Tall Tales

Episode 37 (Season 2, Episode 15)
Directed by Bradford May
Written by John Shiban
Original air date: February 15, 2007

---

if you see, you die ~
if they don't live to tell tale
how does tale get told?

what are you drinking? ~
I don't know, man, I think they're
called purple nurples?

this is serious
investigation — no time
for blah blah blah blah

whole life I've never   they probed me again
found evidence of a real   and again and again, then
abduction — just pranks   they made me slow dance

brave little soldier —
I acknowledge your pain; you're
too precious for world

you've got a trickster:
creates chaos and mischief,
easy as breathing

come on, those people
got what was coming to them:
hoisted on petard

63

SEASON 2

Roadkill

Episode 38 (Season 2, Episode 16)
Directed by Charles Beeson
Written by Raelle Tucker
Original air date: March 15, 2007

---

isn't argument
a little archaic? men
can ask directions

last thing said to him:
I called him a jerk — oh, god
— what if that's last thing?

"House of Rising Sun"
this song: it was playing when we
crashed ~ she's mine... she's mine...

we were already
out here, hunting ~ for what? ~ ghosts
~ don't sugarcoat it

the ghosts can't let go;
they're trapped in loops, replaying
the same tragedies

you're like a walking   15 years ago,
encyclopedia of   you hit Jonah Greely with
weirdness ~ yeah, I know   car; David survived

David already
said goodbye — Molly, it's *your*
unfinished business

Heart

Episode 39 (Season 2, Episode 17)
Directed by Kim Manners
Written by Sera Gamble
Original air date: March 22, 2007

---

if I didn't know
better, I'd say the guy was
attacked by a wolf

a human by day,
a freak animal killing
machine by moonlight

a few scotches in,
he'd hit on anyone in
five-mile radius

the old-fashioned way —
Dean, always with the scissors
~ shut up — two of three?

creature takes over,
she blacks out ~ like really hot
Incredible Hulk

Sam, she's a monster —
you're feeling sorry for her?
~ I understand her

I can't live like this,
this is how you can save me
— I'm asking you to

Sam, I got this one ~
I'll do it; she asked me to —
Dean, please just wait here

SEASON 2

Hollywood Babylon

Episode 40 (Season 2, Episode 18)
Directed by Phil Sgriccia
Written by Ben Edlund
Original air date: April 19, 2007

---

weird crap is bound to
happen ~ Frank here thinks the stage
is haunted, for real

to right: Stars Hollow —
if we're lucky, we might catch
one of the show's stars

swimming pool weather?
I mean it is practically
Canadian, Dean

Latin chant summons,
but if the ghosts are in Hell,
can they hear chanting?

not married to salt,
what do you want? still want to
stick with condiments?

the invocation: heart, soul into it —
necromantic summoning   they crap all over it and
— why in a movie?   want you to smile

there's an afterlife?
there's an afterlife alright:
mostly pain in ass

Folsom Prison Blues

Episode 41 (Season 2, Episode 19)
Directed by Mike Rohl
Written by John Shiban
Original air date: April 26, 2007

I call this one the
"Blue Steel" — wait, who looks better:
me, or Nick Nolte?

I'll have cheeseburger ~
you think you're funny? ~ I think
I'm adorable

you are mine, baby! ~
don't worry, Sam — promise I
won't trade you for smokes

this is, without a doubt, the dumbest, craziest thing we've ever done	just because people are in jail, it doesn't mean they deserve to die

cop in Baltimore:
these boys saved her life and helped
her catch a killer

why you inside, kid? ~ idiot for a brother ~ yep, that'll do it	self-esteem issues: old man treated me like crap 'til the day he died
you don't even smoke ~ are you kidding me? this is currency of realm	Dean, does it bother you at all how easily you seem to fit in?

SEASON 2

What Is and What Should Never Be

Episode 42 (Season 2, Episode 20)
Directed by Eric Kripke
Written by Raelle Tucker
Original air date: May 3, 2007

---

you think that wishes…?
forget it, I'm just happy
to see you, that's all

a wish you never
even said out loud: a loved
one never died or…

you want to mow lawn? ~
are you kidding me? I would
love to mow the lawn

cheeseburger later? ~
how did I end up with you?
~ I got low standards

you work nights at the
hospital? I'm dating nurse:
so respectable

your happiness for
those people's lives: no contest
why is it my job?

kill yourself? ~ pretty
sure… like 90% sure,
but I'm sure enough

perfect fantasy? ~
it was just wish: Mom alive
we never hunted

I wanted to stay:
all I think about is how
much this job has cost

All Hell Breaks Loose (Part 1)

Episode 43 (Season 2, Episode 21)
Directed by Robert Singer
Written by Sera Gamble
Original air date: May 10, 2007

---

don't forget extra
onions this time — hey, see if
they got any pie

a town so haunted,
every resident fled: Cold
Oak South Dakota

what the hell? you see
Ellen? ~ no… no Ash either ~
finds watch Ash — damn it!

it was a vision ~
that was about as fun as
kicked in the jewels

appreciate what
you're doing: keeping them calm
— I know you're freaked, too

you ruined my life;
you killed everyone I love
~ the cost of business

gonna patch you up,
I'm gonna take care of you:
watch out for brother

SEASON 2

All Hell Breaks Loose (Part 2)

Episode 44 (Season 2, Episode 22)
Directed by Kim Manners
Story by Eric Kripke & Michael T. Moore, Teleplay by Eric Kripke
Original air date: May 17, 2007

---

hate to bring this up,
I do, but don't you think it's
time we buried Sam?

something big going
down — it's end-of-the-world big
~ well, then let it end

• *Dean's speech to dead Sam* •

when we were little —
couldn't have been more than five
— you just asked questions

why no mom? why do
we move around? where'd Dad go
when he'd leave for days?

I had *one* job, and
I screwed it up; I blew it
— for that I'm sorry

begged you: quit asking:
don't want to know — just wanted
you to be a kid

guess that's what I do:
I let down the people I
love — I let Dad down

I always tried to
protect you, keep you safe — Dad
didn't have to tell

and now, I guess I
am just supposed to let you
down, too — how can I?

it was just always
my responsibility —
like, I had one job

how am I supposed
to live with that? what am I
supposed to do, Sam?

SEASON 2

All Hell Breaks Loose (Part 2) (cont.)

have to give me a
moment — sometimes you gotta
stop and smell roses

give one year only —
welch or weasel out of it:
deal off, Sam drops dead

what's with Winchesters?
you're both just itching to throw
yourselves down the pit

life can mean something
~ it didn't before? you got
low self-opinion

Colt wasn't trying
to keep demons out — trying
to keep something in

oh no, it's Hell — take
cover ~ that's a devil's gate:
a damn door to Hell

how certain are you
what you brought back is hundred
percent pure Sammy?

don't know what to say ~
I do: that was for our mom
you son of a bitch

don't get mad at me —
look out for you: it's my job
~ and what is my job?

hope you boys ready,
'cause the war has just begun
~ we got work to do

SEASON THREE

SEASON 3

The Magnificent Seven

Episode 45 (Season 3, Episode 1)
Directed by Kim Manners
Written by Eric Kripke
Original air date: October 4, 2007

---

deserve to have fun ~
well, I am in violent
agreement with you

cheeseburger breakfast? ~
year to live; I ain't sweating
the cholesterol

you seem nice enough,
but this ain't "Scooby-Doo" — we
don't play with others

seven deadly sins
in the flesh ~ what's in the box?
Brad Pitt? Se7en? no?

you are animals:
horny, greedy, hungry, and
violent creatures

who the hell are you? ~
I'm the girl who saved your ass
— see you around, Sam

blade can kill demon? ~
yesterday, I would have said
there was no such thing

it's like there's a light
at the end of the tunnel
~ it's hellfire, Dean

what do you say we
kill evil sons of bitches,
raise a little hell

The Kids Are Alright

Episode 46 (Season 3, Episode 2)
Directed by Phil Sgriccia
Written by Sera Gamble
Original air date: October 11, 2007

---

yoga teacher: the
bendiest weekend of life
— it's my dying wish

moon bounce is epic
who else thinks they're awesome? chicks
it's hot chick city

knife you had — you can
kill demons with that thing? where'd
you get it? ~ Skymall

yellow-eyed demon's
celebrity death match: you're
the sole survivor

don't — only bitches
send a grown-up ~ you're not wrong
~ and I'm not a bitch

what? somebody had
to teach him how to kick the
bully in the nads

you disappointed? ~
I'll be gone one day — what am
I leaving behind?

what? I had a type:
leather jacket, a few scars,
no mailing address

just for the record:
got a great kid — would've been
proud to be his dad

you're a demon ~ don't
be racist — I'm here because
I want to help you

SEASON 3

Bad Day at Black Rock

Episode 47 (Season 3, Episode 3)
Directed by Robert Singer
Written by Ben Edlund
Original air date: October 18, 2007

---

she's lying, you got
to know that — she knows what your
weakness is: it's me

searching dad's storage
it's my first sawed-off; I made
it myself — sixth grade

rabbits foot is real —
hoodoo old world stuff, luck charm:
a curse made to kill

I can read people:
you're a thief, a scumbag, but
you're not a killer

again, just look out for your brother, you idjit ~ what? ~ I lost my shoe	I procure unique items, select clientele ~ a thief ~ a *great* thief

all going to Hell,
might as well enjoy the ride
~ agree with you there

it's my lucky day —
my god, did you see that shot?
amazing: Batman

SEASON 3

Sin City

Episode 48 (Season 3, Episode 4)
Directed by Charles Beeson
Written by Robert Singer & Jeremy Carver
Original air date: October 25, 2007

---

dead factory town ~
can't be demons in South Beach?
~ sorry Hef, next time

we open up the
devil's gate, this town becomes
Margaritaville

I gotta hit the
head, release the hostages
— be back in a few

take best shot — gonna
stand there like pantywaist, or
are you gonna shoot?

how you like bowing
down before lesser creatures?
~ Lucifer is real?

not easy — there'll be
collateral damage, but
it has to be done

bright side: I'll be there
with you, that little fallen
angel on shoulder

Bedtime Stories

Episode 49 (Season 3, Episode 5)
Directed by Mike Rohl
Written by Cathryn Humphris
Original air date: November 1, 2007

---

normal eyes and teeth —
killed brothers — how would *you* feel?
~ can't imagine worse

like Cinderella:
pumpkin coach and mice horses
~ could you *be* more gay?

it's Snow White? yeah, I
saw that movie — or the porn
version, anyway

I'm gonna stop the
big bad wolf, which is weirdest
thing I've ever said

your daughter Callie   I know truth — time for
is still here — she's a spirit   you to let go — it's time for
~ so, you've seen her too?   me to let you go

said some good advice ~ is
that what you want me to do,
Dean? just let you go?

tired of Dean's mess?
that broken psyche of his?
being bossed around?

SEASON 3

Red Sky at Morning

Episode 50 (Season 3, Episode 6)
Directed by Cliff Bole
Written by Laurence Andries
Original air date: November 8, 2007

you're my brother, Dean —
I'm gonna try to save you,
won't apologize

see the ship: a few
hours later, pucker up,
kiss your ass goodbye

he's cannon fodder,
can't be saved in time ~ we have
souls, we're gonna try

when this is over
we should have angry sex ~ don't
objectify me

oh, searching for a
witty rejoinder? ~ screw you
~ very Oscar Wilde

ten grand: easier
than thank you? you're so damaged
~ takes one to know one

want you to worry
about you; want you to give
a crap you're dying

SEASON 3

Fresh Blood

Episode 51 (Season 3, Episode 7)
Directed by Kim Manners
Written by Sera Gamble
Original air date: November 15, 2007

Sam Winchester's the
anti-Christ ~ I heard that from
the Easter Bunny

Harmony was drugged:
he put a few drops in drink
~ was it red and thick?

nice move, Dean: running
right at weapons ~ what can I
say? I'm a badass

sick and tired of
stupid kamikaze trip
~ more like a ninja

looking up since four,
know you better than any:
you are terrified

you charged a super
vamped-out Gordon, no weapons:
a little reckless

it's time you should know
how to fix her; you're gonna
need for the future

SEASON 3

A Very Supernatural Christmas

Episode 52 (Season 3, Episode 8)
Directed by J. Miller Tobin
Written by Jeremy Carver
Original air date: December 13, 2007

---

gonna sound crazy ~
what's gonna sound crazy to
me? ~ evil Santa

s-silent night… holy…
night, all is well… all is dry —
bright — round… the table…

wreaths, huh? sure you don't
want to ask her about her shoes?
saw some nice handbags…

she didn't charge you? ~
nope ~ did you sell them for free?
~ hell no, it's Christmas

I don't get it, you
haven't talked Christmas in years
~ this is my last year

all of a sudden,
this Jesus character's the
hot new thing in town

swear by saying "fudge" ~
you fudging touch me again,
I'll fudging kill you

for Dad ~ Dad lied to
me — I want you to have it
~ thanks, Sam, I love it

skin mags, shaving cream ~
fuel for me, and Baby —
Merry Christmas, bro

SEASON 3

Malleus Maleficarum

Episode 53 (Season 3, Episode 9)
Directed by Robert Singer
Written by Ben Edlund
Original air date: January 31, 2008

---

witches — they're always
spewing bodily fluids
— unsanitary

why does the rabbit
always get screwed in the deal?
the poor little guy

why are you part of
conversation? ~ 'cause he's my
brother, black-eyed skank

if gonna make it,
I gotta change ~ into what?
~ gotta be like you

you saved my life — what
was that stuff? god, it was ass;
it tasted like ass

let me serve again;
I have wanted it — I have
wanted *you* so long

all of them — every
damn demon was human once
— every one I've met

Dream a Little Dream of Me

Episode 54 (Season 3, Episode 10)
Directed by Steve Boyum
Story by Sera Gamble & Cathryn Humphris, Teleplay by Cathryn Humphris
Original air date: February 7, 2008

---

because you don't want
to be saved — how can you not
care about yourself?

dreaming with noises
who about? Angelina
Jolie? ~ no ~ Brad Pitt?

you shoved that knife in
again and again — you watched
me bleed, watched me die

not gonna die — not
gonna *let* you die — you're like
a father to me

I've never had this
dream before — stop *looking* at
me like that ~ sorry

• *Dean's Dean vs. :: Dean :: nightmare* •

I get it, my own
nightmare — like Superman III:
mano y mano

:: you can't lie to me, ::
:: I know the truth — I know how ::
:: dead you are inside ::

:: how worthless you feel, ::
:: how you look in a mirror ::
:: and hate what you see ::

Dream a Little Dream of Me (cont.)

sorry, pal — it's not
going to work — you're not real ~
:: sure I am — I'm you ::

it's my siesta —
all I gotta do is snap,
and you go bye-bye

:: you're going to Hell ::
:: won't stop — low self-esteem — not ::
:: a life worth saving ::

:: nothing besides Sam — ::
:: mindless and obedient ::
:: as an attack dog ::

:: car? jacket? music? ::
:: dad's — do you even have an ::
:: original thought? ::

:: watch out for Sammy ::
:: you can still hear your dad's voice ::
:: in your head can't you? ::

:: all he did was train ::
:: you, boss you around — but Sam ::
:: he doted on, loved ::

:: dad knew: good soldier ::
:: and nothing else — Daddy's Blunt ::
:: Little Instrument ::

Dream a Little Dream of Me (cont.)

:: own father didn't ::
:: care whether you lived or died, ::
:: so why should *you*, Dean? ::

my father was an
obsessed bastard — all that crap
of protecting Sam

all of that was *his*
crap — *he's* the one who couldn't
protect family

he's the one who let
Mom die, who wasn't there for
Sam — *I* always was

I didn't deserve
what he put on me, and I
do not deserve Hell

:: you can't escape me; ::
:: you're gonna die — *this* is what ::
:: you're gonna become ::

I don't want to die
I don't want to go to Hell
~ find way to save you

SEASON 3

Mystery Spot

Episode 55 (Season 3, Episode 11)
Directed by Kim Manners
Story by Jeremy Carver & Emily McLaughlin, Teleplay by Jeremy Carver
Original air date: February 14, 2008

---

heat of the moment ~
rise and shine, Sammy ~ Asia?
~ come on, love this song

Tuesday: pig in poke —
I'll have special with side of
bacon and coffee

you die today, Dean —
twice now I've watched you die — I
won't do it again

more archery range;
you are a terrible shot
~ how do you know that?

maple syrup for
past hundred Tuesdays — *now* he's
having strawberry?

we have killed one of
your kind before ~ actually
bucko, you didn't

Sam watching brother
die every day, forever
~ you son of a bitch

killing Dean is *fun?* ~
one: yes it's fun, two: this is
so not about Dean

isn't supposed to
happen today — come on, I'm
supposed to wake up

they have never seen
you with sharp object — holy
full metal jacket

keep sacrificing
yourselves for each other — no
good comes out of it

SEASON 3

Jus in Bello

Episode 56 (Season 3, Episode 12)
Directed by Phil Sgriccia
Written by Sera Gamble
Original air date: February 21, 2008

---

why sourpusses?
we are not the ones you should
be scared of, Nancy

seeing you in chains ~
you kinky son of a bitch —
we don't swing that way

coming right for us
like we got contract on us
— it's 'cause we're awesome

you in there? ~ I shot
the sheriff ~ but you didn't
shoot the deputy

they'll protect you from
possession ~ how long you had
those? ~ not long enough

world will end bloody —
doesn't mean we shouldn't fight
— we do have choices

when this is over,
I'm gonna have so much sex
— but not with you — move

87

Ghostfacers

Episode 57 (Season 3, Episode 13)
Directed by Phil Sgriccia
Written by Ben Edlund
Original air date: April 24, 2008

Ed's obsessed — then meets
Harry at computer camp,
and love at first geek

he shows up early,
does his job — but I think he's
got the hots for Ed

basic EMF,
EVP, temp-flux sweep: looks
like ducks in a row

listen, chisel-chest: salt in my duffle:
we were here first, already   make a circle, get inside
set up — we beat you   ~ inside the duffle?

you gotta be gay
for that poor, dead intern — send
him into the light

teach about how gay
love can pierce through the veil of
death and save the day

we're Ghost… Ghostfacers —
face ghosts when others will not,
in kitchen when hot

SEASON 3

Long Distance Call

Episode 58 (Season 3, Episode 14)
Directed by Robert Singer
Written by Jeremy Carver
Original air date: May 1, 2008

---

you two talking case? ~
no, talking about feelings
and favorite boy bands

six employee code
violations — partner says
run number, run it

grandma having phone
sex with dead husband — rocked some
necrophilia

no hard proof here, Dean —
still just going on blind faith
~ all I got, okay?

think stuff gets erased?
surprised how much just *out* there
waiting to be plucked

just make a phone call —
you're all so connected, but
really so alone

staring down barrel —
Hell: for real, forever, and
I'm really scared, Sam

SEASON 3

Time Is on My Side

Episode 59 (Season 3, Episode 15)
Directed by Charles Beeson
Written by Sera Gamble
Original air date: May 8, 2008

---

thing in the paper ~
stripper suffocates dude with
thighs? ~ the *other* thing

notice some teeth marks?
~ can I see your badges? so
you're cops *and* morons

when they found our guy,
body was stuffed with maggots
~ dude, I am eating

he dumps the bile —
lost your appetite? ~ baby,
can't stay mad at you

there's something else down
the road — folks like us… there ain't
no happy ending

I'll try anything
once, but I don't know — that sounds
uncomfortable

you think I'm monster —
I have never done one thing
I did not have to

why you telling this? ~
maybe you can kill the bitch
~ I'll see you in Hell

SEASON 3

No Rest for the Wicked

Episode 60 (Season 3, Episode 16)
Directed by Kim Manners
Written by Eric Kripke
Original air date: May 15, 2008

---

don't care what it takes —
you're not gonna go to Hell
— not gonna let you

just 'cause I gotta
die, doesn't mean you have to
— go smart or don't go

manipulative
is in the job description:
I am a demon

wish could hear you scream ~
I wish you'd shut your pie hole
— don't get what we want

Sam, you're my weak spot,
and I'm yours, and evil sons
of bitches know it

go after Lilith
our way, and if we go down,
we go down swinging

should have been jamming
"Eye of the Tiger" right there
~ I rehearsed that speech

got the knife ~ going
without me? do I look like
ditch-able prom date?

this isn't your fight ~
hell it isn't — family
don't end with blood, boy

No Rest for the Wicked (cont.)

• Bon Jovi rocks, on occasion •

you know what I do
want ~ on a steel horse I ride
wanted ~ Bon Jovi?

rocks, on occasion ~
and I walk these streets, loaded
six-string on my back

play for keeps ~ come on ~
cause I might not make it back
— I've been everywhere

oh yeah — I'm standing
tall, seen a million faces,
and I've rocked 'em all

cause I'm a cowboy:	or alive, dead or
on a steel horse I ride — I'm	alive, dead or alive, dead
wanted — wanted — dead	or alive, dead or…

you're piercing the veil,
glimpsing the "B" side — Hell's bitch:
see other bitches

what am I supposed
to do? ~ keep fighting and take
care of my wheels, Sam

SEASON FOUR

SEASON 4

Lazarus Rising

Episode 61 (Season 4, Episode 1)
Directed by Kim Manners
Written by Eric Kripke
Original air date: September 18, 2008

---

after 40 years
of pain, waking in coffin,
Dean digs his way out

whatever Sam did
was bad mojo — grave like nuke,
and this: *shows handprint*

name: Wedge Antilles ~
how'd you know that? ~ what *don't* I
know about that kid?

you think I made deal? ~
don't lie to me — I'm off the
hook and you're on it?

Dean, what's Hell like? ~
must have blacked it out — I don't
remember damn thing

that's an iPod jack ~
were supposed to take care of
her, not douche her up

conjure and command:
show me your face, Castiel
— I don't scare easy

what makes you special? ~
I like to think it's because
of perky nipples

traps and talismans,
stakes, iron, silver, salt, knife:
catch, kill anything

Lazarus Rising (cont.)

• *Castiel's first appearance* •

who are you? ~ I'm the
one who gripped you tight and raised
you from perdition

I mean: what are you? ~
I'm an angel of the lord
~ there is no such thing

this is your problem,
Dean, you have no faith *shows wings*
~ some angel you are

you burned woman's eyes ~
warned her not to spy true form
— it's overwhelming

some special people
can perceive my true visage
— thought you would be one

gas station, and the
motel — that was you *talking*?
lower the volume

now tax accountant?
possessing some poor bastard?
~ devout — prayed for this

why angel rescue? ~
good things do happen ~ not in
my experience

you don't think deserve
to be saved? — God commanded
we have work for you

Are You There, God? It's Me, Dean Winchester

Episode 62 (Season 4, Episode 2)
Directed by Phil Sgriccia
Story by Sera Gamble & Lou Bollo, Teleplay by Sera Gamble
Original air date: September 25, 2008

---

if angels were real,
hunter somewhere would have seen
~ yeah — you just did, Dean

okay, say there *are*
angels — then what, there's a God?
~ Vegas money? yeah

God gives a crap? why
do *I* deserve to get saved?
just regular guy

angels: guardians —
fluffy wings, halos — you know:
Mike Landon, not dicks

it's solid iron,
completely coated in salt
~ you built panic room?

angels: warriors —
I'm a soldier, not here to
perch on your shoulder

apocalypse? road
trip: Grand Canyon, BunnyRanch,
Trek Experience

lord works ~ if you say
"mysterious ways," so help
me, will kick your ass

the 66 seals ~
guessing not show at Sea World
~ broken by Lilith

should show some respect:
I dragged you out of Hell — I
can throw you back in

In the Beginning

Episode 63 (Season 4, Episode 3)
Directed by Steve Boyum
Written by Jeremy Carver
Original air date: October 2, 2008

---

what were you dreaming? ~
get your freak on by watching
other people sleep?

thanks — nice threads — you know
Sonny and Cher broke up, right?
~ Sonny, Cher broke up?

Back to the Future:
"Winchester!" both Winchesters
turn, just like McFlys

so, angels got their
hands on some DeLoreans
~ time is fluid, Dean

this is car you want ~
you know something about cars?
~ yeah, my dad taught me

kill vampires with
wood stakes or silver? ~ neither:
you cut their heads off

the light hit his eyes —
I could have sworn ~ black or red?
~ they were pale yellow

In the Beginning (cont.)

I like that John kid;
think you two are meant to be
— depending on it

worst thing can think of
is for my children to be
raised into this life

November 2nd   if alter future,
1983 — don't get   you'll never become hunters
up, no matter what   — all those people die

these deals you're making —
you don't want these people's souls
— just want their children

still gonna kill you —
you look into my eyes — *I'm*
the one that kills you

I couldn't stop it —
she still made the deal — still died
in the nursery

destiny can't be
changed, Dean — all roads lead to the
same destination

brother headed down
dangerous road — not sure where
— stop it, or we will

SEASON 4

Metamorphosis

Episode 64 (Season 4, Episode 4)
Directed by Kim Manners
Written by Cathryn Humphris
Original air date: October 9, 2008

---

just exorcising
demons ~ with your mind, what else?
~ send them back to Hell

already too far:
Sam, if I didn't know you,
would want to hunt you

got a rugaru ~
is that made up? sounds made up
~ they're nasty suckers

long pig — means human
flesh ~ that's my word of the day
~ hunger grows, can't fight

have you ever been   nice dude, but he's got
really hungry? I mean have   something evil in his blood
not eaten in *days*?   — maybe you relate

demon blood in me —
can't rip it out, scrub it clean
— new level of freak

doesn't matter what
you are — only matters what
you do — it's your choice

99

Monster Movie

Episode 65 (Season 4, Episode 5)
Directed by Robert Singer
Written by Ben Edlund
Original air date: October 16, 2008

---

honest monster hunt:
the Winchesters tackling
a black and white case

new "Raiders" movie ~
saw it ~ without me? ~ you were
in Hell ~ no excuse

I'm a maverick ma'am:
rebel with a badge — I don't
play by the rules *wink*

brother, I have been / Mulder and Scully?
re-hymenated, and the / X-Files are real? ~ no, X-Files
dude will not abide / is a TV show

you and your partner
find some horrible nightmare
to fight? ~ some folks paint

life is small, meager,
messy — the movies are grand,
simple, elegant

hero gets the girl,
monster gets the gank — with a
happy ending, too

Yellow Fever

Episode 66 (Season 4, Episode 6)
Directed by Phil Sgriccia
Written by Andrew Dabb & Daniel Loflin
Original air date: October 23, 2008

Donny's a sweetheart —
it's Marie you gotta look
out for — she smells fear

you're dying again,
loser — are you gonna cry?
baby gonna cry?

I'm not carrying
that; it could go off — I'll man
flashlight ~ you do that

suspicious rattling
opens locker *cat jumps out*
screams that was scary!

this isn't going
to work: these badges are fake
— we could go to jail

we're hunting a ghost ~
exactly, who does that? ~ us
~ that's why our lives suck

and you — you're gassy
— you eat half a burrito
and you get toxic

4 months / 40 years,
remember every second
— you're still gonna die

what did you see, Dean? ~
just the usual — nothing
I couldn't handle

Yellow Fever (cont.)

• *"Eye of the Tiger" bonus scene* •

air drumming solo
rising up, back on the street
— did time, took chances

went the distance, now
back on my feet, just a man
and will to survive

so many times, it
happens too fast, you change your
passion for glory

don't lose your grip on
dreams of past — you must fight just
to keep them alive

stares into your soul	rising up to the
it's the eye of the tiger,	challenge of our rival *starts
the thrill of the fight	jamming leg guitar*

last known survivor
stalks his prey in the night *stands
on Baby's door frame*

and he's watching us
all with eye of the tiger
jumps down to applause

It's the Great Pumpkin, Sam Winchester

Episode 67 (Season 4, Episode 7)
Directed by Charles Beeson
Written by Julie Siege
Original air date: October 30, 2008

---

talking ghosts, zombies,
leprechauns: those little dudes
are scary — small hands

600-year-old
hag, could pick any costume:
cheerleader? *I* would

Castiel, angel ~
oh my god — I didn't mean…
heard lots about you

none more dangerous
than a-hole who thinks he's on
a holy mission

of course you have choice —
never questioned crap order?
couple of hammers?

find this witch — or are
you just going to sit there
fingering your bone?

you've been warned twice now ~
you know, my brother was right
about you — you're dicks

you misunderstand —
praying you would save the town
— people: works of art

I'm not a hammer
I have questions, doubts — don't know
whether passed or failed

Wishful Thinking

Episode 68 (Season 4, Episode 8)
Directed by Robert Singer
Story by Ben Edlund & Lou Bollo, Teleplay by Ben Edlund
Original air date: November 6, 2008

---

what are you calling
your book? ~ working title is
"Supernatural"

it's terrible world —
why am I here? tea parties?
is that all there is?

jonesing for some hooch:
amaretto, Irish cream —
he's a girl-drink drunk

okay, follow lead…
I wouldn't mess with this kid
anymore — stay back

• *Dean won't talk about Hell* •

I do remember
everything happened in pit
— won't lie anymore

won't talk about it ~
you can't shoulder this alone
— got to let me help

little heart-to-heart?
sharing, caring gonna change
anything? heal me?

I am not talking
about bad day here — the things
I saw, there aren't words

is no forgetting,
is no making it better
— right here, forever

wouldn't understand,
never make you understand,
so, I am sorry

I Know What You Did Last Summer

Episode 69 (Season 4, Episode 9)
Directed by Charles Beeson
Written by Sera Gamble
Original air date: November 13, 2008

---

we've driven farther
for less — got something to say?
~ saying it: this sucks.

you're pissed Ruby threw
us the tip ~ as far as you're
concerned: family

that's revelations ~
since when have jack-o-lanterns?
~ older translation

hell of a right hook
to knock out a guy that's got
80 pounds on her

angels talk of you —
Castiel pulled out of Hell
— you can help save us

angel radio —
first words, clear as a bell: Dean
Winchester is saved

you recognize me?
wearing pediatrician —
we were close... in Hell

Ruby sits up who
do I have to kill to get
French fries around here?

socially conscious
body; I recycle ~ you
grabbed coma patient?

Sam, too much info ~
told you I was coming clean
~ now I feel dirty

SEASON 4

Heaven and Hell

Episode 70 (Season 4, Episode 10)
Directed by J. Miller Tobin
Story by Trevor Sands, Teleplay by Eric Kripke
Original air date: November 20, 2008

---

you're heartless sons of
bitches, you know that? ~ as a
matter of fact, yes

thank you, Pamela —
I remember who I am
~ who? ~ I'm an angel

why want to be us?
crapping, confused, afraid, pain
~ love, chocolate cake, sex

on the road, orders
from unknowable father?
it's... I can relate

kiss what was that for? ~
our last night on earth, all that
~ stealing my best line

angel and demon
in back seat — setup to joke,
or Penthouse Forum

where's boss? ~ Castiel?
he's not here — see, he has this
weakness: he likes you

maybe don't deserve
to be saved: I disobeyed
— it's our "murder one"

give back angel juice ~
committed serious crime
~ thinking for herself?

Anna kisses Dean
did your best — I forgive you
Cas looks heartbroken

Heaven and Hell (cont.)

• *Dean describes time in Hell* •

I know you heard him:
what he said about how I
had promise ~ I heard

I'm damn curious —
you're not talking about Hell,
and I'm not pushing

it wasn't four months
down there — time is different
— more like forty years

they sliced and carved and
tore at me in ways… until
there was nothing left

suddenly I would
be whole again like magic,
then start all over

every day, offer
to take me off of the rack
if I put souls on

if *I* did torture —
every day I told him to
stick it where sun shines

for 30 years I
told him, but then I couldn't
do it anymore

I got off that rack,
god help me, and I started
ripping them apart

I lost count of how
many souls — the th… the things
that I did to them

Dean, look, you held out
for 30 years — longer than
anyone would have

Dean wipes tears away
how I feel — this inside me
harder to speak now

I wish I couldn't
feel anything — I wish I
couldn't feel damn thing

SEASON 4

Family Remains

Episode 71 (Season 4, Episode 11)
Directed by Phil Sgriccia
Written by Jeremy Carver
Original air date: January 15, 2009

---

chased cases nonstop
for like a month — we need sleep
~ can sleep when we're dead

three bedrooms, two baths,
and one homicide — this place
will sell like hotcakes

this is what we do,
just trust us ~ you hunt ghosts? ~ that's
right ~ like Scooby-Doo?

backwoods hillbilly —
sit and wait for her to go
all "Deliverance"

it's not a ghost, it's
just a girl: psycho Nell — I'm
telling you, *humans*

not going down there…
please nobody grab my leg
please don't grab my leg

well, why doesn't he
come inside? ~ because I had
to carry him out

lock the baby up ~
daddy was *baby-daddy?*
~ dude was a monster

they were animals
defending territory
I enjoyed it, Sam

Criss Angel Is a Douchebag

Episode 72 (Season 4, Episode 12)
Directed by Robert Singer
Written by Julie Siege
Original air date: January 22, 2009

---

his misdirect is
shaking his ass like an Eighth
Avenue hooker

offends me, you know:
playing at magic — real thing
will kill you bloody

listen: pathetic,
bitter old men, glory days
— he's not joke: we are

working to pull ace
from middle of deck for *years*
— now I can pull three

the exact address? ~
426 Bleeker — ask for
"Chief" ~ what's your safe word?

we con people for
a living — takes more than fake
badge to get past us

still chasing demons
when we're 60? ~ no, I think
we'll be dead for good

I shilled for Barnum —
he gave me something: Grimoire
— book of real magic

I'm in ~ what changed mind?
~ don't want to be doing this
when I'm an old man

SEASON 4

After School Special

Episode 73 (Season 4, Episode 13)
Directed by Adam Kane
Written by Andrew Dabb & Daniel Loflin
Original air date: January 29, 2009

---

greatest game ever —
skill, agility, cunning —
one simple rule: dodge

could have torn apart ~
I don't want to be the freak,
want to be normal

aside from werewolf,
that how describe family?
father seems driven

maybe three or four
choices shape someone's whole life
— you're one that makes them

I've seen real evil —
we were scared, miserable
— but it gets better

cool: it's just an act —
we both know you're just a sad,
lonely little kid

you took an interest ~
all that matters: you're happy
— are you happy, Sam?

Sex and Violence

Episode 74 (Season 4, Episode 14)
Directed by Charles Beeson
Written by Cathryn Humphris
Original air date: February 5, 2009

---

oxytocin: how
it feels when first fall in love
— whole "weak in knees" thing

strippers Sam, strippers
— actual case involving
strippers — finally!

what floats the guy's boat,
that's what they look like? ~ yeah, see,
sirens can read minds

last time I checked, son,
D.C. has jurisdiction —
waste my time — idjits

did you sleep with her?
middle of "Basic Instinct,"
you bang Sharon Stone?

focus on naked
girls ~ not doing this for you,
doing it for girls

could be saliva —
really should have wiped the lip
before you drank, Dean

haven't you ever
loved someone and still kinda
wanted to bash head?

and now he loves me,
he'd do anything for me
— best feeling in world

thinking about you —
your lips: very distracting
— it is a problem

get bored, we all do —
wanna fall in love again,
again… and again

SEASON 4

Death Takes a Holiday

Episode 75 (Season 4, Episode 15)
Directed by Steve Boyum
Written by Jeremy Carver
Original air date: March 12, 2009

---

don't see irony?
all we do is ditch death ~ but
the rules don't apply

how to ice reaper?
you can't kill death ~ I don't know,
maybe demons can

am I making you
uncomfortable? ~ get out
of me! ~ such a prude

learn some ghost moves ~ by
tonight? I'll meet you back at
Mr. Miyagi's

you're the one that got
away — you'd be surprised how
little that happens

inside that angsty
noggin of yours *lighting strikes*
~ the hell? ~ guess again

angels on shoulder ~
you know about that? most I've
met are dicks with wings

why didn't you ask? ~
because you seem to do the
exact opposite

done horrible things;
upstairs decided to give
me a second chance

everything: season ~
but you made an exception
for me ~ you're different

okay to be scared ~
I am not scared ~ that's the big
secret: we're all scared

SEASON 4

On the Head of a Pin

Episode 76 (Season 4, Episode 16)
Directed by Mike Rohl
Written by Ben Edlund
Original air date: March 19, 2009

---

knew what was at stake ~
saving the world — tired of
burying friends, Sam

psychic Pamela?
Cas, you should remember her:
you burned her eyes out

black belt in torture ~
you are the most qualified
interrogator

this too much to ask,
I know, but have to ask it
~ talk to Cas alone

he's the funniest
angel in the garrison,
you ask anyone

getting too close to
the humans in my charge: you
— expressed emotions

if open that door
and walk through it, you will not
like what walks back out

spill your guts one way
or another — just don't want
to ruin my shoes

John: unique, stuff of
heroes — but Dean Winchester:
he broke in 30

could still dream in Hell,
and I dreamt of this moment:
got a few ideas

apocalypse, burn
earth down — we'll owe it all to
you, Dean Winchester

for first time, I feel ~
choose your own course of action;
must think for yourself

it's not blame, it's fate —
righteous man who begins it:
one who must finish

I'm not strong enough;
not who either of our dads
wanted me to be

SEASON 4

It's a Terrible Life

Episode 77 (Season 4, Episode 17)
Directed by James L. Conway
Written by Sera Gamble
Original air date: March 26, 2009

---

saved a grim reaper ~
you're a hero! saved us from
the apocalypse!

you think about ghosts? ~
never given it much thought
~ vampires? weird dreams?

ghosts responsible
for all the dead bodies, that's
what you're telling me?

should go check this out? ~
right now? ~ no, it's getting late
~ dying to check out

don't like own last name —
something in my blood, destined
for something different

pack shell with rock salt:
effective ~ Winchesters still
suck major ass, though

details: everything —
don't want to fight ghosts without
some health insurance

other work to do;
hard to explain — this not who
I'm supposed to be

some sort of lesson?
very creative ~ should see
my découpage ~ gross

it is what you are:
you'll find your way to it in
the dark every time

change things, save people
while you drive a classic car
— isn't curse, it's gift

SEASON 4

The Monster at the End of This Book

Episode 78 (Season 4, Episode 18)
Directed by Mike Rohl
Story by Julie Siege & Nancy Weiner, Teleplay by Julie Siege
Original air date: April 2, 2009

---

woman in white lures… ~
gonna need all copies of
"Supernatural"

as in: Sam-slash-Dean ~
they know we're brothers, right? ~ does
not seem to matter

one explanation:
obviously I'm a god —
cruel, capricious god

gonna go park her —
you behave yourself, would you?
no homework — watch porn

probably psychic —
you're just focused on our lives
— like, *laser*-focused

Dean, let him go — this
man is to be protected:
prophet of the lord

one day, these books: they'll
be known as the Winchester
gospel ~ you're kidding

please, I need some help —
I'm praying, okay ~ prayer
is a sign of faith

if prophet threatened,
most fearsome wrath of Heaven
rain down on demon

Jump the Shark

Episode 79 (Season 4, Episode 19)
Directed by Phil Sgriccia
Written by Andrew Dabb & Daniel Loflin
Original air date: April 23, 2009

---

sorry, John died more
than two years ago — who is
this? ~ I am his son

he took you to a
baseball game? ~ what'd Dad do with
you on *your* birthday?

so every nightmare
that I've ever had, that's all
real? ~ Godzilla's not

so, Agent Nugent,
thought about eternity? ~
nods all the damn time

cut out, don't look back —
there's only one thing you can
count on: family

our brother, he died
like a hunter — he deserves
to go out like one

you are just like Dad ~
take as compliment ~ take it
any way you want

SEASON 4

The Rapture

Episode 80 (Season 4, Episode 20)
Directed by Charles Beeson
Written by Jeremy Carver
Original air date: April 30, 2009

I'm dreaming, aren't I? ~
not safe here — someplace private
~ we're inside my head

I'm not Castiel,
I'm Jimmy ~ where the hell is
Castiel? ~ he's gone

angel inside of
you — it's kind of like being
chained to a comet

you used to be strong,
now you can't even kill "stunt
demon number three"

you promised you were going to take care of them — gave you *everything*	you won't die or age — last year was painful, picture thousand more like it

I learned my lesson:
I serve Heaven, not man, and
certainly not *you*

go inside, want to
show you something ~ what's the big
demon problem? ~ you

SEASON 4

When the Levee Breaks

Episode 81 (Season 4, Episode 21)
Directed by Robert Singer
Written by Sera Gamble
Original air date: May 7, 2009

Sammy, you just bought
yourself benchwarmer seat to
the apocalypse

phone rings hello? suck
dirt and die Rufus — you call
again, I'll kill you

gonna tell something:
you got ass-reamed in Heaven,
but not of import?

:: how could you do this? ::
:: we were gonna be normal ::
~ it didn't pan out

Sam doesn't have to? ~
if it gives comfort that way
~ you're a dick these days

love that boy like son —
here instead of battlefield
'cause we love too much

correct if wrong: you
signed on to be angels' bitch?
you prefer "sucker"?

won't let him do this —
found my line: won't let brother
turn into monster

look, my whole life you
take the wheel, you call the shots
— asking you: trust me

it's not something that
you're doing, it's what you are
— means you're a monster

118

SEASON 4

Lucifer Rising

Episode 82 (Season 4, Episode 22)
Directed by Eric Kripke
Written by Eric Kripke
Original air date: May 14, 2009

---

he's your brother and
he's drowning ~ I tried, look what
happened ~ try again

you are a better
man than your daddy ever
was, so don't be him

we have been through much
together, you and I — sad
it ended like this

well, how about this?
the suite life of Zack and Cas
— it's a… never mind

what is worth saving?
pain, guilt, anger, confusion
— paradise, with Sam

want to take a walk ~
I'll go with you ~ alone ~ no
~ screw this noise, I'm out

I'll take pain and guilt,
I'll even take Sam as-is
— better than Stepford

when you've won: rewards —
peace, happiness, 2 virgins
and 70 sluts

you spineless, soulless
son of a bitch — what do you
care about dying?

you are not in this
story ~ yeah, well, we're making
it up as we go

first demon: last seal —
guess who's coming to dinner
~ my god ~ guess again

SEASON FIVE

SEASON 5

Sympathy for the Devil

Episode 83 (Season 5, Episode 1)
Directed by Robert Singer
Written by Eric Kripke
Original air date: September 10, 2009

---

smote crap out of him —
exploded — like a water
balloon: chunky soup

your number one fan:
I'm samlicker81 ~
I'm sorry, you're what?

that's Michael: toughest
sumbitch they got ~ tough? that guy
looks like Cate Blanchett

you're sorry? this kind
of thing don't get forgiven;
should lose my number

I'm front of the line,
baby *kisses Dean* ~ what is
that, peanut butter?

hand-delivered it
to us — it's you, chucklehead
— you're the Michael sword

Michael must defeat
serpent; is written ~ on the
other hand, eat me

in case you dicks showed
up — learned that from my friend Cas,
you son of a bitch

an Enochian
sigil: hide you from angels,
carved into your ribs

I am Lucifer ~
do me a favor, *Satan*:
remind not to drink

what I *do* have is
a GED and a "give
'em hell" attitude

was demon talking —
I ain't cutting you out, boy
— never ~ thanks, Bobby

hard time forgiving —
can never be what we were
— don't think I trust you

SEASON 5

Good God, Y'All!

Episode 84 (Season 5, Episode 2)
Directed by Phil Sgriccia
Written by Sera Gamble
Original air date: September 17, 2009

---

cell phone, Cas? really?
since when do angels need to
reach out, touch someone?

try New Mexico,
on tortilla ~ no, he's not
on any flatbread

I killed two angels:
my brothers — I am hunted;
did it all for you

may I borrow it?
Dean give it to me ~ all right
...now I feel naked

what kind of demons?
no anti-possession charms,
holy water, salt

four horsemen — which rides
red horse? that cherry Mustang:
it's the way I'd roll

save protests for bro,
I can see inside your head —
one-track: blood, blood, blood

that's a sweet little
knife, but come on, you can't kill
War, kiddos ~ we know

know you don't trust me —
now I realize something: I
don't trust me either

SEASON 5

Free to Be You and Me

Episode 85 (Season 5, Episode 3)
Directed by J. Miller Tobin
Written by Jeremy Carver
Original air date: September 24, 2009

---

here about patients:
the exsanguinated ones
fangs eat it, Twilight

starts god, don't do that! ~
hello, Dean ~ we've talked about
this: personal space?

Raphael killed me ~
wasted by Teenage Mutant
Ninja Angel, Cas?

Thelma and Louise:
we'll just hold hands and sail off
this cliff together?

last time you zapped me
someplace, I didn't poop for
a week — we're driving

when I win, you buy
dinner, tell life story ~ fair
bullseye 1, 2, 3

because we're humans,
and when humans want something
really bad, we lie

SEASON 5

Free to Be You and Me (cont.)

Alonzo Mosely:
FBI, this is partner:
Eddie Moscone

last night on earth, what
are your plans? ~ I just thought I'd
sit here quietly

telling me you have
not been up there doing a
little cloud-seeding?

Zachariah gave
cancer; he doesn't have my
imagination

Bert and Ernie: gay,
you are not gonna die a
virgin on my watch

where's Steve? ~ oh Steve's good
— guts are laying roadside by
Hawley five-and-dime

you full-on rebelled
'gainst Heaven — iniquity
is one of the perks

warning: will find you ~
maybe one day, but today
you're *my* little bitch

no one has ever
done anything so bad they
can't be forgiven

your crusade is nuts,
but I *do* know a little
about missing dads

had more fun with you
than had with Sam in years, and
you're not that much fun

you need my consent;
I will kill myself before
~ I'll just bring you back

SEASON 5

The End

Episode 86 (Season 5, Episode 4)
Directed by Steve Boyum
Written by Ben Edlund
Original air date: October 1, 2009

---

taken time out to
think about God's plan for you?
too friggin' much, pal

this isn't funny,
Dean, the voice says I've almost
run out of minutes

I just need like four
hours once in a while ~
I'll just... wait here then

so, you're his vessel?
Lucifer's wearing you to
prom? ~ that's what he said

weaker together —
love, family: will always
use it against us

Rhonda Hurley — tried
on her panties: satiny
— we kinda liked it

don't have to cuff me —
come on, you don't trust yourself?
~ :: absolutely not ::

:: excuse me, ladies — ::
:: need to confer with leader ::
:: — wash up for orgy ::

SEASON 5

The End (cont.)

what are you, hippie? ~
:: I thought you'd gotten over ::
:: trying to label ::

:: I'm not gonna lie ::
:: me and him: a pretty messed- ::
:: up situation ::

:: I want you to see: ::
:: Sam didn't die in Detroit, ::
:: brother — he said "yes" ::

don't get me wrong, Cas,
happy stick is out of ass,
but what's going on?

gonna feed your friends
into meat grinder? Cas too?
something is broken

:: whatever you do, ::
:: you will always end up here ::
:: — see you in five years ::

pretty nice timing,
Cas ~ we had an appointment
~ do not ever change

I just know we're all
we've got — more than that, we keep
each other human

Fallen Idols

Episode 87 (Season 5, Episode 5)
Directed by James L. Conway
Written by Julie Siege
Original air date: October 8, 2009

---

slam into windshield:
force of 80 mile per
hour crash? ~ drugs maybe?

shot to head — no gun,
no gunpowder, no bullet ~
nothin' strange 'bout that

two super-famous,
super-pissed-off ghosts, killing
their own super-fans

ultimate hero:
short man in diapers, also
a fruitarian

Paris Hilton's a
homicidal maniac… ~
or we missed something

can't fall into rut —
you're gonna have to let me
grow up, for starters

they worship Lincoln,
Gandhi, Hilton — whatever,
take what I can get

all you wanted: to
be loved — one distant father
figure coming up

we gotta just grab
whatever's in front of us,
kick ass, go fighting

SEASON 5

I Believe the Children Are Our Future

Episode 88 (Season 5, Episode 6)
Directed by Charles Beeson
Written by Andrew Dabb & Daniel Loflin
Original air date: October 15, 2009

---

goggles on ready? ~
hit it, Mr. Wizard *buzz*
electrocutes ham

freak come in my room
while I'm sleeping, take my tooth?
sounds scary; no thanks

a god or trickster
with sense of humor of a
9-year-old ~ or *you*

Jesse: devil's son? ~
Antichrist not Lucifer's
child — just demon spawn

we tell him the truth:
apocalypse — he might make
right choice ~ *you* didn't

a superhero:
you're Superman minus the
cape and go-go boots

can do the right thing —
if you choose wrong, it'll haunt
you for rest of life

The Curious Case of Dean Winchester

Episode 89 (Season 5, Episode 7)
Directed by Robert Singer
Story by Sera Gamble & Jenny Klein, Teleplay by Sera Gamble
Original air date: October 29, 2009

---

how are you doing? ~
you mean my legs? I'm weeping
in my Häagen-Dazs

came in on the case ~
and you beat me here? ~ brains trumps
legs, apparently

buy-in's 25
years ~ make it 50 ~ I like
the cut of your jib

you'll die if you lose ~
what am I living for? the
damn apocalypse?

my elbows: creaky ~
you crybaby ~ pound it up
your ass, ironsides

first witch I've seen did
not spew bodily fluids
all over the place

that whole going out
of head bit: very method,
more than meets the eye

not useless, Bobby —
don't stop being a soldier
'cause you got wounded

SEASON 5

Changing Channels

Episode 90 (Season 5, Episode 8)
Directed by Charles Beeson
Written by Jeremy Carver
Original air date: November 5, 2009

---

what's happening? ~ the
end of the world ~ you're gonna
need a bigger mouth

town to town, two-lane
roads, family biz, two huntin'
bros, living the life

Dr. Sexy wears
cowboy boots, not tennis shoes
~ fan? ~ guilty pleasure

Incredible Hulk ~
Bana or Norton? ~ TV
Hulk ~ Lou Ferrigno?

I need a penknife,
dental floss, sewing needle,
fifth of whiskey, STAT

Mr. Trickster does
not like pretty-boy angels
commence Nut Cracker

you arrogant dick,
you don't know me — don't work for
either S.O.B.

too powerful to
be trickster ~ I think I know
what we're dealing with

Michael: loyal to
absent father, Lucifer:
the younger rebel

nobody gets that
angry unless talking 'bout
their own family

isn't about some
prize fight between brothers — you
won't stand up to fam

SEASON 5

The Real Ghostbusters

Episode 91 (Season 5, Episode 9)
Directed by James L. Conway
Story by Nancy Weiner, Teleplay by Eric Kripke
Original air date: November 12, 2009

---

did you take my phone? ~
just borrowed it from your pants
— gonna want to see

in every fight scene:
gun or knife knocked away — use
some kind of bungee?

hotel is haunted
must hunt down clues — first team wins
gift card to Sizzler

heard that line all night
from dudes, but you seem different:
not scared of women

their pain is not for
your amusement ~ I don't think
they care ~ oh, they *care*

there's no such thing as
Croatoan for "down there"
— you should see doctor

"Supernatural"
makes digging graves seem easy
— I'm gonna throw up

maybe guy was right:
maybe we ought to put these
things on a bungee

Sam and Dean wake up
every morning, save the world
— who *wouldn't* want that?

my favorite movie
was Beaches — Hillary and
CC: just so brave

SEASON 5

Abandon All Hope…

Episode 92 (Season 5, Episode 10)
Directed by Phil Sgriccia
Written by Ben Edlund
Original air date: November 19, 2009

---

cling to six decades
of your homophobia,
or just give it up

the demon Crowley
making deal — it's going down
~ okay, Huggy Bear

we are just servants —
Lucifer exterminates
humankind: we're next

alright big boy, let's
go ~ *drinks several shots* I'm
starting to feel it

you giving me "last
night on earth" speech? ~ what? no — if
I *was*, would that work?

can make this easy ~
when have you known *us* to make
anything easy?

will not leave you here
alone — get goin' now boys
— kick it in the ass

everyone alright? ~
it's Jo, Bobby — it's pretty
bad — I don't think she's…

there's only five things
that gun can't kill — I happen
to be one of them

see you on other
side, probs sooner than later
kisses forehead, lips

we are gonna win
can you feel it? — we're goin'
to Heaven, Clarence

133

SEASON 5

Sam, Interrupted

Episode 93 (Season 5, Episode 11)
Directed by James L. Conway
Written by Andrew Dabb & Daniel Loflin
Original air date: January 21, 2010

---

a little depressed,
probably 'cause I started
the apocalypse

me and him and this
angel — his name's Castiel
— he wears a trench coat

not gonna wallow ~
always do this — can't just keep
this crap in ~ watch me

this place isn't bad
after all ~ dude, you *cannot*
hit that ~ …oh, so torn

what you boys doing
in here? ~ *Dean drops trou* pudding!
~ alright, come on you

all you do is fail —
did you really think *you* were
gonna beat devil?

I *am* angry at
everything — was you, Dad — now
Lilith, Lucifer…

134

SEASON 5

Swap Meat

Episode 94 (Season 5, Episode 12)
Directed by Robert Singer
Story by Julie Siege & Rebecca Dessertine & Harvey Fedor, Teleplay by Julie Siege
Original air date: January 28, 2010

:: we talking 'bout sex? ::
:: *shocked* Crystal, I would *love* to ::
:: have the sex with you ::

uh, bacon burger
turbo, large chili-cheese fry,
Health Quake Salad shake?

think you'd want something
like that? wife, rug rats, whole nine?
~ not really my thing

:: so, this is gonna ::   :: let's get the hell out ::
:: sound crazy, but I think I'm ::   :: of here :: ~ still gotta burn the
:: in the wrong body ::   body, idiot

are we actually
drinking together? ~ :: we don't
do it that often ::

:: this isn't a game — ::
:: you're crossing line you won't come ::
:: back from, believe me ::

:: omnis et secta :: ~   apple pie family
rogamus — adios, bitch   crap: stressful, trust me ~ we don't
~ :: uh, it's "audi nos" ::   know what we're missing

SEASON 5

The Song Remains the Same

Episode 95 (Season 5, Episode 13)
Directed by Steve Boyum
Written by Sera Gamble & Nancy Weiner
Original air date: February 4, 2010

---

what are you doing
with knife? — something not telling
~ kill Sam Winchester

answer still no — Sam
is my friend ~ you've changed ~ maybe
too late, but I have

DeLorean, no
plutonium? ~ I do not
understand reference

I look like doctor?
he is tough for a little
nerdy dude with wings

how you related? ~
Mary's dad: pretty much like
a grandpa to us

so help me, I will
turn this car around (awkward
family road trip)

died before I could
tell him that I understand,
and I forgive him

November 2nd
1983 — wake up,
take Sam, and you run

true vessel, but not
only one — it's a bloodline
back to Cain, Abel

I gotta believe
I can choose what I do with
unimportant life

not random: a plan —
free will's an illusion, Dean
— you're gonna say "yes"

this is Team Free Will:
ex-blood junkie, dropout, and
Mr. Comatose

SEASON 5

My Bloody Valentine

Episode 96 (Season 5, Episode 14)
Directed by Mike Rohl
Written by Ben Edlund
Original air date: February 11, 2010

---

it's Valentine's Day:
"unattached drifter Christmas"
~ I'm not feeling it

room 31-C ~
I'm there now ~ yeah, I get that
~ gonna hang up now

cupid has gone rogue:
stop him before kills again
~ tu sais que tu me plais[†]

are we in a fight? ~
this is their handshake ~ don't like
it ~ no one likes it

it's more than a word —
I *love* love — if that's wrong, I
don't want to be right

why does Heaven care? ~
certain bloodlines, destinies
~ fixed up our parents?

just punched a cupid ~
I punched a dick ~ what has been
up with you lately?

when you start eating? ~
exactly — hunger is clue:
starvation, famine

a taste for ground beef —
I'm an angel, I can stop
anytime I want

these make me happy ~
how many is that? ~ lost count
in the low hundreds

I want drink or sex?
I get it ~ well-adjusted?
~ no, I'm just well-fed

can see how broken
you are, how defeated — you
can't win, you know it

[†] This line appears in the French dub of this episode; syllable-count stretched for artistic purposes. Translation: you know that I like you.

137

SEASON 5

Dead Men Don't Wear Plaid

Episode 97 (Season 5, Episode 15)
Directed by John F. Showalter
Written by Jeremy Carver
Original air date: March 25, 2010

Digger? gave yourself
your own nickname? can't do that
~ who died, made *you* Queen?

Dean, I can explain ~
the zombie making cupcakes?
~ that's my wife, watch it

Death is behind this ~
awesome: another horseman
— it must be Thursday

listen… she used to
hum when she cooked — never thought
would hear it again

that was *not* my son ~
right — focus for me, sheriff
— one minute *gunshot*

remember demon
inside — you killed me ~ that's why
can't do it again

don't you ever get
tired being wrong? ~ making
this up as I go

SEASON 5

Dark Side of the Moon

Episode 98 (Season 5, Episode 16)
Directed by Jeff Woolnough
Written by Andrew Dabb & Daniel Loflin
Original air date: April 1, 2010

---

spend the rest of your
life knowing Dean Winchester's
on your ass? shoot him

go ahead, do it —
warning you: when I come back,
I'm gonna be pissed

I remember this:
4th of July, '96 ~
thanks, Dean — this is great

we're royally boned —
prayer is a last hope of
a desperate man

this isn't a dream ~
I am dead ~ condolences
~ where am I? ~ Heaven

Dad said had perfect
marriage ~ it wasn't perfect
'til after she died

what do you see? some
see a tunnel or river
— for you it's a road

Mom — Dad still loves you,
I love you, never leave you
~ my little angel

if this is SkyMall,
where's the triplets and latex?
come on, guy has needs

what? ~ I just never
realized how long you have been
cleaning Dad's messes

I looked everywhere
for you — I thought you were dead,
and when Dad came home...

139

Dark Side of the Moon (cont.)

this is the night you
ditched us for Stanford — this is
happy memory?

I just don't look at
family the way you do ~ yeah,
but *I'm* your family

you boys die more than
anyone I've ever met;
angels Windexed brains

trapped while angels run
the show? that's lonely ~ attic's
better than basement

everybody leaves:
Mommy, Daddy, even Sam
— it's not them, it's you

after all you've done,
it's more than he's intervened
in long time — he's done

another deadbeat
dad with excuses — used to
that — I'll muddle through

looks toward God you son
of a bitch, I believed in...
— don't need this: worthless

99 Problems

Episode 99 (Season 5, Episode 17)
Directed by Charles Beeson
Written by Julie Siege
Original air date: April 8, 2010

---

not the first prophet
we've met, but you are cutest
…with total respect

no drinking, gambling
premarital sex — outlawed
personality

what the hell happened
to you? ~ I found a liquor
store, and I drank it

angel stuff takes it
out of you ~ I can't complain
— know you have it worse

the hell have you been?
did you say on a bender?
~ he's still pretty smashed

Leah not a real
prophet ~ what is she? ~ the whore
~ tell what really think

Enochian: fake —
actually means, "you breed with
the mouth of a goat"

you're a servant of
Heaven ~ and you're an angel
~ a poor example

you're the great vessel?
pathetic, self-hating, and
faithless — end of world

wanted you to know:
when picture myself happy,
it's with you and kid

SEASON 5

Point of No Return

Episode 100 (Season 5, Episode 18)
Directed by Phil Sgriccia
Written by Jeremy Carver
Original air date: April 15, 2010

---

not hard to figure
out stops on the farewell tour…
— how's Lisa doing?

how could you do that? ~
all you've *ever* done is run
~ was wrong every time

I never do it ~
why? ~ because I promised *you*
I wouldn't give up

wrongly assumed Dean
brave enough to withstand them
~ know what? blow me, Cas

don't have a dad, so
we may be blood — not family;
my *mom* is family

Cas, not for nothing:
last person who looked at me
like that, I got laid

tired of fighting
who I'm supposed to be ~ stop
sacrificing self

Point of No Return (cont.)

co-dependent: Sam
and Dean — psychotically,
irrationally

I rebelled for this?
I gave everything for you
— this what you give me?

you're not so much the
"chosen one" as you are a
clammy scrap of bait

we didn't lie — just
avoided certain truths to
manipulate you

the Winchesters got
one blind spot: family — they're
gonna come get you

groans how you feeling? ~
a word to the wise: don't piss
off the nerd angels

I'm gonna say "yes" ~
no you will not — when push shoves,
you'll make the right call

won't have to watch you
fail — I don't have the same faith
in you that Sam does

so what changed your mind? ~
damnedest thing: I just didn't
want to let you down

if you can find faith
in me, least I can do is
return the favor

screw destiny right
in the face — take fight to them
and do it our way

SEASON 5

Hammer of the Gods

Episode 101 (Season 5, Episode 19)
Directed by Rick Bota
Story by David Reed, Teleplay by Andrew Dabb & Daniel Loflin
Original air date: April 22, 2010

---

how you doing? ~ no ~
oh lady, I'm just, you know
~ I understand — *no*

rules: no slaughtering,
curb your wrath, keep your hands off
the local virgins

when are you lucky? ~
know what? bite me, Gabriel
~ might later, big boy

westerners, I swear:
sheer arrogance — you're not the
only ones on earth

I see right through you:
smart-ass, I-could-give-a-crap
~ takes one to know one

think you own planet —
what gives you the right? ~ no one
gives it — we take it

Lucifer, brother —
I love you, but you are a
great big bag of dicks

they are broken, flawed ~
damn right they're flawed — lots try to
do better, forgive

got War's, nicked Famine's
two rings down — collect all four
— need Pestilence, Death

SEASON 5

The Devil You Know

Episode 102 (Season 5, Episode 20)
Directed by Robert Singer
Written by Ben Edlund
Original air date: April 29, 2010

---

victims shown signs of
homicidal tendencies?
~ it's mild swine flu

thought the colt would work
— honest mistake — all part of
the learning process

how are you gonna
control the devil when you
can't control yourself?

'cause I don't like you,
I don't trust you, and you keep
trying to kill me

it went like clockwork ~
son of a bitch ~ what you get,
working with demon

if Lucifer wins —
when the Morningstar cleans house
— we *all* get the mop

starting to lose you:
becoming mild-mannered,
worthless sack of piss

you and I are in
lovers' league against Satan
— self-preservation

the only difference
between you and a demon:
your Hell is right here

those angels, demons
don't get it: *we're* the ones you
should be afraid of

leave, before I blast
you so full of rock salt, you
crap margaritas

145

SEASON 5

Two Minutes to Midnight

Episode 103 (Season 5, Episode 21)
Directed by Phil Sgriccia
Written by Sera Gamble
Original air date: May 6, 2010

---

where the hell are you? ~
hospital ~ you okay? ~ no
~ please elaborate

thirsty, my head aches,
have a bug bite that itches
— I am just… human

you are not the burnt,
broken shell of a man I
believed you to be

vessel: powerless —
there's not a speck of angel
~ maybe just a speck

did you kiss him? ~ Sam! ~
no — why'd you take a picture?
~ why did you use tongue?

remember when we
used to just hunt wendigos?
how simple things were?

added a little
sub-A clause on your behalf
— I'm an altruist

I'm happy to say,
if that's what you want to hear
— it's not what I think

really? ~ you and Dean
have habit of exceeding
my expectations

this where you kill me? ~
you have an inflated sense
of your importance

how old are you? ~ as
old as God, maybe older
— I will reap him, too

what of Chicago? ~
I suppose that it can stay;
I like the pizza

I got to ask, Dean —
you afraid of *losing*, or
losing your *brother*?

SEASON 5

Swan Song

*Episode 104 (Season 5, Episode 22)
Directed by Steve Boyum
Story by Eric Gewitz, Teleplay by Eric Kripke
Original air date: May 13, 2010*

• *Chuck's narration, part 1* •

April 21st,
1967: the
hundred millionth

GM car rolled off
the line at plant in Janesville:
blue two-door Caprice

speeches, lieutenant
governor even showed up:
big ceremony

then, three days later
another car — no one gave
two craps about her

but they should have… this
'67 Impala
would turn out to be

most important car —
no — most important *object*
in whole universe

she was first owned by
Sal Moriarty — he was
an alcoholic

two ex-wives, three blocked
arteries — weekends he'd give
bibles to the poor

"gettin' folks right for
judgment day," that's what he said
— Sam, Dean would've smiled

she ended up at
Rainbow Motors: a used-car
lot down in Lawrence

a young marine bought
her on impulse (after some
advice from a friend)

so, I guess that is
where this story begins — and
here is where it ends

SEASON 5

Swan Song (cont.)

you'll let me say "yes?" ~
you're a grown man — you want this,
I will back your play

promise not to bring
me back — once cage is shut, you
can't poke at it, Dean

you go find Lisa —	take care of these guys ~
have barbecues, football games	not possible ~ humor me
— live apple-pie life	~ was supposed to lie

• *Chuck's narration, part 2* •

Impala, of course,
has all the things other cars
have… a few they don't

the army man that
Sam crammed into the ashtray
— it is still stuck there

but none of that stuff's
important — this is the stuff
that is important:

legos that Dean shoved
into the vents: heat comes on,
can hear 'em rattle

these are the things that
make the car theirs — really *theirs*
— when Dean rebuilt her

he made sure these things
stayed — it's the blemishes that
make her beautiful

the devil doesn't
know or care what kind of car
the Winchesters drive

Swan Song (cont.)

what do you say, Sam?
a fiddle of gold against
your soul: I'm better

I told you this would
always happen in Detroit
~ *commences panic*

:: exhilaration ::
:: you know why that is? because ::
:: we're two halves made whole ::

what now? ~ we imbibe
copious quantities of
alcohol and wait

• *Chuck's narration, part 3* •

between jobs they would
sometimes get a day — a week
if they were lucky

Sam used to insist
on honest work, but now he
hustles pool like Dean

drove a thousand miles
for an Ozzy show, two days
for a Jayhawks game

and when it was clear:
park in middle of nowhere,
watch stars for hours

maybe never had
a roof and four walls, but they
were never homeless

SEASON 5

Swan Song (cont.)

angels keep secret,
but I saw it anyway:
perks of a prophet

Michael will kill your
brother ~ then I ain't gonna
let him die alone

hey, ass-butt ~ did you
just molotov my brother
with holy fire?

Sammy, you in there?
Sam it's okay, I'm here — I'm
not gonna leave you

it can't end this way —
I have to fight my brother:
it's my destiny

heals Cas, are you God? ~
that's a nice compliment, no
— but he brought me back

• *Chuck's narration, part 4* •

monkey with keyboard
can poop out a beginning
— ends: impossible

try to tie up loose
ends — never can — fans will bitch,
always will be holes

it's all supposed to
add up to something — they're a
raging pain in ass

Swan Song (cont.)

God gives you shiny
set of wings, and suddenly
you're his bitch again

you got what you asked
for: no paradise, no Hell
— just more of the same

• *Chuck's narration, part 5* •

this is the last Dean
and Bobby will see of each
other for long time

and next week Bobby
will be hunting rugaru
outside of Dayton

Dean didn't want Cas
to save him — he wants to die
or to bring Sam back

he isn't gonna
die or try to bring Sam back
— he made a promise

what's it add up to?
this was test for Sam and Dean;
think they did all right

against good, evil,
angels, devils, destiny
— against God himself

they made their own choice:
chose family — isn't that
kinda the whole point?

endings are hard, but
then again, nothing ever
really ends, does it?

SEASON SIX

SEASON 6

Exile on Main St.

Episode 105 (Season 6, Episode 1)
Directed by Phil Sgriccia
Written by Sera Gamble
Original air date: September 24, 2010

Dean's apple pie life:
still keeps holy water and
gun under the bed

don't get me wrong — if
you'd have said, 15 years from
now: suburbia…

crap job: pest control —
what is in some people's walls
could eat 'em alive

think you could keep this?
knew we were coming for you
— can't outrun your past

wanted a family,
and you have for a long time
— maybe the whole time

I know a few things —
stick around — I'll show you tricks
daddy never dreamed

out of head with grief:
drank, nightmares, collected books
— tried to bust you out

close to happiness
as I've seen — you were out, Dean
~ I look out to you?

half-eaten human
hearts, exsanguinated kids
— makes me uneasy

mom wanted normal
life — you remind me of her:
attitude for one

exactly: just went
didn't hesitate — you care,
and that's who you are

SEASON 6

Two and a Half Men

Episode 106 (Season 6, Episode 2)
Directed by John F. Showalter
Written by Adam Glass
Original air date: October 1, 2010

---

you know, sometimes I
wonder about you ~ sometimes
I wonder 'bout me

I know you're trying
to protect us, but scaring
me a little, too

how you know all this?
~ Lisa's got a baby niece;
been on few milk runs

you watch out for them —
asking: how do you do that,
not turn into Dad?

babies: didn't know —
thought they were freaks of nature,
like X-Men style

not every hunter
is head case — a lot like you
~ *I'm* freaking head case

no luck: baby front? ~
not yet ~ you want one? congrats,
it's a boy... sometimes

pretty sure it's not
a myth ~ what the hell was that?
~ may have been alpha

dad was exactly
like this all the time — scaring
the hell out of me

you're white knuckling
it, like what you *are* is bad
awful thing — you're *not*

SEASON 6

The Third Man

Episode 107 (Season 6, Episode 3)
Directed by Robert Singer
Written by Ben Edlund
Original air date: October 8, 2010

---

you're lying — tell your
mom you broke the damn thing, and
take it like a man

were you racing me? ~
no, I was kicking your ass
~ very mature *grins*

blood, boils, locusts ~
popular Egyptian plagues
~ these *ate* their way out

…down to sleep, I pray
to Castiel to get his
feath'ry ass down here

like I said, the son
of a bitch doesn't answer
…he's right behind me

you like him better? ~
we share a more profound bond
— not gonna mention

the staff of Moses ~
I think we can rule Moses
out as a suspect

spent the last "year" as
a multidimensional
wavelength of intent

is no other way ~
you're gonna torture a kid
~ *can't* care about that

what are you doing? ~
this morning had ménage à —
what is French for 12?

following your
footsteps — it's a new era:
no rules, destiny

Castiel are you
gonna let them? ~ I believe
hairless ape has floor

you went to Hell, Sam ~
it tortured *you*, it still does
— but Dean, *I'm* okay

SEASON 6

Weekend at Bobby's

Episode 108 (Season 6, Episode 4)
Directed by Jensen Ackles
Written by Andrew Dabb & Daniel Loflin
Original air date: October 15, 2010

• *"The Gambler" opening* •

warm summer's evening
on a train bound for nowhere,
met up with gambler

both too tired to sleep
so we took turns a-starin'
out window: darkness

boredom overtook,
he began to speak: he said
son, I've made a life

of readin' people's
faces, knowin' what cards were
by way they held eyes

don't mind my sayin'	know when walk away,
can see you're out of aces	and know when to run, and you
— for taste of whiskey	never count money
give you some advice:	sittin' at table —
got to know when to hold 'em,	be time enough for countin'
know when to fold 'em	when the dealin's done

157

SEASON 6

Weekend at Bobby's (cont.)

these monsters lately —
is it me, or is it weird?
~ it's defo something

it's peaty and sharp —
finish: citrus, tobacco
— I know what Craig is

now blend the herbs and
sauté over a high heat
— enjoy the roast, Mom

bamboo dagger blessed
by shinto priest? ~ woodchipper
~ that trumps everything

Crowley owns my soul —
I'll be damned if I'm gonna
sit here and *be* damned

would call in every
marker, hand out few to boot
~ saying there's a chance

word on the street is
you're big kahuna downstairs
~ you've been reading trades

Dean, a deal's a deal ~
don't need you to fight battles
for me, Moose — get bent

SEASON 6

Live Free or Twihard

Episode 109 (Season 6, Episode 5)
Directed by Rod Hardy
Written by Brett Matthews
Original air date: October 22, 2010

I'm bad; you should run ~
I can make own decisions:
I am 17

all about the same
age ~ and *cute* — hey, ice cream comes
in lots of flavors

picks up vampire book
look: he is watching her sleep
— how's that not rapey?

you wearing glitter?
~ only do it to get laid ~
it works? I'll be damned

hey, try "Lautner" ~ how
many Ts are in Pattins…
that is it: we're in

why aren't you freaked out?
'cause I can hear your heartbeat:
pretty damn steady

you let him get turned,
help us find that alpha vamp
~ risk my own brother?

you have stopped nothing
it's much bigger than you, me
~ *gestures: bring it on*

alpha's building an
army, but what's worse: we don't
scare them anymore

You Can't Handle the Truth

Episode 110 (Season 6, Episode 6)
Directed by Jan Eliasberg
Story by David Reed, Eric Charmelo & Nicole Snyder, Teleplay by Eric Charmelo & Nicole Snyder
Original air date: October 29, 2010

I don't want to ride
in same car, much less work a
damn case ~ he's your case

Dean, there's a *worst*-case
scenario ~ what, Satan?
~ other: it's just Sam

got another one:
dentist drilled a guy to death
~ the non-sexy kind

what happened to you,
Cas? you used to be human
— or at least like one

why'm I tellin' you? ~
because I'm cursed — actually
might be the best thing

you two have the most
unhealthy, tangled-up thing
I have ever seen

never be happy —
came out much harsher than I
meant ~ it's not your fault

you know what happens
when you base your life on lies?
truth comes along and…

as of yesterday,
wanted to kill him in sleep
— thought he was monster

you're covered in blood,
until covered in your *own*
blood, about to die

I'm good at slicing
throats — I am not a father,
I am a killer

that should stop me cold,
but I just do not feel it —
I don't know what's wrong

SEASON 6

Family Matters

Episode 111 (Season 6, Episode 7)
Directed by Guy Bee
Written by Andrew Dabb & Daniel Loflin
Original air date: November 5, 2010

---

physically he's
perfectly healthy ~ then what?
~ it's his soul — it's gone

an interesting
philosophical question:
is he even *Sam*?

this is a vessel;
my true form is the size of
your Chrysler building

you're a hell of a
hunter, Sam, but the truth is
sometimes you scare me

dude's hiding something,
I can feel it — if you weren't
Robo-Sam, you'd too

I'm in the middle
of a civil war — of *course*
your problems come first

trying to tell me
that you're a *bigger* knob than
you've been letting on?

you can't assume that
family means the same thing
to him as to us

tell me everything,
important or not —
you can't tell difference

SEASON 6

Family Matters (cont.)

when your kind huddled
around the fire, I was
the thing in the dark

he does as he's told ~
well if the old man's Kermit,
whose hand's up his ass?

not gonna kill him,
but will move a lot slower
without his kneecaps

I've big plans for you:
without pesky soul, you'll be
perfect animal

purgatory's vast,
under-utilized, and Hell-
adjacent: want it

I *was* a punk-ass
crossroads demon, now: King of
Hell — I've got mojo

working with demon?
you're not who I thought you were
~ you don't know me, son

you got two choices:
shoot your grandfather, or step
aside ~ *Sam cocks gun*

All Dogs Go to Heaven

Episode 112 (Season 6, Episode 8)
Directed by Phil Sgriccia
Written by Adam Glass
Original air date: November 12, 2010

Crowley thinks you're just
gonna what? is that Bobby?
give a kiss for me

take job and shove it ~
is that how you talk to boss?
~ not my boss, dick-bag

this is not a deal,	we make *really sure*
it's hostage situation:	before hand him over to
I own your brother	lifetime demon-rape

got us stumped, Lucky —
why shack up with a family?
is it kinky thing?

the only people
who, in your pathetic life,
have showed you kindness

I'd double cross us ~
that's reassuring, Dexter
~ just making convo

don't care about you,
but need your help — should go back
to being old me

Clap Your Hands If You Believe...

Episode 113 (Season 6, Episode 9)
Directed by John F. Showalter
Written by Ben Edlund
Original air date: November 19, 2010

Elwood: a center
of extraterrestrial
action — why I'm here

add glitter to that
glue you're sniffing, but don't dump
wackadoo on us

I'll be your conscience ~   close encounter ~ first?
you'll be Jiminy Cricket?   second? third? you better run:
~ yeah, freakin' puppet   fourth kind is butt thing

brother abducted?
it happened when you were kids?
~ half hour ago

zero data, leads —
considered that you suck at
hunting UFOs?

what were they like? ~ they
were grabby incandescent
douchebags, goodnight *nods*

our reality's
collapsing, and you're trying
to pick up waitress?

Clap Your Hands If You Believe... (cont.)

• *"Space Oddity" / Tinkerbell in the microwave* •

take your protein pills
electricity flickers
put your helmet on

oh no, not again ~
ground control to Major Tom
— commencing countdown

* Tinkerbell appears *
check ignition, may God's love
be with you ~ nipples?

Tinkerbell hits Dean
ground control to Major Tom
— really made the grade

the papers want to
slams fairy in microwave
know whose shirts you wear

turns on it's time to
leave the capsule, if you dare
holds door closed *laughs* *ding*

it was a little,
glowing, hot naked lady
with nipples: hit me

they take first-born sons
~ did you service Oberon,
King of the Fairies?

didn't know better,
I'd say you have a bunch of
elves working for you

you'll have to get near
me eventually, and I
have good reflexes

you think Lucky Charms
could return soul to sender?
~ talked a good game, though

SEASON 6

Caged Heat

Episode 114 (Season 6, Episode 10)
Directed by Robert Singer
Story by Jenny Klein and Brett Matthews, Teleplay by Brett Matthews
Original air date: December 3, 2010

---

your exceptional
good looks aren't gonna buy you
any mercy — talk

look, Sam, a demon
trying to be funny ~ oh,
is *that* what happened?

look at her, Dean, she's
furious — if she could kill
you, she'd have done it

Crowley would hunt down
the Lucifer loyalists —
it's what I would do

gonna untie us? ~
don't pretend you don't enjoy
~ you gonna kiss me?

Sam, where is the box? ~
can't believe you fell for that:
the plot of "Raiders"

if you don't help us,
I will hunt you down, and kill
you ~ will you, *boy*? how?

Caged Heat (cont.)

learn from our mistakes:
how they get us every time
— our Achilles heel

if the pizza man
loves babysitter, why does
he keep slapping rear?

don't watch porn with dudes,
and you don't talk about it
…he's got a boner

abominations? ~
keep talking dirty: makes my
meat suit all dewy

he'll die? ~ or he won't:
paralysis, psychic pain,
locked inside himself

what was that? ~ learned that
from the pizza man ~ A-plus
for you — feel so … clean

I'll get out of here,
trust me: next time you see me,
I'm there to kill you

wish circumstances
were different — much of the time
I'd rather be here

know what? when angels,
demons agree on something:
I pay attention

SEASON 6

Appointment in Samarra

Episode 115 (Season 6, Episode 11)
Directed by Mike Rohl
Written by Sera Gamble & Robert Singer
Original air date: December 10, 2010

---

you've done this a lot?
~ near 75% ~
that's your success rate?

if don't make it back,
nothing I say's gonna mean
a damn thing to him

we've established you
have hubris but no leverage;
what is it you want?

soul can be bludgeoned,   you will be me for
tortured, but never broken   one day ~ serious? ~ no I'm
— not even by me   being sarcastic

it's *my* life, *my* soul —
your head won't explode when this
whole scheme goes sideways

long history of
throwing wrench in everything
— just stick to the rules

dumbest thing ever:
summon angel who wants to
kill you ~ desperate times

Appointment in Samarra (cont.)

to be clear: you need
the blood of your father, your
dad needn't be blood

what does it all mean? ~
everything: dust in the wind
~ that's it? *Kansas* song?

I've spent my whole life
fighting that crap — there's no such
thing as destiny

I thought you wanted
the girl to skate by? ~ no one
really does, do they?

what's with you, cheap food? ~
I could ask you the same thing
— thought I'd have a treat

natural order ~
natural order's *stupid*
~ agree with you there

wrecking natural
order's not such fun when you
mop up mess, is it?

soul: vulnerable,
impermanent, valuable —
stronger than you know

you and brother keep
coming back — an affront to
universe balance

it might be itchy —
don't scratch the wall — 'cause trust me:
won't like what happens

SEASON 6

Like a Virgin

Episode 116 (Season 6, Episode 12)
Directed by Phil Sgriccia
Written by Adam Glass
Original air date: February 4, 2011

---

he gonna wake up? ~
I'm not a human doctor
~ could you take a guess?

soul: like skinned alive —
if you wanted to kill him
you should have outright

daddy always said:
just 'cause it kills your liver,
not *not* medicine

Dean, what did you do? ~
me and Death… ~ Death? the horseman?
~ I had leverage

glad he's better, but
kid went straight-up Menendez
— now it's all erased?

it's gift horse, I'm not
looking for teeth — sending Death
a damn fruit basket

I tried — I was with
Lisa and Ben for a year
— it didn't work out

Penny's diary ~
did you steal that from her room?
~ love that you asked that

Like a Virgin (cont.)

I think it just goes
to show that being easy
is just all upside

not Loch Ness Monster:
dragons aren't real ~ make a few
calls? ~ to who, Hogwarts?

great, back to the lore ~
says they live in middle earth?
you are such a nerd

sword of St. George and
Excalibur — not many
dragon swords — six tops

oh come on, you know
this one: we need a brave knight
willing to kill beast

I'll give it a whirl
heroic music rises
that's really on there

woke up to find out
burnt whole city down, I have
Zippo in pocket

dragons reading tone poems 'bout purgatory ~ no: instruction book	got a name: "mother" ~ mother of what? of dragons? ~ says "mother of all"

SEASON 6

Unforgiven

Episode 117 (Season 6, Episode 13)
Directed by David Barrett
Written by Andrew Dabb & Daniel Loflin
Original air date: February 11, 2011

---

got mysterious
coordinates to a town
from a Mr. X?

if this is a game:
incredibly clever, or
it's very stupid

hate say, "told you so" ~
you *love* to say, "told you so"
~ you're right, I love it

victim connection:
all banged the same dude — *you*, Sam
— it's a trap for *you*

opposable thumbs
and unlimited texting
— it wants to kill you

just dead man walking:
I'm saying we put him out
of his misery

nearly starved — what kept
me going: I dreamed about
ripping your throat out

Mannequin 3: The Reckoning

Episode 118 (Season 6, Episode 14)
Directed by Jeannot Szwarc
Written by Eric Charmelo & Nicole Snyder
Original air date: February 18, 2011

---

how long was I out? ~
two or three minutes ~ felt like
a week, give or take

shove it down, let it
come out in violence and
alcoholism

don't even dissect —
I mean, bigger than Kermit,
they use an iPad

I'm trying to get
over you — what is it that
you're trying to do?

bunch of killer dolls
like Chucky? I mean, come on
— that's freakin' creepy

if I stayed, you would
end up just like me ~ why say
it like you're so bad?

something's wrong with Mom ~
put her on ~ won't come to phone
— don't know what to do

family: people who
love you, care for you, even
when you are a dick

we've been "Parent Trapped"
— Ben sent out a 911;
you're going on date

leave Baby alone:
got nothing to do with this
— so sorry, Baby

I know what I want,
but I can't have it — phone rings
it's you, or you're dead

well, considering
carjacked by a poltergeist,
guess it could be worse

SEASON 6

The French Mistake

Episode 119 (Season 6, Episode 15)
Directed by Charles Beeson
Written by Ben Edlund
Original air date: February 25, 2011

---

no angels, I think ~
should we be killing someone?
~ don't think so ~ running?

who would wanna watch?
~ the interviewer said not
very many do

you're Jensen Ackles,
I'm Jared Padalecki ~
so, now you're *Polish*?

his name is Misha?
Misha? Jensen? what's up with
the names around here?

dear Castiel, who
running his ass from Heaven
so… breaker breaker

J-squared got me good
I'm really starting to feel
like one of the guys

you play Ruby — you're
at Jared's 'cause you're married
…*married* fake Ruby?

thrilled: it's refreshing —
Dean Cain like that on "Lois"
— he's a *real* actor

J & J had a
late one last night, ROT-
FLMAO!

Dean, grimly somehow
no problem with it ~ because
have no other choice

Misha's tweet says it's
a black market organ thing
— I am betting drugs

The French Mistake (cont.)

sorry, mojo-free
zone — no magic — which makes you
nothing but a dick

ever get feeling
someone is in the back seat?
frowny face *screams* ~ drive

not actors: hunters
Winchesters — people don't know
us, but we matter

how do you do it?
live in this grubby desert,
just dirt when you die?

Misha: he's been stabbed
~ *simultaneously* where?
~ *incredulous* *where?*

nothing but a bag
of strings and pulleys — need to
make important call

the scary man killed
the attractive, crying man,
then started to pray

shrugs well I am just
saying: no Hell below us,
above only sky

step away from him,
Raphael — I have weapons
— their power is mine

home, sweet home — chock full
of crap that wanna skin you
~ at least we're talkin'

SEASON 6

...And Then There Were None

Episode 120 (Season 6, Episode 16)
Directed by Mike Rohl
Written by Brett Matthews
Original air date: March 4, 2011

---

apocalypse came
and went: you didn't notice
— mother would never

let's do this: old times
— it's not rocket surgery
~ as long as I drive

it's that obvious? ~
why don't you three get a room?
~ we all pack a snack?

welcome to next time ~
take it you know each other?
~ he's our grandfather

just because you're blood,
doesn't make you family
— you gotta earn that

it was a good plan,
except a monster would not
give up all weapons

wouldn't change a thing
— I will never forgive you,
so change the subject

:: don't wanna kill me — ::
:: haven't you lost enough pals? ::
~ do what we have to

life's short; ours shorter —
gonna spend it wringing hands?
something'll get us

just so you two know:
a blanket apology,
all the way around

My Heart Will Go On

Episode 121 (Season 6, Episode 17)
Directed by Phil Sgriccia
Written by Eric Charmelo & Nicole Snyder
Original air date: April 15, 2011

---

knew Rufus was done
the day I met him; only
question was: who first?

accidents don't just
happen accidentally —
you know what I mean

you threatening me? ~
no — saying that if you don't
watch back, gonna die

what about the boat? ~
nothing special: Titanic
ever heard of it?

you saved cruise liner… ~
because Celine Dion song
made want to smite self

butterfly-effect
history ~ dude, rule one: no
Kutcher references

that other angel —
the one in dirty trench coat
who's in love with you

was she *your* kind or
my kind of librarian? ~
she was wearing clothes

so, we've pissed fate off
personally ~ she won't stop
until you are dead

of course — you need new
friends, Cas ~ I'm trying to save
the ones I have, Dean

sorry, freedom is
preferable ~ this: chaos
how is it better?

if don't go back and
sink that boat, I'm gonna kill
your two favorite pets

killed 50,000
people for us ~ I didn't:
they were never born

don't have to be ruled
by fate, you can choose freedom
— that's worth fighting for

SEASON 6

Frontierland

Episode 122 (Season 6, Episode 18)
Directed by Guy Bee
Story by Andrew Dabb, Daniel Loflin & Jackson Stewart, Teleplay by Andrew Dabb & Daniel Loflin
Original air date: April 22, 2011

---

showdown at high noon
the clock chimes, their fingers twitch
sepia duel

it's here, I know it:
Campbell family library
(almost like bunker)

know something about
phoenix? ~ River, Joaquin, or
giant flaming bird?

whose gun? ~ Colt's — *the* Colt,
from Samuel Colt's journal
~ let's see ~ get your own

March 5th, '61
we will Star Trek IV this bitch
~ I watched Deep Space Nine

series of partial differential equations — you'll be lost to me	aw, come on ~ you know what that is? ~ yeah, it is horse… ~ authenticity
can recite every Clint Eastwood movie ever ~ even monkey ones?	Marshall Clint Eastwood, this here is Walker, he is a Texas Ranger

178

Frontierland (cont.)

looking for a man ~
I'll bet ~ what's wrong with my shirt?
~ you are very clean

hook up with posse:
I am a posse magnet
— make that into shirt

giant from the future
with some magic brick doesn't
give me the vapors

but you're a hunter ~
retired ~ there's no such thing;
there's no getting out

human soul is pure
energy; if siphon some
off, can bring them back

most creatures I meet
can't get it up for iron
~ hunter? ~ slash-sheriff

showdown at high noon
the clock chimes, their fingers twitch
yip' ki-yay motherf—

this thing's been laying
around since… saying bring it
today ~ it's from Colt

what this means? ~ didn't
get a soulonoscopy
for nothing: we fight

SEASON 6

Mommy Dearest

Episode 123 (Season 6, Episode 19)
Directed by John F. Showalter
Written by Adam Glass
Original air date: April 29, 2011

---

why I have to call?
not like Cas lives in my ass
— get out of my ass

we need inside man:
something with claws, sympathy
~ like friendly monster?

he turned into a
vampire; I chopped his head off
~ with razor wire

you're not like the rest ~
I fed, I couldn't help it
— I'll do it again

I will search the town ~
Cas, we can still see you — just
looks like you're pooping

if she's here, glad we
got Smite-y McSmiterton
with us on our squad

without your power,
just baby in a trench coat
~ you hurt his feelings

what kind of doctor
calls the CDC and then
goes AWOL next day?

what kind of doctor
calls the CDC and then
stashes gooey corpse?

Mommy Dearest (cont.)

silver bullets ~ I'm
unpracticed with firearms
~ know who whines? babies

what do you call these? ~
you discovered, you name it
~ Jefferson Starships

Joe, Ryan in back seat:
both Sam and Dean recognize
the brotherly bond

what I'd like to do
is save a couple of kids,
if you do not mind

highlight crippling
and dangerous empathy
with some "sarcasm"

don't *let* Sam and Dean
Winchester do squat — they do
what they gotta do

mom defends children ~
mother of the year defense?
~ if I look like this?

phoenix ash: one shell,
one ounce of whiskey, down hatch
— musty afterburn

how Crowley escape?
not like Cas to make mistakes
— unless he *meant* to

Cas, how many times
am I going to have to
clean up your messes?

SEASON 6

The Man Who Would Be King

Episode 124 (Season 6, Episode 20)
Directed by Ben Edlund
Written by Ben Edlund
Original air date: May 6, 2011

• *Castiel's monologue, part 1* •

you know, I've been here
for a very long time — I
remember a lot

remember being
at shore, watching small gray fish
heave itself on beach

older brother said,
"don't step on fish, Castiel
— big plans for that fish"

I remember the
Tower of Babel, tall at
37 feet

impressive at time —
it fell, howled "divine wrath"
— dried dung stacked so high

remember Cain and
Abel, David, Goliath,
Sodom, Gomorrah

and of course the most
remarkable event that
never came to pass

it was averted
by two boys, an old drunk, and
a fallen angel

we ripped up ending
and the rules, leaving nothing
but freedom and choice

but what if I've made
the *wrong* choice? I mean, how am
I supposed to know?

ahead of myself —
let me tell you my story,
tell you everything

The Man Who Would Be King (cont.)

what is that good for? ~
apart from the obvious
erotic value?

see, the stench of that
Impala's all over your
overcoat, angel

• *Castiel's monologue, part 2* •

Crowley had a point —
my interest was conflicted:
still Winchesters' guard

taught me to stand up,
what to stand for, also what
happens when you do

I was done, over —
and then a thing happened — most
extraordinary

I was put back, and
we won — stopped armageddon
at terrible cost

once again I went
to harrow Hell to free Sam
from Lucifer's cage

arrogance, hubris —
because hadn't truly raised
Sam — not all of him

near impossible,
but I was just so full of
confidence, mission

sometimes we're lucky
to be given a warning —
this should have been mine

SEASON 6

The Man Who Would Be King (cont.)

only game piece who
doesn't underestimate
denim-wrapped nightmares

he is the Balki
Bartokomous of Heaven:
he can make mistake

Superman: dark side —
we gotta be cautious, smart,
stock up kryptonite

• *Castiel's monologue, part 3* •

worst part: Dean trying
to be loyal with instinct
telling otherwise

hiding, lying, sweep
away evidence — motives
used to be so pure

demon counterpart
to Bobby Singer: Ellsworth
double smites demons

returned to Heaven —
not one — each soul generates
its own paradise

had no choice — did it
to protect boys, or myself
…don't know anymore

favor eternal
Tuesday of autistic man
who drowned in bathtub

no one leads us now —
all free to make own choices,
and choose our own fates

God wants you to have
freedom ~ but what does he want
us to do with it?

The Man Who Would Be King (cont.)

• *Castiel's monologue, part 4* •

simple: freedom is
length of rope; God wants you to
hang yourself with it

explaining freedom
to angels is like teaching
poetry to fish

I'm not ashamed to
say that my big brother knocked
me into next week

he has gone to mat
cut and bleeding for us; when
we were stuck: broke ranks

• *Castiel's monologue, part 5* •

I knew they would have
questions I couldn't answer,
because was afraid

another choice: could
reveal myself, smite demons
— Crowley wouldn't like

Crowley sent his best —
was caught as much by surprise
as the rest of them

other hand, they were
my friends — for a brief moment
I was me again

SEASON 6

The Man Who Would Be King (cont.)

could have just asked me ~
never should have doubted you,
hope you can forgive

• Castiel's monologue, part 6 •

wonders never cease:
they trusted me again, but
just another lie

a little absurd:
Superman going dark side?
still just Castiel

• Castiel's monologue, part 7 •

of course I didn't
realize at the time: it was
all over right then

good Cas, righteous Cas —
as long as they believe it,
you get to believe

SEASON 6

The Man Who Would Be King (cont.)

• *Castiel's monologue, part 8* •

what was I doing
with this vermin? as if I
didn't know answer

Raphael was much
stronger than me — I wouldn't
survive a straight fight

so, I went to ask
an old friend for some help, but
watching him, I stopped

everything that he
sacrificed — I was about
to ask him for more

I want to help you
help me help ourselves ~ speak plain
~ business transaction

happy endings for
all of us, all possible
entendres intend

SEASON 6

The Man Who Would Be King (cont.)

• *Castiel's monologue, part 9* •

smart, stronger than him —
see now that I was prideful
— likely I was fool

lots of "thank you, sir,
can I have another hot
spike up the jacksie?"

what else can I do?
submit or die ~ what are you
French? how 'bout resist?

experts: I know two
eerily-suited Teen Beat
models with some time

• *Castiel's monologue, part 10* •

I wish I could say
I was clean of pride at that
moment, or the next

and so went the long
road of good intentions, the
road that brought me here

The Man Who Would Be King (cont.)

look me in the eye,
tell me you're not with Crowley
— *betrayed* — son of bitch

I am still your friend — Sam, I am the one who raised you from perdition	it sounds so simple; where were you when I needed to hear? ~ I was there
did you bring me back from Hell soulless on purpose? ~ how could you think that?	you taught me free will ~ just because you *can* do it doesn't mean you *should*
when crap comes around we deal with it, like always — not deal with devil	look, you and Bobby: closest things to family — like brother to me

• *Castiel's monologue, part 11* •

so that's everything — I believe it's what you would call a tragedy	asking you, Father, am I doing the right thing? am I on right path?
human perspective — maybe human perspective limited — don't know	you have to tell me give me a sign — gonna do whatever I must

SEASON 6

Let It Bleed

Episode 125 (Season 6, Episode 21)
Directed by John F. Showalter
Written by Sera Gamble
Original air date: May 20, 2011

I made a copy —
glad to meet, Bobby Singer:
paranoid bastard

jump out the window —
bones you break won't compare to
what they're gonna do

your chocolate's been in
my peanut butter too long
— tell you how this goes

I was drinking out
of a soprano's navel:
'75 Dom

kill enough demons,
eventually gonna tell
me where Crowley is

Lisa, Ben — that is
100% on me,
and if they are hurt…

can I ask question?
are you in flagrante with
the King of Hades?

thought you said we were
like family — I think that too
— can't trust run both ways?

Let It Bleed (cont.)

I do everything
you ask, always come when you
call — I am your friend

despite lack of faith
and threats, I saved you again
— any else done more?

asking me: stand down?
same ransom note from Crowley
— can both kiss my ass

from purgatory?
never thought to mention the
whole time slept with me?

going to regret,
but I'm officially on
your team, you bastards

I said I'm sorry ~
I wish this changed anything
~ I know, so do I

glad your life can get
back to normal, anyway
— take care of your mom

you ever mention
Lisa, Ben to me again,
I will break your nose

The Man Who Knew Too Much

Episode 126 (Season 6, Episode 22)
Directed by Robert Singer
Written by Eric Kripke
Original air date: May 20, 2011

---

ground floor, corner room,
nearest to fire escape:
quickest getaway

I could have handled
demon, but then the angel…
I told everything

this is what Cas wants:
for you to fall to pieces —
think what Sam would want

:: we're inside grapefruit — ::
:: you've been juiced — your BFF ::
:: Cas brought Hell-wall down ::

:: I'm not handicapped, ::
:: saddled with soul — souls are weak, ::
:: liability ::

I'm rethinking terms:
you get nothing, not one soul
~ unfairly weighted

have you forgotten:
bottom in relationship
— either flee or die

The Man Who Knew Too Much (cont.)

:: I remember Hell — ::
:: first you have to go through me ::
:: — I am the last piece ::

you know me, know why —
I'm not leaving my brother
all alone out there

I'm doing my best:
impossible circumstance,
friends abandon me

fool — Raphael will
deceive, destroy you ~ right 'cause
you're such straight-shooter

I'm not finished yet:
Raphael had followers
— I must punish them

think I would let you?
if anyone going to
be new God, it's me

we were family once —
I would have died for you — I
almost did few times

you can't imagine
what it's like — they're all inside
— millions of souls

please, I've lost Lisa,
I've lost Ben, now I've lost Sam
— don't make me lose you

just saying that 'cause
you're afraid — you're not family;
I have no family

angel blade won't work:
not an angel anymore;
I'm new God, bow down

SEASON SEVEN

Meet the New Boss

Episode 127 (Season 7, Episode 1)
Directed by Phil Sgriccia
Written by Sera Gamble
Original air date: September 23, 2011

---

what's the point if you
don't mean it? you fear me — not
love, not respect — fear

what a brave little
ant you are — you're powerless
— wouldn't dare again

you need a firm hand,
a father — I'm father now
— be obedient

gonna fix this car —
can work on her 'til she's mint
— we'll work on Sam, too

indifferent
to orientation — cannot
abide hypocrites

we saw him: no beard,
no robe — was young and sexy
— he had a raincoat

FBI believes
Ku Klux Klan forced to disband
~ can't argue with that

Meet the New Boss (cont.)

back as King of Hell,
but *I* choose where each soul goes;
I control the flow

new boss will kill me for talking to you ~ new boss? ~ Castiel, giraffe	Death is our bitch: we ain't gonna die, even if God pulls the trigger
excuse me, you got any Grey Poupon? ~ Poupon? ~ it popped in my head	long before God made angel and man, he made first beasts: leviathans

'less I take you first ~
really bought own press, this one
— you, sir, are no God

try to bind again, and you'll die before you start — nice pickle chips, though	you're same open book — I gotta find out from Death? hallucinations?

gonna stuff pie hole,
gonna drink, watch cartoon porn,
act like world will end

want to make amends ~
does it make you feel better?
~ no, you? ~ not a bit

you never left, Sam: you're still in the cage with me — my best torture yet	they held on inside — leviathans: they're so strong — I can't hold them back

Hello, Cruel World

Episode 128 (Season 7, Episode 2)
Directed by Guy Bee
Written by Ben Edlund
Original air date: September 30, 2011

---

come back with no soul —
Dean glues you back together:
magic amnesia

okay, so he's gone —
rest in peace, if that's in cards
— dumb son of a bitch

'cause you can't torture
someone who has nothing for
you to take away

seeing him right now?
you know that he's not real, right?
~ he says same of you

not under the sink ~
just sitting there, silently
field-stripping weapon

just lost your best friend,
your brother's in the bell jar,
purgatory's free

want couples yoga?
or you wanna get back to
hunting the big bads?

Bobby's running hub,
I'm 5150'd — leaves
you to follow lead

can't call deputy —
you and I killed zombies once,
you handle these things

you don't know what's real?
torture feels different than *this*
— stupid, crappy *this*

flesh-and-blood brother
— I can legitimately
kick ass in real time

you got away: you
got to make that stone number
one, and build on it

if you're gone, I swear:
going to strap brother in car
and drive off the pier

SEASON 7

The Girl Next Door

Episode 129 (Season 7, Episode 3)
Directed by Jensen Ackles
Written by Andrew Dabb & Daniel Loflin
Original air date: October 7, 2011

---

dude: Ricardo ~ what
happened? ~ *suicidio*
~ adiós, ese

round up library ~
those books were one-of-a-kind
~ why I stashed copies

Sam's working a case
identical to one he
had worked as a kid

Sam, you *are* a freak —
so was Hendrix, Picasso
— coolest people are

mom's not good person —
sometimes I don't think I'm a
good person, either

I'm a mortician;
I quietly take what I
need — no one gets hurt

you are a monster ~
you are a hunter, so you're
supposed to kill me

Sam opens the door
Dean punches Sam new rule: steal
my baby, get punched

she's dropping bodies
which means we gotta drop her
— it is that simple

next time you should change
plates — keeping the same tags makes
you easy to track

the only person
I'm going to kill is *you*
~ find me in a few

199

SEASON 7

Defending Your Life

Episode 130 (Season 7, Episode 4)
Directed by Robert Singer
Written by Adam Glass
Original air date: October 14, 2011

---

feels wonky working
a regular case ~ we're due
for some cut and dry

not on *us* to judge ~
except that is complete crap:
everyone judges

nothing but ground ball —
just got to put your mitt down
— you're Dean Winchester

(preparing to pick
up a chick — why the sudden
lack of confidence?)

weren't you happily
out of the family racket
'til Dean showed back up?

hunters: never kids —
I never was — I didn't
even stop to think

brother dragged you back
into catastrophic mess,
not to be alone

right thing would have been
send your ass back home to Mom
~ like to see you try

where will you find one? ~
Synagogue? ~ you're gonna steal
from temple? new low

you carry all kinds
of crap you don't have to, Dean
~ I am mostly crap

Shut Up, Dr. Phil

Episode 131 (Season 7, Episode 5)
Directed by Phil Sgriccia
Written by Brad Buckner & Eugenie Ross-Leming
Original air date: October 21, 2011

---

other guy boiled
in a hot tub ~ you do not
see a lot of that

no pockets in robes ~
didn't know you were expert
~ observe with my eyes

from a freaking flask?
really? on the job? ~ we are
always on the job

a "Bewitched" reference? ~
Nicole Kidman in remake
— a redhead, *hello*

tiny beating hearts —
that's never happened before
— hearts in my cupcakes

FBI agents
came on by asking questions
~ they're *hunters*, sweetheart

chicken feet not chilled? ~
you won't be leaving this room
— well, just not alive

domestic dispute:
if can't kill them, counsel them
~ not my area

punishment: kinky,
erotic, "clamps and feathers"
~ too deep there, cowboy

800 years of
this: remember renaissance?
~ oh, you're one to talk

just saved your marriage
~ to be fair, you also tried
to kill her, you know

there's *always* something
eating at me — I *always*
feel responsible

SEASON 7

Slash Fiction

*Episode 132 (Season 7, Episode 6)
Directed by John F. Showalter
Written by Robbie Thompson
Original air date: October 28, 2011*

---

used pattern-recog
software, basic heuristic
algorithm *shrugs*

you can't stop any
of us; we cannot be killed,
you stupid chew toys

wearing our faces,
Bobby, this is personal
~ I am with Dean here

psycho Butch, Sundance —
you're on CNN right now
— got teleporter?

I'm gonna enjoy
eating you, right down to hat,
everyone you know

I love life and its
infinite mysteries, but
you want to be dumb

they were out of "thanks
for saving me from liver-
eating surgeon" cards

lockdown — nobody
puts Baby in a corner:
Swayze gets a pass

• *Dean tries to pretend he doesn't love Air Supply* •

you want some tunes or
something? *turns on radio*
~ and what would you say

if called on you now,
and said that I can't hold on
~ sorry ~ just leave it

probably gonna
be the only thing that's on
~ there's no easy way

Slash Fiction (cont.)

it gets harder each
day, please love me or I will
be gone, I'll be gone

I'm all out of love —
I am so lost without you
— I know you were right

believing so long —
I am all out of love, what
am I without you?

I can't be too late
to say that I was so wrong
— what you thinking of?

• *Leviathan Sam and Leviathan Dean go all Pulp Fiction in a diner* •

:: he has one of these ::
:: every day — and he thinks that ::
:: they're as good as sex ::

:: plants with creamy goo — ::
:: like eating self-righteousness ::
:: — tell me which is worse ::

:: a hero complex ::
:: applications for sainthood ::
:: no relationships ::

:: he thinks he's funny :: ~
:: who has two thumbs and full-blown ::
:: bats in the belfry? ::

SEASON 7

Slash Fiction (cont.)

:: it is nothing but ::
:: Satan-vision on inside — ::
:: how he walks around… ::

:: do you wanna trade? :: ~
:: I like this one's hair better, ::
:: you stay in big one ::

:: fire up camera :: ~
:: everybody be cool, this ::
:: is a robbery ::

:: anybody moves, ::
:: I will execute every ::
:: last one of you *aims* ::

they hit St. Louis:
Pumpkin and Honey Bunny'd
Connor's diner there

you a Browning fan?
"man's reach should exceed his grasp"
~ :: that's lovely, Browning? ::

little SNAFU here
bobby kisses jody was
not expecting *that*

:: could be anything — ::
:: you're strong, uninhibited ::
:: you are smart enough ::

:: but you're so caught up ::
:: in *being good* and *taking* ::
:: *care of each other* ::

:: wasting perfectly ::
:: good opportunity to ::
:: subjugate the weak ::

to steal every last
soul, you mean — don't roofie me
and call it romance

The Mentalists

Episode 133 (Season 7, Episode 7)
Directed by Mike Rohl
Written by Ben Acker & Ben Blacker
Original air date: November 4, 2011

---

spirits of further,
will I win the Powerball?
I'm gonna be rich

you are a virile
manifestation of the
divine ~ what the hell?

sweetheart, look at them
they're FBI — I'm Russian:
we can spot the law

looking for something? ~
we're looking for a necklace
~ oh, how romantic

not good for siblings:
working together, being
around each other

they were not really
brothers — that was just cover
for their lifestyle

Ellen is concerned —
tell someone how bad it is,
or she'll kick your ass

if I've learned one thing,
it's that if something feels wrong,
it probably is

it's the pawn shop guy —
he goose-chased me to friggin'
pregnant yoga class

just a refill — if
you affirmate me, gonna
punch you in the face

I didn't trust her —
since Cas, I'm having hard time
trusting anybody

I don't like lying
to you — it doesn't feel right
— been climbing the walls

if I learned one thing
from that museum, it's that
sibling acts are tough

grading on a curve
has got me past everything
since kindergarten

Season Seven, Time for a Wedding!

Episode 134 (Season 7, Episode 8)
Directed by Tim Andrew
Written by Andrew Dabb & Daniel Loflin
Original air date: November 11, 2011

I'm in love and I'm
getting married — say something
~ congratulations

shouldn't she ask for
permission or…? ~ you want her
to ask for my hand?

met in erotic
horror section at book store
~ Becky, *T.M.I.*

don't know what mojo
you're working but I'll find out
~ Dean, that is my wife

that's what's bugging you:
I don't need you anymore,
moving on with life

Bobby said you'd be
all surly and premenstrual,
but hey, sticks and stones

trying to save you
from really bad accident
~ you threatening me?

Season Seven, Time for a Wedding! (cont.)

dosed with love potion
~ used a social lubricant
~ so, you roofied me

you're so pathetic,
it actually loops around
again back to cute

Sam would gank your ass ~
protective of my ass: one
of my best features

"Supernatural"
not exactly popular —
gonna show you off

I'm not a cheater,
I am an innovator —
it's called a loophole

not wall street — it's Hell —
we have a little something
called "integrity"

I gotta say man,
you don't suck ~ nicest any
ever said to me

I gotta say man,
for wack-job, pulled together
~ nicest ever said

SEASON 7

How to Win Friends and Influence Monsters

Episode 135 (Season 7, Episode 9)
Directed by Guy Bee
Written by Ben Edlund
Original air date: November 18, 2011

---

if didn't take belt
and pens, whole enchilada
would have offed itself

ranger for 12 years —
to tell you the truth, we have
no idea what's there

respect Mom Nature —
she'll string you up, eat your ass
right through the Gore-Tex

hostess will seat you —
do I *look* like a hostess?
~ *want* to look like a…?

that is good sandwich:
new pepperjack turducken
slammer — limited

bunch of birds shoved up
inside each other: top-three
most edible birds

talking 'bout Bambi ~
you don't shoot Bambi, jackass
— shoot Bambi's mother

ranger called in his
10-20 — his own will find
— we got crap to do

I could give two shakes
of a rat's ass — is that right?
do rats shake their ass?

I don't even care
anymore, and what's better?
don't *care* that I don't

all my crazy is
under just one umbrella
~ you always were deep

don't go Sigmund Freud
on me now okay, just got
drugged by a sandwich

I've been to enough
funerals — you die before
me, and I'll kill you

he almost took your
freaking head off — Bobby, your
hat — Bobby?… oh god…

SEASON 7

Death's Door

Episode 136 (Season 7, Episode 10)
Directed by Robert Singer
Written by Sera Gamble
Original air date: December 2, 2011

Karen? ~ who were you
expecting, Farrah Fawcett?
~ she always calls first

you're in a coma —
what happens: I climb in your
custard, fish you out

each time I opened
the door: another chapter
— the good, bad, bloody

crap you don't want to
think about — you bury it,
don't go there, *ever*

worst regret of life:
never got to get past this
— I'd say anything

he's not gonna die —
it's one bullet — he'll be fine
'cause he's always fine

laughing because scared,
or laughing because stupid?
~ I'll see you soon, Dick

you got handed a
small, unremarkable life,
did something with it

you have done enough,
believe me ~ I don't care ~ why?
~ because they're my boys

kids ain't supposed to
be grateful — supposed to eat
your food, break your heart

fate: I adopted
two boys and they grew up great;
they grew up heroes

did what had to do —
you learn that they never say
"thanks" when you save 'em

last memory, huh?
glad I saved the best for last
~ Bobby? stay or go?

SEASON 7

Adventures in Babysitting

Episode 137 (Season 7, Episode 11)
Directed by Jeannot Szwarc
Written by Adam Glass
Original air date: January 6, 2012

---

not leviathan! ~
oh sure, Dick Roman's not one,
Gwyneth Paltrow's not…

is no pill for *my*
situation, sweetie-pop
— you think it's easy?

Bobby didn't give
us coordinates to some
Cheeseville patch of weeds

well go out and kill   decide to be fine
something, or whatever you   until the end of the week,
kids do — blow off steam   and make yourself smile

now hand it over ~
I burned it — lucky for you:
memorized it first

Sam went to college? ~
you could, too: be hunter slash
pediatrician

did you ever know
anyone who left the life?
~ they all get killed first

Time After Time

Episode 138 (Season 7, Episode 12)
Directed by Phil Sgriccia
Written by Robbie Thompson
Original air date: January 13, 2012

---

how does sheriff in
Sioux Falls get Ohio case?
~ I'm just that nosy

I hope you're watching
cartoon smut ~ called anime,
and it's an art form

you gonna look up
more anime, or are you
strictly into Dick?

you are the same, just
68 years before me:
demons, ghosts, shifters

took him: ball of light ~
you guys get that a lot? ~ yeah,
more than most people

gotta get you in
some new clothes — you look like some
kind of bindle stiff

from future — gas costs
four bucks, cheese comes in spray can,
president: black guy

Time After Time (cont.)

awesome! ~ awesome? you
some religious kook? ~ no, he
just likes saying that

the "Biff strategy"
— betting races already
knows the outcome of

used to, 'cause that's what
family did, but they just
seem to keep dying

if he doesn't kick
in a skull every couple
of days, gets touchy

hunting's the only
clarity you're gonna find
— luckier than most

I'm gonna stay here
and keep my peepers on the
sheik and the sheba

1944
ain't so bad — go to Europe,
punch Hitler in neck

Dean picks up some mail
Back to the Future III — need
to borrow paper

something tells me you
used to kill three saps just for
change of scenery

want to know future?
your future's covered in thick,
black ooze — everywhere

SEASON 7

The Slice Girls

Episode 139 (Season 7, Episode 13)
Directed by Jerry Wanek
Written by Eugenie Ross-Leming & Brad Buckner
Original air date: February 3, 2012

---

actually call her?
she gave you her number ~ they
always give number

telling you: I've been
eating at the buffet of
strange all afternoon

Harmonia and
Ares produced Amazons
~ like Wonder Woman?

so, maybe you're ~ don't
say it ~ look, if that kid's yours
~ I said *don't say it*

in trouble — you're the
only person I can trust,
'cause you're my father

walk away right now,
and I won't go after you
~ I don't have a choice

don't care how you deal,
really — but just don't get killed
~ I'll do what I can

SEASON 7

Plucky Pennywhistle's Magical Menagerie

Episode 140 (Season 7, Episode 14)
Directed by Mike Rohl
Written by Andrew Dabb & Daniel Loflin
Original air date: February 10, 2012

---

find something quick — this
whole protocol du jour thing's
really creeping cheese

look for octovamp?
vamptopus? ~ that is crazy
even for us, right?

if fears run wild,
then it will affect kids long
into adulthood

what'd they do to you?
99.9%
of clowns can't hurt you

Billy drew me this ~
now unicorns are evil?
~ yeah, *obviously*

theory? they think the
ball-washer did it ~ the what?
~ ball-washer ~ what? ball-…

shark bite: 20-foot —
"shark week" — how do you *not* watch
a whole week of sharks?

land shark, dractopus,
seabiscuit the impaler
— srsly, what's next?

huge robot: it shoots
destructo-beams out of eyes
~ I'll see it coming

we used to come in
after hours… you ever
shroom in a ball pit?

getting my ass kicked
by those juggalos tonight
was therapeutic

Repo Man

Episode 141 (Season 7, Episode 15)
Directed by Thomas J. Wright
Written by Ben Edlund
Original air date: February 17, 2012

---

drunk tank, psych eval,
forced hold, a nice long stay at
an institution

why would you bring back
a demon in the first place?
~ not demon — Jeffrey

loved being possessed —
loved the connection, power
— him: love of my life

know you pretty well:
watched you torture innocent
man to get demon

you were so desperate
to fix the world — kills you that
people still get hurt

a life well-lived comes
from the structured pursuit of
meaning, happiness

suddenly there's a
devil's trap on the ceiling
(where did it come from?

who painted it? this
continuity error
has always bugged me)

got you, bunk buddy —
got my finger wiggling
'round in your brainpan

SEASON 7

Out with the Old

Episode 142 (Season 7, Episode 16)
Directed by John F. Showalter
Written by Robert Singer & Jenny Klein
Original air date: March 16, 2012

---

    no leviathan   dancers are toe-shoes
activity in Tromso ~   full of crazy — saw Black Swan:
where hell is Tromso?   tutu-on-tutu

you know, having a   getting the strong urge
cranky, total paranoid   to Prince Siegfried self into
as your go-to guy…   oblivion? yes

I wonder how old
porn kills you ~ pretty sure you
do not want to know.

live your life the way
you think would make her proud, or
not embarrass her

sleep deprivation   leviathans, here? ~
interrogation technique: lookin' at big, old, giant
trust me, it's torture   nesting doll of Dick

think you can crack it? ~   there's a bucket of
can a dog play poker? ~ I   that stuff you love throwing at
don't… ~ the answer's yes   us *right there* — dunk me

gooey son of bitch —
gonna tell what you're building,
or wash mouth with soap

The Born-Again Identity

Episode 143 (Season 7, Episode 17)
Directed by Robert Singer
Written by Sera Gamble
Original air date: March 23, 2012

---

longest human gone
without sleep? eleven days
— you wanted normal

we have pumped him as
full of sedatives as we
safely can so far

it's all snake oil:
last faith healer we found had
reaper on a leash

screw Cas! quit being
Dali frickin' Yoda 'bout
this, okay? — get pissed!

scale of 1 to 10 ~
not bad: 3 ~ your 10 must be
astronomical

I'm talking about
truly elegant torture
I've prepared for you

I saw his real face:
he was a demon ~ wack loads
of them walk the earth

Emanuel has
very special gifts ~ I've heard
you can heal people

SEASON 7

The Born-Again Identity (cont.)

keeping together
better than I thought — kind of
like pinned under bus

who gave you the name? ~
bouncybabynames.com
~ it's working for you

dude broke my brother's
head ~ he betrayed you — this dude
was your friend? ~ he's gone

don't know if he's dead,
I just know that this whole thing
can't be messier

of course it matters ~
no, you're not a machine, Dean
— you are a human

see if you can't turn
harmless little Cas into
angel-sized weapon

he bled on it? good —
question: any chance in hell
you got a lighter?

you just met yourself —
known you *years* — you're an angel
~ is that flirtation?

you got juice — you can
smite every demon in lot
~ don't remember how

can't make disappear,
but may be able to shift
— get Sam back on feet

beautiful, Clarence ~
I remember *everything*:
what I did, became

it's mutually
assured destruction — it is
not a demon deal

218

Party on, Garth

Episode 144 (Season 7, Episode 18)
Directed by Phil Sgriccia
Written by Adam Glass
Original air date: March 30, 2012

---

we got another
body up here ~ how is that
possible? *Garthed* her!

are you allergic
to a suit? ~ no, I just look
good in uniform

I'll can uniform,
go fed, and see you at the
brewery in 40

sad for brewery dudes —
now two kids get ganked by an
unknown freak-a-deek

no beer is worth, what
eight food awards? beer's not food
— it's what water is

Garth chugs beer ~ Garth are
you drunk? ~ I just drank a *whole*
beer — of *course* I'm drunk

Mr. Fizzles wants
to help ~ Mr. Fizzles will
go where sun don't shine

(on IMDB,
Fizzles is credited as
being played by self)

you even *get* drunk
anymore? it's kind of like
drinking vitamin

bottle holds shōjō —
alcohol spirit — not known
for being friendly

what happened in the
brewery? ~ nothing, was just my
imagination

who knows more about
being a ghost than Bobby?
instant Swayze, right?

SEASON 7

Of Grave Importance

Episode 145 (Season 7, Episode 19)
Directed by Tim Andrew
Written by Brad Buckner & Eugenie Ross-Leming
Original air date: April 20, 2012

---

you know she, Bobby
had a thing right? foxhole thing:
very Hemingway

she and I kind of
went Hemingway, too ~ you, *too?*
~ a lot of foxholes

better: even though
wish we could see him again,
doesn't mean we should

for the record, I
hated that Swayze movie:
romantic bullcrap

I'm Bobby, a ghost
hoping for a little ghost
orientation

is it me, or am
I being checked out? ~ no, stud,
I'm being checked out

dead, ghost, me: three words
don't want to use in sentence
— feel like I was drugged

I can kill werewolves,
fix a pinto, bake cornbread
— damned if can't get zen

Annie's here too — she
says you both look uglier
than she remembered

could be in Heaven
right now, not… ~ stuck here with you?
still have work to do

SEASON 7

The Girl with the Dungeons and Dragons Tattoo

Episode 146 (Season 7, Episode 20)
Directed by John MacCarthy
Written by Robbie Thompson
Original air date: April 27, 2012

• *Charlie dancing in the elevator* •

used to think maybe
you loved me, baby, I'm sure
— and I just can't wait

'til the day when you
knock on my door — every time
go for the mailbox

gotta hold self down,
'cause I just can't wait 'til you
write me: coming 'round

walking on sunshine,
I'm walking on sunshine, whoa
and don't it feel *good*

how'd it go last night?
moral imperative: live
vicariously

if can't score at a
reproductive rights function,
simply cannot score

historically had
problem with authority
~ you're completing me

how about a nice
game of chess? ~ War Games? shall we
play a game, bitches?

SEASON 7

The Girl with the
Dungeons and Dragons Tattoo (cont.)

Springsteen, Manning, our
own Charlie — know what they are?
irreplaceable

how long to crack drive?
~ a day ~ anything you *can't*
hack into? ~ not yet

didn't volunteer ~
totally… exactly… but,
now I volunteer

steal our resources?
make us some slaves? ~ planet-wide
value meal: we're meat

said if took longer
to hack, she deserved to be
eaten ~ I like her

did Hermione
run? ~ of course not — she kicked ass
— *I'm* gonna kick ass

Leia, bikini,
straddling d20 — drunk,
it was comic-con

one in a million:
you invent guns and iPads,
viruses — crafty

Dean gives Charlie a
Cyrano de Bergerac
-esque flirting lesson

this ain't the first time —
you think my name is really
Charlie Bradbury?

peace out, bitches ~ she's
kinda like the little sis
I never wanted

Reading is Fundamental

Episode 147 (Season 7, Episode 21)
Directed by Ben Edlund
Written by Ben Edlund
Original air date: May 4, 2012

---

and one day, college
will not matter anymore
~ you're out of your mind

that sound like someone
saying, "no, wait, stop" to you?
~ yeah ~ *Dean shrugs* oh, well

baffled? frankly I'm
offended — this is not the
way weather behaves

look: walking, talking ~
hello, Dean — pull my finger
...my finger, pull it

been like naked guy
at the rave since he woke up:
totally useless

today in garden,
I followed a honeybee:
saw route of flowers

all that thorny pain
~ I do not like poetry
— put up or shut up

cat's penis sharply
barbed along its shaft — females
were not consulted

I don't like conflict
Cas zaps away *tablet breaks*
~ in the dayroom now

SEASON 7

Reading is Fundamental (cont.)

what the hell *are* you? ~
Kevin Tran — I'm in advanced
placement — don't kill me

neanderthals — their
poetry was amazing:
perfect tune with spheres

shoves game off table
forget the game ~ I'm sorry
~ no: *playing* "Sorry"

you smote thousands, then
gave a big speech — what was that?
~ well, *rude* for one thing

all right, we'll go to
the cabin — the kid can do
his book report there

screw the garrison —
we need the tablet to end
Dick's *Soylent Us* crap

you're in our corner ~
no, I don't fight anymore,
I just watch the bees

angels: they don't care —
they don't have the equipment
— just breaks them apart

figured one thing out:
you find a cause and serve it;
it orders your life

very touch of you
corrupts: when Cas laid a hand
on you, he was lost

well, you know me — I
am always happy to bleed
for the Winchesters

SEASON 7

There Will Be Blood

Episode 148 (Season 7, Episode 22)
Directed by Guy Bee
Written by Andrew Dabb & Daniel Loflin
Original air date: May 11, 2012

---

might want to slow down:
don't look so hot ~ I'm in veil
— Brad Pitt days: over

keep your friends close, and
enemies blah, blah — needless
to say: I keep tabs

gonna go into
toxic shock — I need road food
~ Roman's banking on

I cannot do this —   so, now you want to
I can't live on rabbit food   prevent extermination
— I'm a *warrior*   of vampire race?

any way you slice:
Pac-Man, True Blood in same room,
and that is bad news

hate having to wait   (self-awareness: these
and try again next season   characters know this is a
~ I'm looking forward   television show?)

225

SEASON 7

Survival of the Fittest

Episode 149 (Season 7, Episode 23)
Directed by Robert Singer
Written by Sera Gamble
Original air date: May 18, 2012

I suppose you want
it in writing? ~ I don't kiss
on the mouth ~ your loss

on my car, he showed
up naked — covered in *bees*
~ not sorry missed *that*

emo boy zaps me
back here ~ why? ~ go ask *him*, he
was *your* boyfriend first

cosmetics testing
needed? how important is
lipstick to you, Dean?

no insects up there —
here: trillions making silk,
honey, miracles

prefer insects to
angels — offer: honey — I
collected myself

now, please accept this
sandwich as a gesture of
solidarity

shifty, what's problem? ~
do we need a cat? this place
feels one species short

so what's it feel like? ~
what, going vengeful? it's an
itch you can't scratch out

don't do it to scratch —
do it 'cause it's the job, and
when it's your time, *go*

here's running into
you guys on the other side
— not too soon, all right?

I see now it's a
punishment resurrection:
it's worse every time

bottom of the ninth,
I'd rather have you, cursed or
not ~ we are *all* cursed

don't want to make you
uncomfortable — I detect
note of forgiveness

Survival of the Fittest (cont.)

well I'm probably
gonna die tomorrow, so…
~ well, I'll go with you

what's the plan? ~ Dick knows
we're coming, so we're gonna
announce ourselves *big*

• *Baby's back and "Born to be Wild"* •

get motor runnin'
and head out on the highway,
look for adventure

whatever comes our
way — go and make it happen
take the world in a

love embrace — fire
all of your guns at once and
explode into space

every soul here is
a monster ~ telling me we're
in purgatory?

this is where they come
to prey upon each other
for eternity

how do we get out? ~
afraid we're much more likely
to be ripped to shreds

SEASON EIGHT

SEASON 8

We Need to Talk About Kevin

Episode 150 (Season 8, Episode 1)
Directed by Robert Singer
Written by Jeremy Carver
Original air date: October 3, 2012

• *Dean revives Benny after purgatory, "Man in the Wilderness"* •

another year has
passed me by — still I look at
myself, and I cry

what kind of man have
I become? all the years spent
in search of myself

and I am still in
the dark, 'cause I can't seem to
find the light alone

I feel like a man
in the wilderness — lonely
soldier off to war

sent away to die,
never knowing why, sometimes
makes no sense at all

it makes no sense at
all ~ this better be you, you
son of a bitch *digs*

standing too close to
exploding Dick sends your ass
to purgatory

Cas is dead? you saw? ~
I saw enough ~ you're not sure?
~ *said* I saw enough

ditched the phones — something
happened to me this year, too:
don't hunt anymore

always ignored that
'cause of our deep, abiding
love for each other

voice mails span 6 months
our responsibility —
couldn't answer phone!

no visible signs
of douchery… *sniffs* does it
smell like dog to you?

We Need to Talk About Kevin (cont.)

take a breath, calm down —
where's the angel? ~ you're human
~ the angel? ~ don't know

did what I promised
we'd do: I moved on, lived life
~ yeah, I'm getting that

the rules are simple:
don't take joint from guy named Don,
and no dogs in car

was bloody, messy —
bottom-dwelling nasties, but
being there felt pure

I show you the door,
hump my soul to other side
~ looking for soul train?

wouldn't protect *him* ~
you two had a thing ~ yeah, when
going to Princeton

prophet has not shown
his face, but you should know: Dean
Winchester is back

told Crowley: Hell gate —
instead: destroying demons
~ you son of a bitch

what happened to you? ~
Cliffs Notes: Sam hit dog, I went
to purgatory

he's in it, whether
he likes it or not ~ free will:
that's only for you?

where's your angel? ~ ask
your mother ~ there's that grade-school
zip — really missed it

Channing, there is a
demon in you; you're going
to your safety school

purgatory was
pure — I'm kinda wishing I
appreciated

SEASON 8

What's Up, Tiger Mommy?

Episode 151 (Season 8, Episode 2)
Directed by John F. Showalter
Written by Andrew Dabb & Daniel Loflin
Original air date: October 10, 2012

---

she's bait, man, plain and
simple — and you want to swim
right up, bite the hook?

we need to find the
tablet, whip up the spell: boom
— sun, sandy beaches

you've seen exorcist? ~
is *that* what you've been doing?
watch *television*?

pull out of fire,
jump right back in ~ like *I* can
tell her what to do

have to get inked up —
you too — keeps the demons out
~ not my first tattoo

hey, how'd you do that
reverse-exorcism thing? ~
said the verse backward

pawn shop: first and main ~
three days' journey: follow stream
— you'll find angel there

What's Up, Tiger Mommy? (cont.)

what's it going to be?
the tablet, or that piece of
crap you call a car?

God's right hand: Plutus
~ that a planet anymore?
~ it's the god of greed

course he can swing it,
if bumper stickers on my
car mean anything

heart was in right place ~
think too much heart was always
Castiel's problem

purgatory hug
damn it is good to see you —
nice peach fuzz ~ thank you

94%
of psychotics think they're sane
— ask selves "what is sane?"

I prayed to you, Cas ~
I'm an angel in land of
abominations

buddy, I need you;
not leaving here without you
~ it's too dangerous

you're bidding the moon? ~
think man named Buzz goes to space
without making deal?

about sacrifice —
her soul is most valuable
thing: it's everything

Winchesters have a
habit of using people,
watch them die bloody

it would have sucked, and
I would have hated myself —
what's one more nightmare?

SEASON 8

Heartache

Episode 152 (Season 8, Episode 3)
Directed by Jensen Ackles
Written by Brad Buckner & Eugenie Ross-Leming
Original air date: October 17, 2012

---

guy gets heart ripped out
~ I'm guessing literally
~ way that interests me

innocent people
supposed to die so that you
can shop for produce?

ritual, or some
sort of heart-sucking, possessed
satanic, crack-bat

don't know about you,
but this last year has given
me new perspective

when things happen that
aren't supposed to, they are called
accidents, I think

you're seriously
talking 'bout hanging it up?
~ looking at options

used to say the heart
was key — that was the focus
of sacrifice

could be the same guy?
for a 95-year old,
Brick Holmes could take hit

*boys enter locker
room of the strip club* smell that?
~ you're gross *Dean shrugs, nods*

if I go real slow,
can show you your own beating
heart before you die

when this is over:
finished with Kevin, tablet
— I'm done — I mean that

never had normal,
got to see what that felt like
— I want that, had that

SEASON 8

Bitten

Episode 153 (Season 8, Episode 4)
Directed by Thomas J. Wright
Written by Robbie Thompson
Original air date: October 24, 2012

I bet one of these
girls would let you partake in
their awkward-guy phase

in 5 years, I will
be in middle of ocean,
my girl by my side

come on, we both know
he has nobody else to
do this with — rain check

is it just me, or
are you getting a workplace
romance vibe from them?

bit by alien? ~
maybe mutant ~ am I a
superhero now?

could be dealing with
another Mayan God ~ other
one was such a joy

started talking 'bout
you, I saw red — next thing I
remember: ran home

Bitten (cont.)

eat heart: self defense?
who you trying to convince,
Kate, me or yourself?

I didn't eat for
like a year — clear eyes and clogged
arteries, can't lose

he just sets up shop:
everything's wine, roses and
animal tickers

not FBI — I'm
sure FBI agents don't
say "awesome" that much

impossible to
control the monster inside;
I fell off wagon

done living in your
shadow — have always lived in
it — now we're equals

I just wanted you
to know that Michael wasn't
always a monster

I didn't choose this —
I've never hurt anyone;
please give me a chance

Blood Brother

Episode 154 (Season 8, Episode 5)
Directed by Guy Bee
Written by Ben Edlund
Original air date: October 31, 2012

---

if you kill me, I
know where I'm going, who I'll
see when I get there

was trying to kill
Crowley, who happened to be
wearing Kevin's mom

Sam, last I counted
you took a year off from the
job — I need a day

most wounds will mend up,
vampirically speaking — soon
100%

I am not your aunt —
no possible relation
to sibling offspring

gonna shove your ass
back through eye of that needle
if kills all of us

vampire pirates:
vampirates ~ can't believe no
one ever thought that

Blood Brother (cont.)

we are real, Benny,
this is real — it's the only
way to play this game

stalk helpless women,
break into their motel room,
and fix their plumbing?

you don't know him, he's
a friend ~ you don't have any:
all your friends are dead

you didn't hide it
from me, Benny — I chose you
~ why'd you stay with them?

all I could salvage
from my wayward son — wanted
to remember you

I saw something in humanity — I drink blood, I don't drink people	evil, after all — at least I've had that much to keep me cold at night
come from nowhere and quote "seen a lot of stitches" — it's pretty creepy	what I loved ain't here — snuffed out a long time ago by monsters like me

why resurrect me?
Dean, you could have drained my soul
into a culvert

Southern Comfort

Episode 155 (Season 8, Episode 6)
Directed by Tim Andrew
Written by Adam Glass
Original air date: November 7, 2012

---

think Benny's different?
says he's not drinking live blood?
and you believe him?

I can't help but ask
myself: when is my thing *not*
decapitation?

hold up — are you the
new Bobby? ~ you shut your mouth
~ yes ~ *you* shut your mouth

ectoplasm is
usually black, right? *Garth tastes*
~ it's ectoplasm

in purgatory ~
the purgatory? ~ no the
one in Miami

hillbilly hankies?
civil war: over ~ that's a
touchy subject here

you were a dentist? ~
yeah, for just a hot minute
— where I got first case

SEASON 8

Southern Comfort (cont.)

---

you killed the tooth fairy? ~
yeah, not my proudest moment;
I felt terrible

what do we got, a
ghost with oedipus complex?
don't know what that means

easy there, flyweight —
last time drank a beer, had to
pick you up off floor

we do this tonight? ~
burn confederate soldier
in town of rednecks

Bobby belonged to
all of us — not just you, Sam
— using what he taught

send this joker home ~
Karl sniffs Dean seductively
the specter likes you

:: you never even ::
:: wanted this life — always blamed ::
:: me: pulling you in ::

:: drinking demon blood, ::
:: cahoots with ruby, lost soul, ::
:: running with Samuel ::

:: those aren't mistakes, Sam ::
:: those are choices — might have lied, ::
:: *never* betrayed you ::

:: Cas let me down, you ::
:: let me down — the only one ::
:: who hasn't: Benny ::

why didn't penny
jack you? ~ I let all that go
with help of yogi

240

SEASON 8

A Little Slice of Kevin

Episode 156 (Season 8, Episode 7)
Directed by Charles Robert Carner
Written by Eugenie Ross-Leming & Brad Buckner
Original air date: November 14, 2012

---

*Crowley torturing
Samandriel* this hurts you
more than it hurts me

no reason to *keep*
torturing — once get going
really hard to stop

I hired a witch:
scrappy, reliable, and
she's willing to kill

if it doesn't work,
thank you for everything ~ no
one gets left behind

had to scratch, claw, kill,
and bleed to find that portal
— almost finished me

lie — don't get lied *to* —
aren't you all about faith? ~ not
particularly

always deliver
the goods, and *then* you get paid
— even hookers know

Kevin a prophet? ~
not sure what happened to Chuck,
but he must be dead

SEASON 8

A Little Slice of Kevin (cont.)

---

don't quite understand
your hesitation ~ well, you
just killed my mother

I did everything
I could do to get you out
— I did not leave you

humans can't possess
this thing — what was God thinking?
we'll get back to that

which is it, madman,
or megalomaniac? ~
Kevin comes with me

can get it up, but
can't keep it up — you're bluffing
~ want to take that chance?

failed you, like I've failed
every godforsaken thing
that I care about

nothing you could have
done would have saved me, because
didn't want to be

report in to me;
you will never remember
~ no, I won't do that

Hunteri Heroici

Episode 157 (Season 8, Episode 8)
Directed by Paul Edwards
Written by Andrew Dabb
Original air date: November 28, 2012

Garth has a safe-house-
boat? ~ dude, I don't even ask
questions anymore

what is the word, Cas? ~
it's a shortened version of
my name ~ yes, I meant…

turned radio off:
block subsonic frequencies
— could draw diagram

what's word on the word?
any tablet chatter on
angel radio?

so what now? move to
Vermont and open up a
charming B&B?

I could be third wheel ~
that's not a good thing ~ a third
wheel adds extra grip

he suffered from a
mild bladder infection ~
stop smelling dead guy

freaking suburbs, man ~
so, she is not a witch ~ just
the best wife ever

just do not use the
words "moist" or "irregardless"
~ there goes opener

Bugs Bunny ~ some sort
of insect-rabbit hybrid?
how do we kill it?

I have one question
for you: *slams table* why did
you kill your husband?

bird represents God;
coyote: man — endlessly
chasing the divine

Hunteri Heroici (cont.)

I need four hours ~
I don't — I'll watch over you
~ not gonna happen

you boys chase crazy,
or does the crazy chase you?
~ depends on the day

I devastated
Heaven, vaporized thousands
— I cannot go back

because if I see
what Heaven's become, afraid
I might kill myself

it's wabbit season ~
I do not think you pronounced
that word correctly

you cannot tell me
that this place doesn't give you
the heebs and/or jeebs

worst thing can happen
to a guy that's got a mind
like mine? losing it

the cat talks sometimes
~ I'll interrogate the cat
...I've almost cracked him

been dealing with this
crazy for months — you bring a
gun to a gag fight?

trying to keep that
dream alive will destroy you,
destroy everything

Citizen Fang

Episode 158 (Season 8, Episode 9)
Directed by Nick Copus
Written by Daniel Loflin
Original air date: December 5, 2012

---

vamps in Carencro ~
it's been a while since I've
had some étouffée

Occam's razor: keep
it simple, stupid — it's not
that complicated

found someone to hold
myself accountable to:
my great-granddaughter

what in the world could
a *Winchester* possibly
owe a vampire?

each relationship
I have ever had has gone
to crap at some point

I got a body
with two holes in it, and just
heard you went fishing

the one thing I can
say about Benny: he has
never let me down

I will respect her
decision — if you love her
you will do the same

guys like us, we don't
get a home, you know, we don't
get a family

tell her about all
the dead — tell her about the
monster that you are

SEASON 8

Torn and Frayed

Episode 159 (Season 8, Episode 10)
Directed by Robert Singer
Written by Jenny Klein
Original air date: January 16, 2013

---

like it or not, that
is the truth — there was a time
when that meant something

you save a vampire
by making me think that the
woman I love: dead?

Cas watches Dean sleep
how many times I gotta
tell you: it's creepy

torture an angel,
it screams — that kind of pain makes
a ripple effect

I am gonna need
exact words ~ you serious?
~ that's serious face

not just manifest
through shrubbery, but to burn
— we have to find him

you've every torture
instrument known to man but
Neil Diamond album

Torn and Frayed (cont.)

I mean, come on — how
long does it take to get a
calf skull from Egypt?

I can't enjoy a
world I need to save — right now
none more important

I need both of you,
as they say, to "stow your crap"
— able to do that?

protecting the word
of God seems to be hardwired
into these dingbats

what did I just do? ~
you killed a traitor ~ I was
trying to atone

could not separate
from job — it's time for one of
us to be happy

both feet in or both
out — anything in between
is what gets you dead

everything you've done
for me, will never forget,
but this is the end

SEASON 8

LARP and the Real Girl

Episode 160 (Season 8, Episode 11)
Directed by Jeannot Szwarc
Written by Robbie Thompson
Original air date: January 23, 2013

---

working on a case —
long as waiting on Kevin,
that'll be our fun

she heard a TV,
or was having a bad dream,
or was high as balls

"you shall bleed for your
crimes against us," followed by
skull emoticon

"I will destroy you"
oh, these kids today with their
texting and murder

what I want in a
duel is *un*-magic wand
— fake wands! it's a game!

besides creepy mark,
only thing these guys have in
common is LARPing

take your leave to my
medical tent, and attend
to your severed limbs

why do I have such
bad luck? what am I, some kind
of monster magnet?

ME said that he
was killed by belladonna
~ the porn star? ~ poison

you sent Sam a phantom
text from his ex? dick move, sir
~ not finest hour

are we still talking
about Sam, or did *you* break
up with someone, too?

here, I am a queen —
a hero — out there I am
just hacking out code

if not for you, Dick
wins — out there in the real world
you *are* a hero

I see a lot of
these maidens checking you out
~ I can't shut this down

LARP and the Real Girl (cont.)

may I have a moment?
handmaiden? take phone, find Sam
— we'll find shadow dorks

just an IT girl,
standing in front of monster,
asking not to kill

dark magic ~ my eyes!
the stinging of your attack
burns my very soul

Gilda, my name is
Charlie Bradbury, and I'm
here to rescue you

wow, real magic — that's
really cool, if not mostly
terrifying *gulp*

can't bang a fairy,
about to lose crown, but yeah
— I'm totally good

• *Dean's Braveheart speech* •

dying in your beds
many years from now, would you
be willing to trade

all the days, from this
day to that day for one chance ~
isn't that speech from?

only one he knows ~
just one chance to come back here,
tell our enemies

they may take our lives
but they will never take ~ hold
~ my bad ~ our freedom!

demigods, druids,
and chamber pot servants who
gave their lives fighting

this episode is
dedicated to the men,
women, elves, magi

for the Queen of Moons
— go bravely into the next
world, fallen soldiers

SEASON 8

As Time Goes By

Episode 161 (Season 8, Episode 12)
Directed by Serge Ladouceur
Written by Adam Glass
Original air date: January 30, 2013

---

when one of *us* falls
out of *your* closet, then you
can ask the questions

looks at Baby's tags
2013 — my god,
the Mayans were wrong

alpha male monkey
violence will not help you
to comprehend this

dudes time traveling
through motel room closets: that
is what we've come to

H.G. Wells left Dad
high, dry when he was a kid
~ maybe he got stuck

Dad made up for that
by being father of year
~ always there for us

you'd need an ancient
demon-killing knife of Kurds
~ that is what this is

our father taught us
how to be hunters ~ you're not
hunters are you? apes?

As Time Goes By (cont.)

we are preceptors,
beholders, chroniclers
what can't understand

we share with a few
trusted hunters: the elite
~ Yodas to Jedis

symbol for speaking
to the dead — you boys ever
exhume a body?

John was legacy:
I was supposed to teach him
ways of the letters

learned things the hard way:
wife taken by a demon,
killed by one himself

gonna whip up a
blood spell, Marty McFly back
to 1950s

when Dad died, couldn't
save him — I never want that
to happen to Sam

you are Winchesters —
as long as you are alive
there is always hope

Winchesters, Campbells:
brains and brawn ~ family tree:
a whole lot of dead

would have made difference
if own father was around?
~ did the best he could

Everybody Hates Hitler

Episode 162 (Season 8, Episode 13)
Directed by Phil Sgriccia
Written by Ben Edlund
Original air date: February 6, 2013

---

the alarm call that
ended the Men of Letters ~
think we found the bat cave

you know damn well we
could use a break — what if we
finally got one?

your sinister friend ~
don't believe being followed?
no one ever does

necromancers? ~ yeah
from world of whatever-craft
brother always plays

• *Dean's "gay thing"* •

I'm Agent Bolan ~
really? wow, I thought you were
like a headhunter

this is maybe *third*
time I'm seeing you today
— why you following?

oh, so we, um, we
didn't have a thing back there?
~ back where? w-what now?

sorry, thought we had
thing back at quad: a little
"eye magic" moment

and I saw you here,
and I figured I would wait
until you were done

then maybe we might ~
yeah, okay, but no moment
— this is a federal

investigation ~
is that supposed to make you
less interesting?

no, I'm sorry man,
I hope I didn't freak you
out or anything

SEASON 8

Everybody Hates Hitler (cont.)

I-I'm not freaked out,	you have a good night ~
it's just a federal thing	you-you *Dean runs into chair*
— okay, citizen	have a… uh, okay

you being followed? ~	what you're saying is:
I thought I was, earlier —	we didn't have a moment?
turned out: a gay thing	~ I was tailing you

he was my gay thing —
that was good, really had me;
that was very smooth

shaped from clay, brought to
life by rabbis to protect
the Jewish people

Thule Society —
Nazi necromancers — dark
magic with the dead

*Sam and Dean salt and
burn the corpse* ~ oh my god, these
guys are psychopaths

these thin vellum-y	how about: you screw
pages: perfect for rolling	yourself, you Nazi bastard
— clay man instructions	~ talk about this? ~ pass

SEASON 8

Trial and Error

Episode 163 (Season 8, Episode 14)
Directed by Kevin Parks
Written by Andrew Dabb
Original air date: February 13, 2013

Kevin's hideout called
"Fizzles' Folly" — named after
a damned sock puppet

never had own room —
I'm making this awesome; got
my kick-ass vinyl

I've got this killer
mattress — it's memory foam
— it remembers me

and it is clean, too:
there's no funky smell, there's no
creepy motel stains

a real kitchen now ~
you know what a kitchen is?
~ I'm nesting, okay?

gonna feel dirty
saying this, but you might want
salad and shower

God wants us to take
SATs ~ works in douchey,
mysterious ways

kid should eat something
not ground hooves, pigs' anuses
— nothing wrong with that

between claws and teeth
and invisibility,
those bitches: bitches

should we talk to her? ~
so she can lie to us and
then call the cops? no

gotta man the grill ~
impressed? ~ I like a man who
can handle his meat

you're hot — you want to
go to my room and have sex?
I'm feeling my oats

see if I can't gank
Huckleberry Hound before
he makes his next move

Trial and Error (cont.)

• Dean tries to convince Sam that Dean ought to be the one to do the trials, because he doesn't see his own self-worth •

both know where this ends
one of us dies or worse ~ just
decided it's you?

I am a grunt, Sam —
you've always been the brains of
this operation

you see a light at
the end of this ugly-ass
tunnel — *I* do not

wife, kids, and grandkids —
living 'til you're fat, bald, and
chugging viagra

gonna die with a
gun in my hand — that's all I
have waiting for me

that is my perfect
ending, and it's the only
one I'm gonna get

want you to get out,
have a life, become Man of
Letters, whatever

gonna do trials,
I'm gonna do them alone
— that's end of story

you are staying here
I'm going out there — land shark
comes knocking, call me

and if you try to
follow me, gonna put a
bullet in your leg

SEASON 8

Trial and Error (cont.)

stupid move, Ellie ~
did it for my mom — what would
you do for *your* mom?

you need to go to
a hospital ~ I've had worse
~ yeah, he has had worse

---

*• Sam tries to convince Dean that Sam ought to be the one
to do the trials, because dammit, Dean,
you're not as worthless as you think •*

I'm closing the gates
— it's a suicide mission;
I want to *survive*

I want to live, and
so should you — you have friends here,
you have family

I mean, hell, you have
even got your own room now
— you were right, okay?

I'm smart, so are you —
you're not a grunt, you're genius
when it comes to lore

light at the end of
tunnel — if you come with me,
can take you to it

you are the best damn
hunter I have ever seen:
better than me, Dad

I believe in you
(Sam's always believed in Dean)
please believe in me

SEASON 8

Man's Best Friend with Benefits

Episode 164 (Season 8, Episode 15)
Directed by John F. Showalter
Written by Brad Buckner & Eugenie Ross-Leming
Original air date: February 20, 2013

---

total episodes:
three hundred twenty seven
— this one is halfway

of all the lame-ass
things you've ever said, gotta
be lame-assiest

Shemp was funnier ~
Curly was freaking genius
~ he's too obvious

just showed up at door;
she wanted her belly scratched
~ she can stay the night

lose the ignorant
bigotry for two seconds
~ that was pretty hot

we don't fit ~ how do
you reconcile what you
are with what you do?

rookie detective
to lieutenant overnight?
booga on his side

it's not a sure thing ~
anything we *ever* do
a sure thing? ~ well, no

it is not that you
don't trust me — it is that you
can only trust *you*

meet Phillippe LeChat ~
Dean sneezes weird, that only
happens around cats

what I told you last
night: how you're imagining
it ~ what? no, that's… yes

I'll hand it to you:
not one bestiality
joke's come out of you

the only way we've
made it through it all is by
hanging together

257

SEASON 8

Remember the Titans

Episode 165 (Season 8, Episode 16)
Directed by Steve Boyum
Written by Daniel Loflin
Original air date: February 27, 2013

---

no Cas, Kevin is
taking his time, you're acting
cagey — need a lead

guts pecked out, frozen
face — people don't walk away
from that — *zombies* do

holy crap that's him ~
that's the dead guy? ~ dead, my ass
— that's a zombie, boys

I'm disappointed ~
you wanted to shoot zombies?
~ damn straight, shoot zombies

your son currently,
but temporarily: dead
— I'll let that one slide

I die once a day —
after few hours, I'm back
~ a real-life Kenny?

summon the bastard,
work him over until he
un-does what he did

what has Jason Bourne
skills, dies a lot, violent
women? ~ don't know, you?

the Men of Letters:
a secret society
— we are legacies

didn't he steal fire? ~
he Ocean's Eleven'd Mt.
Olympus, stole flames

it just goes to show
that we must all leave room for
happy accidents

alright, we've never
battled a god-curse before
— hope we can break it

she has lost a step:
not really worship-worthy
~ trash-talking a god?

Remember the Titans (cont.)

so, Artemis loved
Prometheus? how did you
know? ~ intuition

long Clark Griswold life,
full of prostate exams and
colonoscopies

not on my watch — if
you die, gonna be because
of something normal

• *Dean prays to Cas for help with Sam* •

Cas, you got ears on?
know I'm not one for praying,
because in my book

it's same as begging —
this is about Sam, so I
need you to hear me

going into this
deal blind, don't know what's ahead
…what it'll bring Sam

now, he's covering
pretty good, but I know that
he is hurting *nods*

supposed to be me —
so, for all that we've been through,
I am asking you

you keep a lookout
for little brother, okay?
where the hell are you?

SEASON 8

Goodbye Stranger

Episode 166 (Season 8, Episode 17)
Directed by Thomas J. Wright
Written by Robbie Thompson
Original air date: March 20, 2013

---

no hesitation:
quick, brutal — everything's in
order, finally

would it have killed these
asshats to label boxes:
not hieroglyphics?

we should leave in 5 —
need time with Miss October?
~ oh yeah, make it 10

heard me, didn't you? ~
you prayed to him? ~ yes, I heard
— that's not why I'm here

would be more helpful
if they knew everything ~ lie
— they can't be trusted

hoping demon more
knowledgeable than others
interrogated

he puts "ass" in Cas —
hasn't been right since got back
from purgatory

if sketchy, why pray? ~
I can hear you both; I *am*
a celestial

the hostage is in
there ~ aren't you a little short
for a stormtrooper?

innocent people
died to buy yourself some time?
~ I'm Meg, a demon

saw you Zero Dark
Thirty that demon — you were
more than persuasive

really know how to
make a girl's nethers quiver,
don't you? ~ I'm aware

why are you so sweet
on me Clarence? ~ I don't know,
nor who "Clarence" is

kill you to read book? ~
with proper spells, book could kill,
theoretically

Goodbye Stranger (cont.)

    yes, I remember
the pizza man, and it is
     a good memory

      miss simplicity:
I was bad and you were good
     — life was easier

I'm kind of good, which
sucks; you're kind of bad, which is
all manner of hot

    subatomic and
electromagnetic field
~ bottom line, Bill Nye

kill him — you've done this
a thousand times, Castiel;
you're ready — kill him

you want to live a
long, normal life away from
creepy things like me

I laughed, I cried, I
puked in my mouth a little
— I kind of get it

   got you off hunting?
that's one rare creature — how'd you
   meet this unicorn?

Cas, this isn't you —
it's me, we're family — we
need you — *I* need you

Castiel? so that's
who's been poking my boys, and
not in sexy way

love it when you get
all tough — touches me right where
my bathing suit goes

   can't carry burden
that comes with these trials, but
    I can carry *you*

you just quoted "Lord
of the Rings" ~ Rudy hobbit
always gets a pass

SEASON 8

Goodbye Stranger (cont.)

• *"Goodbye Stranger" — Cas takes the tablet on the road, alone* •

undisputed truth:
have to have things my own way,
keep me in my youth

ship without anchor,
slave without chain — just the thought
of those sweet ladies

sends a shiver through
my veins — and I will go on
shining like brand new

I will never look
behind me, troubles will be
few — goodbye stranger

it's been nice, hope you
find your paradise — tried to
see your point of view

hope your dreams come true—
goodbye Mary, goodbye Jane
— will we meet again?

feel no sorrow, shame —	it's not for me — just
come tomorrow, feel no pain	give me motion, set me free
— it's sweet devotion	in land and ocean

Freaks and Geeks

Episode 167 (Season 8, Episode 18)
Directed by John F. Showalter
Written by Adam Glass
Original air date: March 27, 2013

---

make sure you're okay ~
like my feelings? ~ if that's what
you want talk about

get some herbal tea,
find Cowboy Junkies on the
dial ~ eat me, Dean

sneaking out to hunt
with the Apple Dumpling Gang?
do for kicks these days?

never too young to
kill monsters — especially
ones killed family

kids' school for hunters? ~
don't be such a dweeb, okay?
we're not the X-Men

what, after soccer
practice and the bake sale, they
chop vampires' heads off?

when I found them, they
were lost, confused, angry — I
gave them family

SEASON 8

Freaks and Geeks (cont.)

next generation
hunters have to be better
~ better than what? ~ us

once they get revenge,
they'll be better hunters than
any of us dreamed

kids don't have to live
how we did: crappy motels
no life, family

we don't kill people ~
not a person — a monster
~ Krissy, this ends bad

you think he's lying? ~
or wrong ~ never trust a guy
who wears a sweater

gonna let him live? ~
yeah, all alone with himself:
no family, no friends

why care about her? ~
hunting not always about
killing, like I said

alright for old guy ~
I am really not that old
~ keep telling yourself

I know, you'll kill me
if I hurt her, blah, blah, blah
~ no, no — *she'll* kill you

they are hunters now —
there is only one way out
and it ain't pretty

maybe if we shut
that hell-hole once and for all,
can have a real life

SEASON 8

Taxi Driver

Episode 168 (Season 8, Episode 19)
Directed by Guy Norman Bee
Written by Eugenie Ross-Leming & Brad Buckner
Original air date: April 3, 2013

---

an innocent soul
has to be rescued from Hell,
delivered: Heaven

if cross the border
into Hell: visitors pass
~ you want *into* Hell?

this isn't what I
paid for — I booked the Hell tour
~ it's Hell-adjacent

patience isn't one of my virtues — well, I don't *have* any virtues	cute when they're little — they turn into teenagers and party's over
your free pedicure: made Dean swear to never tell how it changed your life	don't try to spin this — you think I don't know that you told him to kill me
Winchester jumbo breaking into mothership; prophet translating	hoping Cas returns — admire your loyalty — wish he felt the same

Bobby stabs a Sam ~
you *knew* somehow, right? ~ took a
chance: 50/50

265

SEASON 8

Taxi Driver (cont.)

guess I let you down ~
just happy to hear from you ~
you might change your mind

when Dean Winchester
asks you for a favor, he's
not screwing around

you got access to
the place ~ by "access" you mean
"getting beheaded"

you're right, it's too much ~
you know I love a challenge
~ you are serious?

you tell Dean "goodbye"
— I was never any good
up there anyway

I'm not a good fit —
not with vampires, and for
sure not with humans

Benny got us out —
a bunch of vamps showed, and he
used himself as bait

we had agreement ~
I know that agreement — that's
a non-agreement

all things considered —
ornery as hell, of course
~ well, as he should be

bureaucrat — fighting
outside your weight class ~ don't call
me a bureaucrat

yeah, moms are like that,
so we killed her and got your
address off her phone

SEASON 8

Pac-Man Fever

Episode 169 (Season 8, Episode 20)
Directed by Robert Singer
Written by Robbie Thompson
Original air date: April 24, 2013

Dean tosses a beer
Sam watches as it sails by
why don't have nice things

make, receive phone calls
and nobody can track us?
man I *love* this place

invite to dungeon,
or do I gotta answer
your questions three, first?

find every single
copy of those books, burn them
~ online now — good luck

• *Charlie goes shopping for FBI clothes: a montage* •

if gonna do a
ride along, then you gotta
lose novelty shirts

son of a pantsuit ~
used to think maybe loved me,
now baby, I'm sure

just can't wait 'til the
day when you knock on my door
kills music ~ …montage

I'm sorry, I froze —
couldn't control-alt-delete
— real-life role-play: hard

Charlie why don't you
go talk to the witnesses?
~ I'll miss the bro-ment!

Charlie tied to chair
you're not going anywhere ~
whimper Wilhelm scream

my manly man-friend
is gonna get you, creepy
power-suit lady

Pac-Man Fever (cont.)

need sleep fast — punch me
punches little off your game...
re-punches, harder

"come with me if you
want to live" — I have always
wanted to say that

a War Games callback —
I think the only way to
stop this: not to play

an infinite loop,
like Pac-Man without level
256 ~ what?

got scared, I called — they
should never have been driving
~ it wasn't your fault

I sneak into the
hospital whenever I
can, and read to her

want to tell her that
I love her, have her hear it
~ game over kiddo

she would read me "The
Hobbit" — she's the reason I
love the stuff I love

you should dig through our
archives — you're definitely
Woman of Letters

• *Charlie reads The Hobbit to her mom* •

one last time, okay?
reads in a hole in the ground
there lived a hobbit

nor dry, bare, sandy
hole, with nothing in it to
sit down on or eat

not nasty, dirty,
wet hole, filled with the ends of
worms and oozy smell

was a hobbit-hole
and that means comfort *Charlie's
mom knows that she's loved*

SEASON 8

The Great Escapist

Episode 170 (Season 8, Episode 21)
Directed by Robert Duncan McNeill
Written by Ben Edlund
Original air date: May 1, 2013

---

your slang: "Special K"
"nose to the god-stone" — that's Dean;
Sam is more basic

you gotta let me
take care of you, let me help
you get your strength back

I'm dead, you bastards,
so screw you, screw God, and screw
everyone between

before you brewed it,
you'd just chew the berries — you
learned it from the goats

trapped in a quantum
superposition — there's so
many Biggerson's

slew every firstborn
whose door wasn't splashed with blood
— that was just P.R.

how many times torn
into my head, washed it clean?
~ frankly, too many

269

SEASON 8

The Great Escapist (cont.)

spanner in the works:
you came off the line with a
crack in your chassis

you have never done
what you were told ~ in the words
of a friend: bite me

what did great spirits'
sacred messenger ask for?
~ he asked for stories

told us where half was —
dab of crap tricked us — sent us
to hunter mousetrap

remember thinking:
could never go on a quest
because I'm not clean

your storytelling:
the true flower of free will
as you've mastered it

haven't heard of us?
what kind of angel *are* you?
we're the Winchesters

you create stories,
become gods of intricate
dimensions themselves

Sam, Dean wouldn't get
me a barbecue dinner
~ demons too polite?

already won: got
deals and plans up the jacksie,
and I don't need you

not an archangel:
in secretarial pool
before God chose me

it's your choice, and that's
what this has all been about:
the choices you make

SEASON 8

Clip Show

Episode 171 (Season 8, Episode 22)
Directed by Thomas J. Wright
Written by Andrew Dabb
Original air date: May 8, 2013

---

bunker: orderly ~
Dean wants a ping pong table
~ that is a game, right?

like bolting off with
the angel tablet because
you didn't trust me?

cram apology ~
thought I was doing right thing
~ yeah, you always do

anybody else:
I would stab them in their neck
~ why free pass? ~ it's Cas

Sam is more damaged
than I am ~ yeah, well, even
banged up, Sam comes through

there is not a doubt
in my mind that he's gonna
cross that finish line

where's the pie? ~ I think
we're out ~ you don't understand:
grabs clerk I need pie

angels are like a
big dysfunctional family
— lock them in a room

got needles, got thread,
we have seen Young Frankenstein
about thousand times

killing everyone:
damsels, innocents, would-be
vampire chow — *all*

you son of a bitch ~
son of a *witch* — my mommy
taught me a few tricks

we will get it done,
kick it in the ass, like we
always do — with me?

271

SEASON 8

Sacrifice

Episode 172 (Season 8, Episode 23)
Directed by Phil Sgriccia
Written by Jeremy Carver
Original air date: May 15, 2013

---

on what grounds? ~ grounds that
you're a douchebag; no douchebag
should have that power

it's a secret lair,
you understand? no keggers
~ don't have any friends

what was he like? ~ God?
larger than life, gruff, bit of
a sexist… but fair

a professional negotiation — you want to talk dangly bits?	your demon ass is gonna be a mortal ass: you're the third trial
your humanity: you always put emotion before common sense	looking for partner in crime, or nurse role-play and light domination?

how are you feeling? ~
for the first time in long time:
like we're gonna win

I'm down with sending
the angels back to Heaven,
just because they're dicks

Sacrifice (cont.)

think it's wise to be
drinking on the job? ~ what show
have *you* been watching?

crud — this is like the
first five minutes of every
porno I have seen

really think you could
kidnap the King of Hell and
no one would notice?

we deserve to be
loved — *I* deserve to be loved
…just want to be loved

    given history,   know what I confessed?
where do I start to even   my greatest sin: how many
  look for forgiveness?   times I let you down

   motivate me with   killed Benny for you,
Magic cards, Skyrim, Aziz   will let sons of bitches who
  Ansari — not sports   killed Mom walk for you

  it was always God's   don't you dare think that
intention — the ultimate   there is *anything* I would
   sacrifice: to die   put in front of you

what is happening?
lights streak down out of Heaven
~ angels: they're falling

SEASON NINE

SEASON 9

I Think I'm Gonna Like It Here

Episode 173 (Season 9, Episode 1)
Directed by John F. Showalter
Written by Jeremy Carver
Original air date: October 8, 2013

---

how many angels
fell? thousands? ~ calling it a
meteor shower

something happened back
there in that church: don't know what
— you are dying, Sam

• *Dean prays to all of the angels asking for help with Sam* •

Cas, you there? Sammy's
hurt pretty bad — I know you
think I'm pissed at you

it doesn't matter,
okay? we'll work it out — please
man, I need you here

but I don't care that
the angels fell, so what you
did or didn't do…

screw it — listen up:
this one goes out to any
angel with ears on

time to make a deal
this is Dean Winchester *cringe*
and I need your help

deal is this: Linwood
Memorial Hospital
in Randolph, New York

no secret that we've
not always seen eye-to-eye;
I'm good for my word

first one who can help
gets my help in return — you
know that ain't nothin'

Gadreel hears his plea
and I wouldn't be asking
if wasn't needing

I Think I'm Gonna Like It Here (cont.)

how about a lift? ~
I would fly, but I have no
wings… not anymore

have something better:
the King of Hell in my trunk
~ that a metaphor?

there's a place I built
when was last here, long ago
— it's a grand canyon

you lost your grace, right?
that means you're human: you bleed,
you eat, and you sleep

angel punches Dean
anyone ever tell you
you hit like angel?

promise: you and me,
come whatever — well, hell if
this ain't "whatever"

no way to save bro's
life? ~ no good ways, I'm afraid
~ what are the bad ones?

gotta let me in,
let me help — there ain't no me
if there ain't no you

you get off on this? ~
consider it an honor
to collect you, Sam

handful of quarters
to wash a bloody trench coat,
or to buy some snacks?

you're capable of
anything — you proved me right
— we got work to do

SEASON 9

Devil May Care

Episode 174 (Season 9, Episode 2)
Directed by Guy Norman Bee
Written by Andrew Dabb
Original air date: October 15, 2013

Cas is human? ~ -ish:
got no grace, no wings, no harp
— whatever hell else

I thought to myself:
what would Sam Winchester do?
~ stab him in the brain

King of Hell might know
a few things ~ Crowley's alive?
~ he's junk in my trunk

we'll hold him down while
you knife him — then go out for
ice cream and strippers

when you opened door
from outside: reset system
~ yeah, let's go with that

check for angel-y,
demon-y, or monster-y
— gonna be busy

you're giving us name
of every demon on earth
~ doesn't sound like me

naked guy in a
luchador mask: real classy
— I'm Kevin Solo

torture? brilliant:
Sam in stilettos and a
leather bustier

you know this is trap —
we're just going to walk right in
~ guns blazing — with me?

whole place is poison?
Dean covers junk with one hand
~ that's not gonna help

Devil May Care (cont.)

we're friends ~ you *tortured*
me ~ I torture all my friends,
it's how I show love

you Winchesters: so
suicidally stupid
and obedient

are we gonna fight,
or make out, 'cause I'm getting
real mixed signals here

an angel? ~ you think
we'd roll up to this mousetrap
without some backup?

:: I am in Sam's head ::
:: and I know that what you did, ::
:: you did out of love ::

I'm trusting you, Zeke —
I just gotta hope that you're
one of the good guys

if you don't think that
we would die for you, I don't
know what to tell you

the fallen angels?	I look around and
Crowley in basement? ~ living	I see friends and family
in freakin' sitcom	— happy with my life

SEASON 9

I'm No Angel

Episode 175 (Season 9, Episode 3)
Directed by Kevin Hooks
Written by Brad Buckner & Eugenie Ross-Leming
Original air date: October 22, 2013

---

can I ask: ever
tire of urinating?
can't get used to it

not all willing can
contain Heaven's grace — have to
expect casualties

often the people
who have the least to give are
the most generous

your lack of faith does
not cancel what I believe
— that's not how it works

that is the name of
a pretty famous angel
— "It's Wonderful Life"

a shame, isn't it?
so much is wasted when so
many are hungry

what if you were to
find out: no one listening;
God has left Heaven

what happened to the
guy who attacked you? ~ I stabbed
him; he exploded

so that was okay?
what I did, that was correct?
~ very much so ~ good

believe me: I've done
a lot of foolish, unwise
things — I'm no angel

I'm No Angel (cont.)

intergalactic
hyperspace x-ray eyeballs
— go find someone else

I'm confused — I know
she stabbed me, but I do not
appear to be dead

wouldn't get kabob'd
if she brought you back ~ you *lied*
~ I did, I do that

much: being human
~ it ain't all just burritos
and strippers, my friend

you look for purpose —
you must not be defeated
by anger, despair

chokes you had sex with
April? ~ that would be where the
hedonism comes in

you have protection? ~
I had my angel blade… ~ oh,
had his angel blade

you know I always
appreciate our talks, Dean,
our time together

SEASON 9

Slumber Party

Episode 176 (Season 9, Episode 4)
Directed by Robert Singer
Written by Robbie Thompson
Original air date: October 29, 2013

---

this dump: the last true
beacon of light in a world
gone topsy-turvy

the epicenter
of the ultimate chess match
between good, evil

so, what do you have
to say for yourself? ~ nothing:
I cut out her tongue

still don't understand
why he left — the bunker is
safest place for him

wait, all by yourself? ~
yes, despite my lady-parts:
captured wicked witch

took down a teenage
vampire and ghost, which sounds
like Y.A. novel

sweet Ada Lovelace!
it's got encryption software
powered by magic

according to the
"Supernatural" books ~ can't
delete those from net?

BeckyWinchester-
176, ring a bell? ~
there are no bells, no

Slumber Party (cont.)

home's not good enough? ~
not our home, it's where we work
~ what's the difference?

where's my volcano
and magic ring to throw in
damn thing? where's my quest?

not secretary?
a Woman of Letters? how
long have I been out?

right now why don't you
rest up, and help the smartest
person in the room

I told you to stay
in the dungeon ~ bet you say
that to all the girls

abandoned buildings
and crappy motel rooms — this
is home, and it's ours

there you are ~ that your
batman voice? definitely
not your batman voice

*Dorothy, Charlie
depart on yellow brick road*
there's no place like home

SEASON 9

Dog Dean Afternoon

Episode 177 (Season 9, Episode 5)
Directed by Tim Andrew
Written by Eric Charmelo & Nicole Snyder
Original air date: November 5, 2013

---

are those bleeding hearts
real witches, or just hippies?
~ what's the difference?

sniffs what is that smell? ~
patchouli, depression from
meat deprivation

always knew I'd find
source of all evil at a
vegan bakery

sees owners know who
wears sunglasses inside? blind
people... and douchebags

well, he doesn't have
what we have — Kevin, how do
we speak to a dog?

you're scratching your head,
you're barking at the mailman,
playing fetch ~ ruh-roh

yep, animals have
a universal language,
like Esperanto

with the help of a
Pawnee shaman and a zoo
membership, found cure

need just one biscuit ~
need a Raquel Welch poster
and a rock hammer

think power you hold
over other people's lives
makes up what you lack?

I want to know what
you are — screw the sharktopus:
you are my main course

I was afraid to
tell you earlier, but I
barfed in your back seat

SEASON 9

Heaven Can't Wait

Episode 178 (Season 9, Episode 6)
Directed by Rob Spera
Written by Robert Berens
Original air date: November 12, 2013

Cas learns how to be
human by watching mundane
daily human tasks

where have you been all
my life? you're not like the other
sales associates

decipher footnotes,
reverse spell, punt those winged
dicks back to Heaven

• *In what world does Nora not think this comes off
as asking Steve out on a date?* •

been afraid to ask — don't want to take advantage of my employee	it's hard enough to get a date, let alone meet a really great guy
and I certainly don't want to jeopardize our work relationship	tomorrow's my night off, and I know you're off too — was just wondering…

if there's any chance
you're free tomorrow night? yes?
kiss you are the best

285

Heaven Can't Wait (cont.)

Crowley's well-rested —
we're not keeping him chained up
for the one-liners

I knew you had to
lay low from the angel threat
— this is some cover

do you have any
idea how hard it was
when I fell to earth?

I lost my powers;
I had nothing — now I'm a
sales associate

inventory, sales,
customer service — and I
even prepare food

you went from fighting
those heavenly battles to
nuking taquitos

like it or not, there's
still a little part of you
that is not a douche

Abaddon: pretty
terrifying — scarier
than you've been in years

you are above this ~
here, at least, I have a shot
at getting things right

guess you can't see it:
dignity in what I do,
human dignity

my dates usually
end when run out of singles,
but yeah, humans date

never had powers ~
you are a hunter ~ and you're
hunter-in-training

yeah, you said I sucked ~
I didn't say that — I said
"room for improvement"

human emotion —
been on earth for a few years,
only start to grasp

okay, lose the vest,
unbutton shirt — far enough,
Tony Manero

always open door,
ask questions — dutch? she's lying
— go get 'em, tiger

Heaven Can't Wait (cont.)

have a policy:
don't give blood to anyone
who murders mother

*• Castiel sings theme song from
"The Greatest American Hero" to calm Nora's baby •*

Cas sings look at what's
happening to me — I can't
believe it myself

suddenly I'm up
on top of the world — should have
been somebody else

believe it or not
I'm walking on air — never
thought would feel so freeee

flyin' away on
a wing and a prayer — who could
it be? believe it

or not, it's just me
believe it or not, it's just
me *lays baby down*

SEASON 9

Heaven Can't Wait (cont.)

• *Castiel waxes philosophical to Nora's baby;*
is this how the baby feels, or how Cas feels? •

nobody told you,
nobody explained — just shoved
out kicking, screaming

into human life,
without any idea
why it feels like this

why this confusion,
which feels like it's a hair's breadth
from terror or pain

when you think you *do*
understand, turns out you're wrong:
didn't understand

I guess that's just how
it is when you're new at this
…wasn't long ago

all I'd need to do
to ease your pain was touch you
— you are *very* warm…

used to admire —
failed more than succeeded, but
at least you played big

I know it's been hard
on you, but you're adapting
— I am proud of you

the part of you that
overreacted, that cares
— it makes you special

we'll deal with angels —
you're human now, it's not your
problem anymore

SEASON 9

Bad Boys

Episode 179 (Season 9, Episode 7)
Directed by Kevin Parks
Written by Adam Glass
Original air date: November 19, 2013

I tried taking the
five-finger discount at the
market: got busted

wasn't on a hunt —
they sent me to a boys' home
~ like a reform school?

you made a mistake ~
yeah, *I* made the mistake — none
of this was Dad's fault

old man called — once he
found out what happened, he said
"let him rot in jail"

where did you get the
shiner? ~ you think that's funny?
~ I think you are slow

*looks at bruises on
Dean's arms* deputy do that?
your old man? ~ werewolf

what are you doing? ~
fighting monsters — all sorts, with
Bruce, monster-smasher

SEASON 9

Bad Boys (cont.)

look me straight in eye,
let me know you mean business
— shake hard as you can

let us barbecue
Old McDonald here, and get
the hell out of Dodge

it's a family thing:
can't really talk about it
~ family left you here

look in the mirror —
you want the guy looking back
to be his own man

gotta do what's best
for you, even if will
hurt the ones you love

I'm not a rock star ~
I don't know about that — you
look pretty rockin'

how'd you know asking
mom to leave was gonna work?
~ total hail Mary

here I was thinking
this was worst part of your life
— turns out was the best

Rock and a Hard Place

Episode 180 (Season 9, Episode 8)
Directed by John MacCarthy
Written by Jenny Klein
Original air date: November 26, 2013

---

next time that junkie's
jonesing for a hit of blood,
we got leverage

Sheriff, laying off
the blind dates, I hope? ~ yeah, you
just bite your tongue, boy

choking on the floor
'cause of witchcraft makes higher
power relevant

angels? you're joking ~
don't get excited, they suck
~ said there was witness?

I'll be a squirrel
in a skirt — be back in a
jiff with the papers

purity pledge? don't
think we can un-ring that bell,
if know what I mean

congratulations,
Sam and Dean Winchester *nods*
— you are both virgins

SEASON 9

Rock and a Hard Place (cont.)

• *Dean describes the joys of sex to a room full of virgins* •

Dean, what sent you on
the path away from sin? ~ hard
to say exactly

yeah, sex has always
felt… I don't know… good, you know?
really, *really* good

sometimes, you feel bad:
you're drunk, you shack up, then it's
the whole morning thing

"hey, that was fun," and
then it's, "adios," you know
…always, "adios"

what's the big deal, right?
there's the touching, the feeling
all of each other

my hands everywhere:	everything just builds,
tracing every inch of her	and builds, and builds, until it
body, two of us	all just… *explosion*
moving together,	whole thing was just a
pressing and pulling, grinding	little too… sticky, so I
— you hit that sweet spot	got my "v" card back

Rock and a Hard Place (cont.)

really think gonna
hit that? she's the chastity
counselor ~ I *know*

dragons off the list ~
sorry, *dragons*? are a *thing*?
~ too many things are

I've seen a lot of
awful things: stuff of nightmares
— but you're the *good* dreams

you sure Dean was here? ~
yeah, I think he crossed someone
off his bucket list

8 pm train out of Sioux Falls, 79 miles an hour	(is this a real life "train traveling" example? of course, Sam's on it)
I'm calling the cops ~ *punch* I *am* the cops ~ what the fudge? ~ wipe your nose, dear	what's wrong with liver? all duct tape and safety pins: how are you *alive*?
Bethlehem hippie: before him they practically *threw* virgins at me	if there's something wrong, it's not your fault — you gotta have a little faith

SEASON 9

Holy Terror

Episode 181 (Season 9, Episode 9)
Directed by Thomas J. Wright
Written by Eugenie Ross-Leming & Brad Buckner
Original air date: December 3, 2013

---

you shouldn't be here ~
just as much right to be here
as you do, brother

there are chunks of time
just missing — like there are times
when I am not here

damn straight the trials —
whacked you — not up to warp speed,
will be: would I lie?

guy here already ~
Cas, the hell are you doing?
~ I still have that badge

you were living the
life, working your way up the
Gas-n-Sip ladder

if the angels are
slaughtering one another,
I just have to help

you sure you're ready
to jump back into all this?
seemed like you'd found peace

Holy Terror (cont.)

the reaper you banged? ~
yeah, and you stabbed ~ she was hot
~ *sighs* so hot... and nice

up to the point she
started torturing ~ not all
hook-ups are perfect

don't feel good about
it, but I don't have a choice:
can't work together

I freed you: I caused
angels to fall, including
the imprisoned ones

no stupid angels —
but maybe some funny ones
— plan: rebuild Heaven

they're a born-again
biker gang ~ that's not something
you hear every day

:: humans: chaotic :: ~
all that emotion, and the
wasted energy

unfamiliar
with this end of the process:
please hear my prayer

great, valued, trusted,
top-of-the-Christmas-tree Cas:
no more than a dupe

I'll need a moment,
and *you* have something I need
Cas steals Theo's grace

need a spell, ASAP ~
everyone always needs a
spell, always ASAP

I *always* trust you,
and I always end up screwed
~ oh come on, *always*?

messed up: almost dead —
no more birthdays, dust to dust
— well that messed me up

:: so, again you thought ::
:: I couldn't handle something, ::
:: so, you took over ::

SEASON 9

Road Trip

Episode 182 (Season 9, Episode 10)
Directed by Robert Singer
Written by Andrew Dabb
Original air date: January 14, 2014

• *Famous Final Scene scene (Dean reacting to Kevin's death)* •

think terms: bridges burned,
think of seasons that must end,
see rivers rise, fall

will rise, fall again —
everything must have an end,
like ocean to shore

like river to stream,
as the light fades from the screen:
famous final scene

booted out of the
penthouse — why be an angel
when you can be God?

Dean, I'm sorry ~ yeah,
sorry don't pay the bills, and
won't bring Kevin back

you were stupid for
the right reasons — sometimes that
is all that matters

in your general
vicinity, people do
not have much life-span

Road Trip (cont.)

I have vehicle —
stopped a few miles from here,
inexplicably

when you betray us,
I'll be one to carve out heart
~ oh, Cas, such a flirt

own epic story —
to make that work, sometimes have
to kill your darlings

Dean Winchester, Cas? ~
without the tie, he's barely
recognizable

so, captain sexy
cuts angel, yoinks his grace, and
gets his mojo back

customer support:
like answering prayers, but
they pay you for it

key to happiness:
getting the *one* thing you want,
never letting go

:: what if there's a price? :: ~
there is always a price, but
it is worth paying

a demon sticking
needles into my brother's
brain — humor me, man

thought life was at stake —
I got played ~ thought was saving
Heaven — got played too

we're a couple of
dumbasses? ~ prefer the word
"trusting" — less dumb, ass

SEASON 9

Road Trip (cont.)

don't want to be in
brother anymore — not one
for sloppy seconds

find him: "Poughkeepsie" —
it's our code word: it means "drop
everything and run"

a demon and an
angel walk into brother:
sounds like a bad joke

I see you again... ~
I'm dead, yes I *know* — I love
you too, as always

think this is a fight?
it's a campaign: hearts and minds
— demons have a choice

everyone gets a say, a virgin, and all the entrails they can eat	Kevin's blood is on *my* hands — I will burn for that — I will end Gadreel
was ready to die ~ I wouldn't let you because that is not in me	I'm poison — people get close to me, they get killed, or worse — can't you see?

I'm not gonna stop
you, but don't go thinking that's
the problem — it's not

SEASON 9

First Born

Episode 183 (Season 9, Episode 11)
Directed by John Badham
Written by Robbie Thompson
Original air date: January 21, 2014

---

sneers you want to hunt?
with *me*? ~ I do love a good
buddy comedy

peanut butter with
grape jelly, not jam — I found
jam unsettling

you're terrible liar ~
not true: I deceived, betrayed
both you *and* brother

can't taste PB, J? ~
I taste every molecule
— it's overwhelming

the file's empty ~
didn't they teach note-taking
at hunters' Hogwarts?

they didn't have a
guinea pig — we do ~ you have
a guinea pig? where?

didn't you grow up
pretty? still in the family
business? ~ born and raised

I'd never leave my
domestic partner in crime
~ can't zap out of here

it's been a pleasure
having company — once a
century's enough

SEASON 9

First Born (cont.)

chose to live rather
than to sacrifice yourself
— you chose each other

this is by far the
dumbest idea you've ever
had ~ well, it's early

being human means
settling your debts — let's start
balancing the books

Dean fights off demons
in kitchen; Cain casually
shucks corn and drinks beer

only person who
screws up more consistently
than you, Sam, is me

PB&J taught
me angels can change — maybe
Winchesters can, too

I offered a deal:
Abel's soul up in Heaven
for my soul in Hell

met Colette — she loved
me unconditionally —
asked one thing: to stop

mark can be transferred
to someone who's worthy ~ you
mean killer, like you?

you have to know, with
the mark comes a great burden
— some call it great cost

your problem is that
nobody hates you more than
you do; I have tried

Sharp Teeth

Episode 184 (Season 9, Episode 12)
Directed by John F. Showalter
Written by Adam Glass
Original air date: January 28, 2014

---

looking for a John doe:
a skinny, Ichabod Crane
looking kind of guy

Gadreel left some grace
in me before he bolted ~
know how wrong that sounds?

did he steal a car? ~
did he steal a car naked?
~ I'll check the cameras

told you we can't hunt
together — for your own good
~ after we find Garth

Dean could start a fight in an empty house — deep down: big ol' teddy bear	Sam can be a bit insecure at times, for good reason — bless his heart

wait, hold on... you said
~ second generation ~ you
were *born* a werewolf?

guns waving, with the
jawlines and the hair — very
intimidating

SEASON 9

Sharp Teeth (cont.)

the road to revenge
is a dark and lonely one;
you never get off

I know this looks nuts —
I found love and family —
who cares where comes from?

Kevin's gone for good ~
what happened? ~ when he needed
me, I wasn't there

human extinction,
full werewolf domination
— freakin' Wisconsin

you've done this countless
times; you're still nervous ~ nothing
wrong with little fear

was bitten, not born
into it — still holds onto
his humanity

I just know that when
we rode together, we split
the crappiness ~ yeah

all a little weird,
we're all a little wacky —
some more than others

I can not trust you —
not the way I thought I could,
not the way I should

somebody's gotta
live to tell this damn story
— who better than you?

whatever happened,
we are family ~ you say
that like some cure-all

shut up and come here —
holds arms open hurry up,
before I change mind

everything that has
ever gone wrong between us:
because we're family

SEASON 9

The Purge

Episode 185 (Season 9, Episode 13)
Directed by Phil Sgriccia
Written by Eric Charmelo & Nicole Snyder
Original air date: February 4, 2014

---

hot dog in pocket ~
I hate to break it to you,
but that's no hot dog

eat all sorts of stuff,
like baked beans, buff wings, butter
~ butter? ~ yeah, deep fried

don't flatter yourself —
I do not break that easy
~ just being honest

lettuce: stomach stretch
~ another reason to stay
away from salads

personal training
brothers — kind of like Hans and
Franz, but less German

they're roofies ~ how do
you know what roofies look like?
~ how do you *not* know?

this isn't what you
think — I am not a killer,
I'm a pishtaco

just once, be honest:
you didn't save me for me,
you did it for you

strictly business — last
I checked we were in business
of killing monsters

was ready to die,
but you couldn't stand the thought
of being alone

what I do, I do
because it is the right thing
— I'd do it again

if I were dying
you'd do same ~ no, I wouldn't,
same circumstances

SEASON 9

Captives

Episode 186 (Season 9, Episode 14)
Directed by Jerry Wanek
Written by Robert Berens
Original air date: February 25, 2014

---

*a wispy spirit
floats toward Sam; Dean shoots it*
yep, bunker's haunted

• *Dean talks to ghost-Kevin, hoping he can hear* •

all right, I cannot
do all this coffee-buzzing,
bump-in-the-night crap

I got serious
things to say to you, I'm not
gonna say to *this*

Kevin, I'm sorry
you did not choose this life, and
you busted your ass

you lost everything,
everyone you've loved — reward?
got killed on my watch

was my fault; nothing
I can do to make that right
— I am so sorry

Captives (cont.)

that's your third voice mail —
do you think maybe he's just
not that into you?

with you by my side —
new boss, ultimate rebel
— working together

unplug ground wire first — if standard U.S. coding, should be the green one	I was never free — my only choice was obey or be killed — I choose…

do it, kill me ~ we're
saving you for someone else
~ do honors, Ms. Tran

he's my son: it is
my job to keep him safe for
as long as I can

go put a blade in
that asshat who possessed you,
and we'll call it square

uninterrupted,
no-escape quality time:
24/7

fighting: it's stupid —
my mom's taking home a ghost
— you are both still here

#THINMAN

Episode 187 (Season 9, Episode 15)
Directed by Jeannot Szwarc
Written by Jenny Klein
Original air date: March 4, 2014

Sam and Dean sit down
"ah, the Winchesters — yay," says
nobody, ever

get in mystery
machine and leave town, or I'll
put holes in your knees

Thinman is the new
Bigfoot ~ Thinman is just a
ghost with a brand name

Winchesters are here,
and I don't want my knees blown
off by Sam and Dean

jockstraps steal glory —
no one cares what they think — don't
even have *Twitter*

won't wait for someone
else to die — will find Thinman
~ where? ~ the woods, obvi

a crossroads demon? ~
demon that likes to stab and
watch YouTube, why not?

rainbows can't happen
without rain ~ do not try to
use science with me

everybody knows
that Batman can't fly ~ not me,
and I broke my arm

I drove you to the
E.R. on my handlebars:
good times ~ yeah, they were

#THINMAN (cont.)

sounds like "Sad Times at
Bitchmont High" — what does this have
to do with the case?

don't tell him, he'll leave
anyway — trust me: secrets
kill relationships

hey, are you okay? ~
Harry shakes his head just got
punched right in the feels

things you can forgive,
and things you can't ~ which is this?
~ figure out yourself

don't want to be a
jellyfish spine anymore
~ they do not have spines

not demons, monsters —
they were just frickin' people
~ well, people are sick

it's Scooby-Doo time:
not Thinman — just a me-me
~ Ed, it's pronounced "meem"

did all this for us —
don't know why you don't see that
~ you did this for *you*

I can't forgive this ~
what does this mean about us?
~ it's complicated

you roll with a guy
so many years, start to think
always will be there

Blade Runners

Episode 188 (Season 9, Episode 16)
Directed by Serge Ladouceur
Written by Brad Buckner & Eugenie Ross-Leming
Original air date: March 18, 2014

---

*voicemail: Crowley speaks
in muffled gibberish* ~ did
he drunk-dial you?

no interests but
sex, pizza, and human blood
— he cannot function

that explains a lot ~
look, Snooki — can I call you…?
~ no, it's Nicole now

not the face, are you
crazy? look, guys, what happens
in Hell stays in Hell

focus, Crowley, get
a grip ~ are you just gonna
let Hell go to hell?

to be human: your　　　　I'm still a little
DNA; my addiction,　　　tainted by humanity:
my cross, my burden　　　I'm sentimental

human Cas: okay —
I should have known Crowley would
be a douche version

SEASON 9

Blade Runners (cont.)

keep locked in closet,
ignore suffering, barge in
and demand my help?

he'll open heart to
you because you're such prizes
~ better: legacies

when you were saying
all of that just now, did it
feel at *all* creepy?

same team, in trenches —   I'm not asking you
when this is over we can   for your cooperation,
get matching tattoos   I'm just taking it

remember: stay close,
do what I say, and shut up
~ I'm growing on you

shaking with power
Dean, hey, it's over: he's dead —
drop the blade, Dean — Dean!

it's Enochian;
message not for you — for me:
"be afraid, your queen"

you are right, Moose, you
can't trust me — but sadly I
can't trust you, either

SEASON 9

Mother's Little Helper

Episode 189 (Season 9, Episode 17)
Directed by Misha Collins
Written by Adam Glass
Original air date: March 25, 2014

---

maybe everyone
has a different reaction
to losing their soul

you're lying to Sam
like he's your wife, which kind of
makes *me* your mistress

I say demons, you
don't bat an eye — everyone
else here thinks I'm nuts

'less Abaddon likes
10-cent wings, stale beer, the clap,
I doubt that she's here

complicated ~ I'm
an ex-nun: complicated
is my middle name

so we're assuming
demonic possession? ~ or
a linguist gone mad

chroniclers of
all man does not understand
~ Woman of Letters?

love: cold ones, jukebox,
good and evil bro-in' down
~ shut pie hole, Crowley

yeah, well, when I kill,
I do it for a reason —
I'm nothing like Cain

demons don't take leaks —
next time you want to shoot up,
find better excuse

ask something? ~ sorry
I never date anyone
under 65

Meta Fiction

Episode 190 (Season 9, Episode 18)
Directed by Thomas J. Wright
Written by Robbie Thompson
Original air date: April 15, 2014

---

what makes a story
work? and who gives it meaning?
the writer? or you?

tonight, thought I would
tell you a little story,
and let you decide

I am no leader,
but I will find Metatron;
I will make him pay

how are you Dean? ~ fine,
how 'bout you? ~ I miss my wings;
life on the road… smells

what's honorable
about a miniature
bar in motel room?

we got some off-the-
menu items, but this ain't
Diagon Alley

I thought you were dead ~
please, you cannot take the trick
out of the trickster

used most of juice to
get back into porn — that came
out wrong — so did *that*

guy who died for sins —
not the cat with the beard and
sandals — the hot one

boy-toy and I are
rolling our way toward your
secret domicile

SEASON 9

Meta Fiction (cont.)

I lied before — I
never watched Downton Abbey;
trying to fit in

I have been you, Sam
Winchester — your insides reek
of shame and weakness

you've been around since
scaly things crawled out of muck
— read book, watch movie?

just gave you every
book, movie, and TV show
that I have consumed

the first rule: steal from
the best — second rule? every
hero needs villain

slaughter those who will
not join my army — let one
live to tell the tale

you did all this to
make me a hero? ~ um, no
you are the *villain*

among God's little
wind-up toys, you were only
one with any spunk

loved humanity ~
sure got a funny way of
showing it, asshat

a scared little boy,
afraid to be on his own,
never loved enough

coward, sad, clingy —
would drag everyone through mud
not to be alone

easy there, tiger —
trade: you have something of mine,
I've something of yours

s'mores? holy fire
always gives them delightful
minty aftertaste

you, brother, feathered
friend, secrets locked away in
bunker can't stop me

Meta Fiction (cont.)

did you understand
Death Star reference? ~ what's that have
to do with Heaven?

that's why we rewrite —
that was God's problem, you know:
published the first draft

ending: how get there
doesn't matter, as long as
everyone plays part

• Metatron plays a record for some writing mood-music •

loneliness is the
coat you wear — a deep shade of
blue is always there

the sun ain't gonna
shine anymore, the moon ain't
gonna rise in sky

the tears are always
clouding your eyes when you are
without love, baby

sun ain't gonna shine,
moon ain't gonna rise — tears are
always clouding eyes

sun ain't gonna shine
anymore when without love,
won't shine anymore

sun ain't gonna shine
anymore — not anymore,
sun ain't gonna shine

SEASON 9

Alex Annie Alexis Ann

Episode 191 (Season 9, Episode 19)
Directed by Stefan Pleszczynski
Written by Robert Berens
Original air date: April 22, 2014

I keep telling you:
you can run and hide, but we
will always find you

that's a vamp alright ~
Jody might not need our help
~ they grow up too fast

wasn't a dental ID, it was a fang check — you two are hunters	not talking because vampiric Stockholm syndrome? ~ protecting the nest

want me to enlist
men in protection detail
against vampires?

I will give you a pass, on account of the whole "raised by monsters" thing	think motherhood's just about blood? you don't know the first thing about it
she's a kid who's been playing "vampire murder" since before braces	ain't about forcing to be like *you* the second she's inconvenient
those human feelings — I can take the pain away; stay a family	"look at me, bitch?" ~ if you've got another snappy one-liner, all ears

SEASON 9

Bloodlines

Episode 192 (Season 9, Episode 20)
Directed by Robert Singer
Written by Andrew Dabb
Original air date: April 29, 2014

I just want a drink ~
want to eat Taylor Swift's heart
— can't get what we want

you werewolves think you're
so special, when really you're
just sons of bitches

thing wasn't human ~
don't know what to tell you: no
such thing as monsters

you ran away to
be a human — always had
a soft spot for 'em

basically, we chase
down evil, cut its head off ~
you're what, monster cops?

I'm a shapeshifter,
we shift our shape — it's kind of
all there in the name

you work with the bad
guys to get to the worse guys
~ dude, I am *right here*

so you're telling me
there are 5 monster families
that run Chicago?

seriously don't —
you get into this too deep,
there's no getting out

315

SEASON 9

King of the Damned

Episode 193 (Season 9, Episode 21)
Directed by P. J. Pesce
Written by Eugenie Ross-Leming & Brad Buckner
Original air date: May 6, 2014

---

done with the rough stuff,
you want us to be your goons?
~ had success before

if you don't want to
do it, I understand ~ who
says I don't want to?

no one's been tortured
with torture like the torture
you'll be tortured with

I will not join you —
except at your death scene, where
I'll burst into song

my father was a
simple tailor, drunk, monster
~ that sounds about right

hot for Metatron,
Bieber, Beckham ~ they don't know
you even exist

priorities change —
I wasn't the bon vivant
that I am now, son

not just a demon:
King of Hell — *you* thought I would
not amount to much

well that's the problem:
I think everyone's lying,
you think *no one* is

I didn't really
have any role models — my
mother was a witch

seen you through Sam's eyes:
you have a reputation
for honor; trusts you

you need to get a
move on: it is a good day's
drive from *Poughkeepsie*

I'll cheer the day when
last trace of humanity
leaves me *sneers* *feelings!*

Stairway to Heaven

Episode 194 (Season 9, Episode 22)
Directed by Guy Norman Bee
Written by Andrew Dabb
Original air date: May 13, 2014

---

because he's a weird
guy, okay — he is a weird,
dorky little guy

powerful magic
comes at a price, and we don't
know what that price is

Spears, Aguilera?
~ aliases usually
names of musicians

just a second ~ gave
you a second ~ you are *such*
an angel sometimes

I mean sure, he's cute —
Castiel has simple charm
— but *I'm* lovable

Winchesters: heard so
much about you ~ what can I
say? Cas is a fan

I know you try to
be a good guy, but what you've
got here is a cult

last time you had this
kind of juice, you killed humans
and angels, and lied

he *does* seem angry
— always a little angry —
now it seems like… more

SEASON 9

Stairway to Heaven (cont.)

I mean, just smell that…
~ old shoes, alcoholism?
~ authenticity

you'd still be you: a
nerd trying to be one of
the popular kids

you play the hero —
you're a killer with oceans
of blood on his hands

you're here, why? you just
love musical theater?
~ only if "Fiddler"

• *Sam solves the Enochian riddle,
and Cas shows off his pop-culture mastery* •

Enochian — some sort of riddle: "why is six afraid of seven?"

seven is a prime number; prime numbers can be intimidating

wordplay: answer is the key, like Doors of Durin in "Lord of the Rings"

know about "The Lord of the Rings?" ~ I'm very pop-culture savvy now

Stairway to Heaven (cont.)

Sam reads on the wall
only the penitent man
shall pass — "Last Crusade"

I look into your
eyes; I don't see an angel
staring back at me

what would make person
want to pop their top? I have
never been *that* low

what do you want? ~ just
tell "Ass-tiel" that I'm still
alive: bomber failed

look, you have seen earth,
you've had a taste of free will
— gotta ask: like it?

the only thing he
cares about is himself and
the Hardy Boys there

you gave us order,
we gave you our trust — don't lose
it over one man

after speech, his true
weakness revealed: he's in love
…with humanity

the point is that while
everyone else is playing
checkers, I'm playing

monopoly, and
I always build a hotel
on Boardwalk and *win*

you really believe
that we three will be enough?
~ we always have been

SEASON 9

Do You Believe in Miracles?

Episode 195 (Season 9, Episode 23)
Directed by Thomas J. Wright
Written by Jeremy Carver
Original air date: May 20, 2014

reunited all
angels under the banner
of Heaven — that's like…

winning a people's
choice award? not quite like the
real deal now, is it?

if wanted soapy
massage from Dr. Phil, would
have speed-dialed "3"

Dean, Crowley have been
bro-mancing over the blade
since Dean got the mark

you said you had plan
how we might convince them to
let us pass ~ Wookiee

never get tired?
get urge to just bugger off,
howl at the moon?

most people don't want
to be cynical — just want
something to believe

"Game of Thrones," shower
sex: that's complicated — Hell
ain't complicated

that big blade and that
douchey tribal tat sure gave
you some super-juice

SEASON 9

Do You Believe in Miracles? (cont.)

save Dean Winchester —
that was your goal, right? I mean
you draped yourself in

flag of Heaven, but
ultimately all about
saving one human

better this way — mark
making me into something
I don't want to be

didn't read enough —
you never did learn how to
tell a good story

• *Crowley explains to Dean that he's not dead yet...* •

brother, bless his soul:
summoning me as I speak —
make deal, bring you back

exactly what I
was talking about — it's all
become... expected

SEASON 9

Do You Believe in Miracles? (cont.)

you have to believe
when I suggested you take
on the mark of Cain

I didn't know that
this was going to happen
— not really, I mean

I might not have told
you the *entire* truth, but
I never lied, Dean

that is important,
fundamental, but… there's one
story about Cain

might have… forgotten
to tell: he, too, was willing
to accept his death

his death, rather than
becoming killer the mark
wanted him to be

he took his own life —
as rumor has it, the mark
never quite let go

you can understand
why I never spoke of this:
mere speculation

it wasn't until
you summoned me — it wasn't
truly until you

left that cheeseburger
uneaten — I began to
let myself believe

maybe miracles
do come true — so, listen to
me, Dean Winchester

what you're feeling right
now — it's not death, it is life:
a new kind of life

open your eyes, Dean,
see what I see, what I feel
— let's howl at moon

SEASON TEN

SEASON 10

Black

Episode 196 (Season 10, Episode 1)
Directed by Robert Singer
Written by Jeremy Carver
Original air date: October 7, 2014

I heard the rumors:
a Winchester? one of us?
it's true, isn't it?

you think there's any
chance at all that he's still… ~ Dean,
even remotely?

told you hurry up
then you had to do that thing
~ :: that you begged me for? ::

what's going on here? ~
:: what's it look like? :: ~ in *my* bed?
~ get a room, you two

when guy was stabbed in
front of me, did I conduct
a field interview?

brother and I were   only demonized
beginning to wonder if   soul that's inside of Dean is
hit another dog   his, and his alone

don't care he's demon —
it's that he's with me, having
the time of his life

Black (cont.)

he is my best friend,
my partner in crime — they'll write
songs, graphic novels

:: you lied :: ~ does tin man
have a sheet metal willy?
me, of course I lied

our professional
future — if I have to spend
one more night in this

fetid petri dish
of broken dreams and B.O.,
will cut off own face

:: deal was we howl ::
:: at the moon — no time stamp, no ::
:: expiration date ::

not ending party;   he is a monster ~
moving it — out club circuit, he *was*, but now he is prey
in stadium tour   — *I'm* the monster now

nothing but chaos —
not all bad: art, hope, love, dreams
~ those are human things

SEASON 10

Reichenbach

Episode 197 (Season 10, Episode 2)
Directed by Thomas J. Wright
Written by Andrew Dabb
Original air date: October 14, 2014

---

not psycho liar ~
well, a psycho liar *would*
say exactly that

she's my cherry pie,
tastes so good, make a grown man
cry — sweet cherry pie

I want to stay and
help — is that wrong? ~ no, it's
just very human

Castiel, I think
the Winchesters are a bad
influence on you

they may be a bit
rough, but they are the best men
I have ever known

death is your drug — you
will spend the rest of your life
chasing that dragon

:: murder 101: ::
:: hire someone to kill your wife, ::
:: don't want to be there ::

Reichenbach (cont.)

:: you got that pervy ::
:: "nail my secretary" look ::
~ it's different for guys

you're punk-ass demon —
you work for me now, get in
there and do your job

you killed the client? ~
:: does it matter? was a douche; ::
:: now he's a dead douche ::

tell me, what are you?
a demon? or a human?
pick a bloody side!

the crazy ones: they're
always good for a fling, not
a relationship

poor little Hannah:
you are so desperate to
be dominated

I have made deals born
of desperation —
always end in blood

you're wrong — not about
the lying part, I am a
terrific liar

:: ever stop to think ::
:: if I wanted to be cured, ::
:: I wouldn't have bailed ::

I don't care because
you are my brother, and I'm
here to take you home

and now here we are,
finally, Dean Winchester
~ :: oh great, a groupie ::

:: just spitballing here — ::
:: maybe you are not as good ::
:: as you think you are ::

doesn't make us square
if I see you again ~ stop,
no one likes a tease

:: it's just a car, Sam :: ~
wow, you really *have* gone dark
~ :: you have *no* idea ::

:: gonna spend whole life ::
:: knowing he had his shot and ::
:: he couldn't beat me ::

Soul Survivor

Episode 198 (Season 10, Episode 3)
Directed by Jensen Ackles
Written by Brad Buckner & Eugenie Ross-Leming
Original air date: October 21, 2014

:: you think you'll fix me — ::
:: occur to you that maybe ::
:: don't want to be fixed? ::

it's what humans do:
I say that I'm fine, and then
you say I look well

:: the lore, hunters, and ::
:: Men of Letters — what a load ::
:: of crap it all is ::

:: that line between us ::
:: and the things that we hunted ::
:: ain't clear, is it? ::

:: if this doesn't work ::
:: both know what you gotta do ::
:: — got stomach for that? ::

your preference to die
for your principles: noble,
but it's meaningless

carry on ~ I'm not
enough ~ sometimes *enough* is
whatever you have

we don't get to quit
in this family — this is
all we've ever had

:: Dad? he brainwashed us ::
:: into wasting lives fighting ::
:: *his* losing battle ::

been around humans,
seen how distractions occur:
feelings: temptations

why can't you people
just sit on clouds and play harps
like you're supposed to?

:: just enough demon ::
:: left in me that killing you ::
:: ain't no choice at all ::

I can see his point —
humans can feel real joy, but
also profound pain

take a lot more than
try to kill Sam with hammer
to make walk away

SEASON 10

Paper Moon

Episode 199 (Season 10, Episode 4)
Directed by Jeannot Szwarc
Written by Adam Glass
Original air date: October 28, 2014

---

you've been kicked, bit, scratched
stabbed, possessed, killed… and you sprain
your friggin' *elbow*?

it was a demon ~
does that sling come with a slice
of crybaby pie?

well, where do we start?
what with the logging ~ ice caps
~ bitcoin… Obama

watched you die, carried
your corpse, put your dead body
on your bed, and then…

he always knew: when
his clock ran out, it wasn't
gonna be pretty

never even said
thank you ~ don't ever have to
say that — not to me

this fleabag ain't done
eating Sons of Anarchy
~ guess she likes bad boys

going after her?
gotta admit: when push came
to kill, she did good

believe me or not:
never hurt anyone who
didn't deserve it

Kate, you keep moving,
keep your nose clean, and we can
stop meeting like this

to protect Tasha? ~
she is family, and worth
eating bullet for

just trying to do
right thing; I'm sick and tired
of doing wrong one

SEASON 10

Fan Fiction

Episode 200 (Season 10, Episode 5)
Directed by Phil Sgriccia
Written by Robbie Thompson
Original air date: November 11, 2014

---

amulet: symbol
of Winchesters' brotherly
love — take one for team

there's too much drama
in the drama department
— it's over, Marie

theater: about life,
truth — where is the truth in
"Supernatural"?

take it you're feeling
back to normal? ~ whatever
that is, in our world

out there hunting: it's
the only normal I know
— we got work to do

Hugh Jackman got cast
off "Oklahoma!" ~ yeah, you
ran tech, Wolverine

John, Mary: husband,
wife — bringing home brand new life:
his name is Sammy

what in the holy? ~
case probably has something
to do with all this

here to look into
the ~ there is no *singing* in
"Supernatural"!

if there *was* singing,
it would be classic rock, not
this Floyd Webber crap

we sing a cover
of "Carry on Wayward Son"
in the second act

gonna need 50
jello shots and hose-down to
get this stink off me

boy melodrama:
the two alone, together,
bonded, united

330

Fan Fiction (cont.)

you know they're brothers
right? ~ yes, but subtext ~ take a
sub-step back, ladies

canonically
no, but it's *transformative* ~
you mean fan fiction?

what are they doing? ~
kids these days call it "hugging"
~ is that in the show?

I just couldn't leave
it the way it was, so I
wrote my own ending

we *do* explore the
nature of Destiel in
act 2 ~ sorry, *what?*

it's just subtext, but
you know, you can't spell "subtext"
without s-e-x

I mean, shouldn't it
be "Dea-stiel"? "Sastiel"?
"CasDean"? ~ shut your face

all real: ghosts, angels,
demons ~ I want to believe
~ real, and so are *we*

willing to accept
monsters are real, but those books
are works of fiction

scary, right? ~ you want
to piñata this asshat? ~
nice, that's very "Dean"

Fan Fiction (cont.)

it's not a tulpa ~
say one more time, but just a
little more Arnold

scarecrow alive, and
we burned my prop for nothing?
~ it needed to burn

fight: especially
my sweet, brave, selfless Sam — there's
nothing he can't do

author inserting	I want you to put
themselves into narrative:	as much *sub* into that *text*
not my favorite	as possibly can

there's no other road,
other way, day, but today ~
did he just quote "Rent"?

he trained us both to
track, hunt and kill — he took from
us our own free will

on the road so far:
saving people, hunting things
— business, back in swing

so, you can pop in	raised from perdition
tomorrow morning ~ yes, so	to be God's ammunition
I'll just wait here, then	— I will wait for you

Fan Fiction (cont.)

• *"A Single Man Tear," song from the musical: Supernatural* •

exorcizamus
omnis immundus, 'zamus
omnis spiritus

because underneath
the manly sheen — it is my
brother: boy named Dean

a single man tear
slips down his face — emotion
shown without a trace

a single man tear,
single man tear, single man
tear — that's all we fear

he hides behind a
mask so strong — he is worried
that he could be wrong

exorcizamus
omnis… a single man tear,
that is all I'll spare

wish he could see way
I see him: perfect brother;
a man without sin

…own man — underneath
this broken mask, it is my
father, all his wrath

a single man tear,
single man tear, single man
— no chick-flick moments!

has it all: life, death,
resurrection, redemption,
family… music

can tap your toe to —
not meandering piece of
genre dreck — epic

Season 10

Fan Fiction (cont.)

    you should leave before
anyone asks questions — thanks
      for saving my friends

        educational:
you know, seeing the story
    from your perspective

    don't need a symbol
to remind me how I feel
    about my brother

you're right, Sammy — out
on the road, just the two of
  us ~ against the world

• *"Carry on Wayward Son," cover from the musical, Supernatural* •

     carry on my son,
there'll be peace when you are done
    don't you cry no more

     once I rose above
noise and confusion, just to
   get a glimpse beyond

    this illusion — I
was soaring ever higher,
   but I flew too high

    masquerading as
man with a reason, charade
    is the event of

   the season, and if
I claim to be a wise man,
surely means don't know

  carry wayward son
lay your weary head to rest
  don't you cry no more

---

    second act: wonky,
the first act has some issues,
 but, what did you think?

SEASON 10

Ask Jeeves

Episode 201 (Season 10, Episode 6)
Directed by John MacCarthy
Written by Eric Carmelo & Nicole Snyder
Original air date: November 18, 2014

---

ready: jump back in —
radio silence ~ Murphy's
Law ~ Murphy's a douche

Bobby had secrets,
like loving Tori Spelling
— Dean cheated on her

find herself ~ ashram
in India? ~ clown college
in Sarasota

you stay here and keep
an eye on Mrs. Peacock
and Colonel Mustard

husband and wife tag-
team killer ghosts? ~ gotta keep
the marriage alive

cut the crap, Wadsworth —
what you doing hiding dead
maids in secret rooms?

Sam finds the butler
dead, while Dean is talking to
him in different room

shapeshifter's using
dead people ~ we can rule out
"the butler did it"

our get togethers
don't end in murder — only
thing different is *you*

rope, lead pipe, wrench, knife,
candlestick, revolver: all
the weapons of "Clue"

we are not the bad
guys, Dash ~ I beg to differ:
you're wearing flannel

I *knew* those boys were
trailer-trash, not to mention
homosexuals

just as my dad was
about to take me, hunter
became the hunted

serious, Izod:
put pin in it, we'll come back
for your preppy ass

335

SEASON 10

Girls, Girls, Girls

Episode 202 (Season 10, Episode 7)
Directed by Robert Singer
Written by Robert Berens
Original air date: November 25, 2014

---

you're on dating app?
"impala67" ~
don't knock 'til you try

I'm taking shower ~
we do not need to shower
~ does this bother you?

I would sooner die
than do business of any
kind with filth like you

it's hardly the most
appetizing process, but
it makes me hungry

you threw me into
the sex trade? I'm evil, but
that is just tacky

on the run from those
fannies — screw the grand coven
and their silly rules

I had to take my
vessel from his family
— twice, actually

here on earth, working
with you, I've felt things — human
things: passions, hungers

were you a demon
when you murdered my father?
you're *still* a monster

those stories that we
tell to keep us going? man,
sometimes they blind us

go to dark places:
I beat the crap out of a
good man just for fun

people who love me
pulled me back from that edge — truth:
I'm beyond saving

know how story ends:
at the edge of a blade or
barrel of a gun

Hibbing 911

Episode 203 (Season 10, Episode 8)
Directed by Tim Andrew
Story by Jenny Klein & Phil Sgriccia, Teleplay by Jenny Klein
Original air date: December 2, 2014

---

hey, we good? ~ aces
I love the smell of parchment
in the morning, yeah

you'd think these eggheads,
with all amassed crap, would have
something important

hiya! looks like you
didn't get partner ~ looks like
~ well, you got one now

she smokes grass under
bleachers, but at least she's not
luring men to deaths

Sheriff Mills? might say
she left her manners back in
Sioux Falls — she's with me

I just met the guy:
Doug seems like kind of a dick
~ but, he was *my* dick

got any gems on
how to handle teenage girl,
'cause mine is… ~ a dick?

haven't been able
to shake that ray of sunshine
— she's pretty helpful

ain't the first feds to
roll through, come up with nothing
— cute to watch you try

be a little less
defensive of pretend job ~
this badge *means* something

just sayin': I make
mean bowl of chowder if you
ever need to talk

ever think there are
things out there that don't end up
in police blotter?

if you want pointers
how to fight this crazy crap,
I can fill you in

SEASON 10

The Things We Left Behind

Episode 204 (Season 10, Episode 9)
Directed by Guy Norman Bee
Written by Andrew Dabb
Original air date: December 9, 2014

I'm not your father ~
right — those were the first words you
ever said to me

you took everything
from me; what do you want now?
~ I came to help you

what is it you do? ~
I fight certain deadly threats
to humanity

Castiel I met:
wanted to punch him in his
stupid angel face

I was not that bad ~
you were — now you're just… nicer,
and kind of a doof

people trying to
do their best in world where too
easy to do worst

appreciate meal,   a midlife crisis? ~
and felony, but don't need   I'm extremely old, I think
a babysitter   I am entitled

SEASON 10

The Things We Left Behind (cont.)

---

people you let down:
can't save — you gotta forget
'em for your own good

is that what you do? ~
opposite of what I do
— ain't a role model

Cas, promise something:
if I *do* go dark side, you
gotta take me out

knife, smite, throw into
the sun — don't let Sam get in
the way, 'cause he'll try

I can not go down
that road again, man — I can't
be that thing again

horrible mother —
almost traded for three pigs
— worth five pigs *at least*

want to talk to me
about wrong? you killed my dad
wrong enough for you?

used to pray to you,
Castiel: beg you to bring
him home safe ~ I know

King of Hell, bravo —
I always knew that my boy
was meant for big things

never knew father —
did you love *your* father? ~ with
everything I had

won't win "number one
dad" awards, but he was there
when we needed him

son, you don't like me?
not my job to be liked — my
job: to raise you right

think Claire's in trouble? ~
hanging with guy named Randy,
she is in trouble

tell me you *had* to
do this, tell me it was them
or you ~ I didn't

339

SEASON 10

The Hunter Games

Episode 205 (Season 10, Episode 10)
Directed by John Badham
Written by Eugenie Ross-Leming & Brad Buckner
Original air date: January 20, 2015

---

you are soaked in the
horror sweat — I haven't seen
that since the plague years

was a massacre —
a time I was a hunter,
not stone-cold killer

lovely room — it's where
you bring the kinky chicks, right?
~ I'll ask the questions

locals were going
to try me for witchcraft, and
that never ends well

he's gone nuclear:
total foaming-at-the-mouth,
balls-out maniac

won't apologize
for being career woman
— can be family

isn't gonna work —
you look like my father — it's
his body, he's dead

Claire, you have seen things,
you have been through things that no
one your age should have

Dean is a monster ~
possible there's a little
monster in us all

nebbishy little
guy, me, always sticking it
to the lunkhead jocks

The Hunter Games (cont.)

why you just assume
I'm not gonna be helpful?
~ 'cause you're a dickwad

wait dinner for you? ~
you don't cook, I do not eat:
perfect arrangement

yeah, well, you know us:
when we screw ourselves, we do
like to go whole-hog

maybe: connection —
extremely messed-up human
to another one

settling a score
that has taken way too long
— gonna enjoy it

Dean Winchester, whose
existence defined by war
on dark and monstrous

I can pick up on
longing — perhaps you wanted
to tell me something

I'm gonna try to
let go of the little bit
of monster in me

SEASON 10

There's No Place Like Home

Episode 206 (Season 10, Episode 11)
Directed by Phil Sgriccia
Written by Robbie Thompson
Original air date: January 27, 2015

---

soon as we get rid
of this demonic tramp stamp,
I am back on booze

you mean *our* Charlie?
yea high? wouldn't hurt hobbit?
practically *sparkles*?

if shrink interviewed
us at that age, wouldn't be
kittens and rainbows

adorable — that's
your problem: all good-guy code
no bite — what a waste

I made a deal with
the wizard… of Oz — wears hood,
creepy mask: a jerk

normally, I'd be
pounding Harvey Wallbangers,
checking out her ass

now, all I want to
do is sip club soda and
send her to college

learned from being dark?
it sets you free, and part of
you knows that's right, too

you hit like a girl
who never learned how to hit
— that's it, let it out

you killed the wizard —
I knew it: the magic was
in you all the time

I forgive you, Dean ~
yeah, well *I* don't ~ I know, that
is kind of your move

SEASON 10

About a Boy

Episode 207 (Season 10, Episode 12)
Directed by Serge Ladouceur
Written by Adam Glass
Original air date: February 3, 2015

---

can't live your life locked
in this room ~ got three hots and
a cot, could be worse

you can beat this, Dean ~
do you really believe that?
~ damn right I believe

believed in Easter
Bunny until you were twelve
~ eleven ~ ...and half

we all know what is
going on here ~ don't say it...
~ aliens ~ said it

can handle questions
with locals — it's a dive bar;
it's my comfort zone

what can I do you? ~
screw it, gonna believe in
myself ~ attaboy

bathroom: "like staring
into the devil's butt" — true
saw it ~ the john, or...

just a drunk ~ prefer
functional alcoholic ~
really, who *are* you?

no grass in infield
and a girl is gonna die
— not in chatty mood

heard Taylor Swift song
on the bus to the motel
...and I *liked* it, Sam

you can drink again
in seven years ~ not funny
~ that's *kind of* funny

now, you filet one
rugrat, people get angry
~ I blame Obama

three ex-husbands and
50 grand in debt: I was
a crappy adult

343

About a Boy (cont.)

mark and everything
else: we'll figure it out, we
always do ~ damn right

• *Formerly teenage Dean now appreciates Taylor Swift* •

players gonna play,
play, play, play, play *Sam winces*
the haters gonna

hate, hate, hate, hate, hate,
baby I am just gonna
shake, shake, shake, shake, shake

shake it off, shake off
Dean shrugs heartbreakers gonna
break, break, break, break, break

Impala peels out
and the fakers are gonna
fake, fake, fake, fake, fake

baby I am just
gonna shake, shake, shake, shake, shake,
shake it off, shake off

SEASON 10

Halt & Catch Fire

Episode 208 (Season 10, Episode 13)
Directed by John F. Showalter
Written by Eric Charmelo & Nicole Snyder
Original air date: February 10, 2015

---

don't you think: if Cain
knew how to get rid of mark,
he would have *done* it?

Trini is nav app —
it is like a talking map
— you are Gen X, right?

got Italian,
Chinese, froyo — college is
better than Vegas

if died, I drove car
you'd kill me? ~ if you stunk her
up with taquitos

now I am going
through her deleted files
~ wait, you can do that?

I've made more mistakes
than I can count — mistakes that
haunt me, day and night

ask for forgiveness —
can't just bury stuff like this
— gotta deal with it

keep killing, become
something you won't recognize
— or, you can move on

I gotta know where
I stand — otherwise, I am
gonna lose my mind

my peace is helping
people, working cases — that's
all I want to do

gonna fight it 'til
I can't fight it anymore,
then go down swinging

345

SEASON 10

The Executioner's Song

Episode 209 (Season 10, Episode 14)
Directed by Phil Sgriccia
Written by Robert Berens
Original air date: February 17, 2015

I've gone by many
names in this life — the *Father*
of Murder is one

did I come here to
punish you, or to save you?
I'm here to do both

fishing, needlepoint?
hobbies — serial killer
stats? that's an illness

that's why I never
gave in when you asked for sweets,
no matter how cried

mark thirsts for all kinds	the blade against Cain —
~ this is a *massacre* ~ and	win or lose, you may never
soon a genocide	come back from that fight
well, *of course* I was	if he's not a threat
manipulating you — I'm	to your life, he's a threat to
mother after all	credibility

I said I would go
down swinging — at peace with that
— didn't know: so soon

The Executioner's Song (cont.)

take out whatever
comes out of there, and I mean
whatever comes out

not all killers are
my descendants, not all my
descendants: killers

but enough *are* to
know that extinguishing them:
least I owe this world

no resisting mark
or the blade — there is only
remission, relapse

my story began
when I killed my brother — that's
where *your* story ends

tell me that you will
stop — tell me that you *can* stop
~ I will *never* stop

you're not a mother —
you can't know what that pride felt
like, how *huge* it was

you've got the crown, but
you're no ruler, not *really*
— a sad, bored, wee boy

flop ass-up, second
Winchesters ask you to — you're
no king, you're their bitch

SEASON 10

The Things They Carried

Episode 210 (Season 10, Episode 15)
Directed by John Badham
Written by Jenny Klein
Original air date: March 18, 2015

---

there's that point when we
have to face the truth, even
if we don't like it

agents, I gather ~
suits? or do we give off some
sort of a fed-stench?

gonna keep doing
what we do, and I'd like you
to be there with me

look, I know what you
two are thinking, but we will
not hunt my best friend

you save people from
things they can't wrap minds around
— no one notices

almost took you off
the map — who'd save me now? ~ don't
get sentimental

you say that like it
is just another Tuesday
~ it's only Monday

you'd be a hostile
environment — well, more than
you already *are*

it was a real-life,
actual, honest-to-god
monster: what you saw

I hope I don't see
two of you anymore, no
offense ~ none taken

Dean-o, will you do
me the honor of tying
me to this chair, here?

couldn't save this one ~
can do everything right... still
sometimes the guy dies

Paint It Black

Episode 211 (Season 10, Episode 16)
Directed by John F. Showalter
Written by Brad Bucker & Eugenie Ross-Leming
Original air date: March 25, 2015

---

yes, one expects to
suffer in Hell — but, I fear
I've reached my limit

how do you quit one
life for something different,
and *believe* in it?

felt I had no choice:
my life had become painful,
there was hopelessness

making fun of me? ~
FBI believes in *ghosts*?
I'm afraid *I* don't

how long since my last? ~
never been to confession
~ well, that is *too* long

I do not grovel
before she who lay with a
non-magic, hatched spawn

finally confessed —
said words out loud: "I love you"
— I waited, dying

in shadows: dicking
around with black cats, broomsticks
instead of greatness

• *Dean's confession with Father Delaney gets real* •

what if I didn't
want to die… I'm not ready
~ you expecting to?

life, the work I do —
I pretty much just figured:
all there *was* to me

jam the key in the
ignition, and haul ass 'til
I ran out of gas

go out: way I live —
pedal to the metal, that
would be it ~ but now?

SEASON 10

Paint It Black (cont.)

recent events make
me think I might be closer
to that than I thought

I'm just starting to
think that maybe there's more to
it all than I thought

I don't know… there's things,
people, feelings that I want
to experience

learning there's more to
universe than tiny world
can be frightening

differently than I
have done before, or maybe
even for first time

you truly believe
in God, agent? because that
can be a comfort

I believe there *is*
a God, but I'm not sure he
still believes in us

a spiritual
person: accepted many
planes of existence

my relationship
with Winchesters: my business
— I'm not killing them

it's the Winchesters —
again with the Winchesters
— perpetually…

who mixes their blood
and bones in *paint*? no woman
ever did for *me*

:: business to forgive ::
:: you pigs, when what you do is ::
:: *unforgivable* ::

don't buy that the mark
is terminal — don't make peace
with that idea

350

Inside Man

Episode 212 (Season 10, Episode 17)
Directed by Rashaad Ernesto Green
Written by Andrew Dabb
Original air date: April 1, 2015

Bobby's in Heaven,
having a drink, and reading
'bout Tori Spelling

I say we get drunk
and shoot crap ~ yeah, except we
do that every day

you can be damned *and*
a conscientious worker
~ sure you're a demon?

hippie here? seeing
some creep-ass hobbit fella
in a prison cell

I am an angel ~
can't be — I'm an atheist
~ well, not anymore

hustled me? ~ pretty
quick for a guy who's all hair
gel and body spray

so, you can hear thoughts? ~
well, not yours — all I'm getting
from *you* is colors

mark gone, or *demon*?
just another day at the
office for you boys

remember when job
was just chopping up some fang,
tossing back cold one?

so, while I'm playing
Steve McQueen, will anyone
be looking for me?

SEASON 10

Inside Man (cont.)

what's a nice girl like you doing in a place like this? I'm sorry did	I say *nice girl?* I meant evil skank ~ you say that like it's an insult

snap: he comes running —
you're good influence on him;
why you need to die

a wise man once told me,
"family don't end in blood" — does
not start there either

trying to kill him ~
been there: never seems to work
out the way you want

family's there through the
good, bad, all of it — got your
back, even when hurts

Bobbys are fighting
back — they're surly — I repeat,
the Bobbys: surly

he looks like Fraggle ~
take as compliment — that was
excellent program

Winchester playbook ~
Dean: given up ~ you idjits
haven't? ~ no, would you?

just trying to buy
time 'til I screw you over
— what? it worked before

here I am playing
Dr. Phil to King of Hell:
not see that coming

you may have brought me
into this world, but you were
never my mother

why you letting her? ~
because we're family, we're blood
~ that's not the same thing

I'm bloody *Crowley* —
I'm King of Hell: I do what
I want, when I want

352

Inside Man (cont.)

• *Bobby's letter to Sam* •

just wanted to say:
Cas told me what you're doing
for Dean, and I'm not

asking you to stop —
but maybe going behind
his back ain't the best

your brother — well, he
can be stubborn, but I think
he would understand

I know it's the life —
doing a *little* bad so
can do *lot* of good

sometimes bad's real bad,
and the good — it can come at
one hell of a price

ain't there on the ground —
whatever you do, I know
you'll make the right choice

you're a good man, Sam
Winchester — one of the best;
I'm damn proud of you

I was content here,
but getting the call from you:
happiest I've been

no matter what it
costs — stay safe, keep fighting, and
kick it in the ass

SEASON 10

Book of the Damned

Episode 213 (Season 10, Episode 18)
Directed by P. J. Pesce
Written by Robbie Thompson
Original air date: April 15, 2015

---

are you always so
condescending when someone's
pointing blade at you?

you're right: inclement
weather for nuptials and
the wrong cutlery

at inopportune
times is hardly ironic
— but *sure* is catchy

can I kill him now? ~
you know I can *hear* you, right?
~ no, need him alive

I'm in a phone booth —
didn't know these existed
outside Bill and Ted's

gonna take time off:
beach, drinking cervezas, swim,
local "wildlife"

this book is old and
scary, and I've never seen
anything like it

last on beach? ~ never ~
sand between our toes, Sammy,
sand between our toes

it has been one crap
sandwich after another
for the past few weeks

used to be human —
don't you miss all this? ~ no, I
don't miss digestion

Book of the Damned (cont.)

you killed my friend ~ Dean
is fine… mostly… can you not
get past that? ~ never

just a cupid — just
an angry, angry cupid
~ I see you're upset

you call yourselves nerds?
~ get our Alan Turing on
and decrypt this bitch

book's calling to me —
it's calling out to the mark
like it is alive

destroy it before
it falls into the wrong hands
— and that includes me

buddy comedy,
without the comedy ~ or
the buddies ~ *come on*

glowing lights filled with
self-loathing or delusions
of grandeur — or both

Cas: swam *so* far just
to drown in shallow waters
— isn't ironic?

life mostly ends in
Sophie's choices, death, or tears;
all of the above

this life: I love it —
can't do it without brother
— don't *want* to do it

oh, the places I'll
go with *this* and your grace — one
out of two ain't bad

your carpal tunnel
and your bullet wound now healed
~ just become besties?

SEASON 10

Book of the Damned (cont.)

• *Sam's deception with the book of the damned is revealed,*
"Behind Blue Eyes" •

no one knows what it
is like to be the bad man,
to be the sad man

behind blue eyes — no
one knows what it's like to be
hated, be fated

telling only lies —
but my dreams aren't as empty
as my conscience seems

to be, have hours ~
I don't trust you, and never
will ~ only lonely

my love is vengeance ~
but I need help, and this is
right in your wheelhouse

that is never free ~
Sam, burn it now ~ when my fist
clenches, crack open

before I use it,
lose my cool — when I smile,
tell me some bad news

before I laugh, act
like a fool — if I swallow
anything evil

silly boy ~ finger
down my throat — if I shiver,
give me a blanket

keep me warm, let me
wear coat ~ family never
stop looking for book

need the mark of Cain
off brother; something tells me
can crack book, find cure

no one knows what it's
like ~ the only question is
~ to be the bad man

will you help me? ~ be
the sad man, behind blue eyes
~ shall we discuss terms?

SEASON 10

The Werther Project

Episode 214 (Season 10, Episode 19)
Directed by Stefan Pleszczynski
Written by Robert Berens
Original air date: April 22, 2015

---

only one thing you
can do for me I can't do
myself: kill my son

you wouldn't have come
if I wasn't last resort
— you are desperate

couldn't have waited? ~
come on, I can handle it
— I *did* handle it

why so small-minded?
already apologized
for that accident

beauty sleep isn't
optional — I am over
300 years old

it's in our wheelhouse
— our responsibility;
it's our legacy

told her not to go —
no one goes in the basement
~ what's in the basement?

don't you see? deals with
witches, opening the box
— *you're* the reckless one

you'll do *anything*
to keep on clinging to that
doomed brother of yours

take this all on by
yourself, but odds *totally*
are stacked against you

SEASON 10

The Werther Project (cont.)

---

can't leave Dean alone ~
well then, we'll just have to tie
up the bonny lad

you gotta wonder:
why *this* place? where you wanna
be — your happy place

"to silence the box,
slake its thirst with blood
of our own" — my blood

all you have to do	no one needs to know:
is be still for one moment	happens in purgatory
— fight will come to *you*	stays purgatory
know you can see it:	always loved it here —
the purity, the honor	as good a place as any
~ no honor in that	to call it a day

do it if had to,
I *would*, but the real Benny
would never let me

this thing on my arm,
for better or worse — the mark:
it wants me alive

the universe is
trying to tell us something:
stronger together

358

Angel Heart

Episode 215 (Season 10, Episode 20)
Directed by Steve Boyum
Written by Robbie Thompson
Original air date: April 29, 2015

Jimmy is that you?
I looked everywhere for you
~ so sorry I left

I don't know any
miracle worker — think I'd
be in dump like *this*?

need help from *both* of
you — you were both troubled teens;
you speak her language

looking for my mom:
want to find her, and tell her
she ruined my life

um… happy birthday
— got it at hot topical ~
right… um, thanks, I guess

gimme something to
punch already — I'm kidding
I'm fine… I'm just… fine

I'm coming with you ~
I am coming with you, too
~ you want in on this?

found in hospital
she'd be better off on own?
~ stronger on her own

cooped up in this room,
will lose mind ~ spoiler alert:
you already have

credit card scams too? ~
yeah, hunting monsters doesn't
exactly pay bills

putts it's in the hole!
it's in the hole! — Bill Murray?
Caddyshack? *classic*

why do you do it? ~
help people, make a difference
~ that's *it*? ~ not enough?

I wasn't watching —
did the ball go in the hole?
~ *sighs* Happy Gilmore

Angel Heart (cont.)

your dad's sacrifice
was not meaningless — he gave
up his vessel, so

Cas could save the world
— your father is a hero;
did not die in vain

souls: little slices
of Heaven — properly kept,
make delicious meals

Jimmy is that you?
is this…? ~ Heaven — I waited
for you for so long

a halfway house for
wayward girls? ~ Jody Mills: good
people — place to crash

sometimes death isn't
always goodbye; goodbyes aren't
always forever

you go down this path —
our path — it's not a long life
~ *you* seem pretty old

gonna be okay? ~
I'll keep fighting, keep swinging
'til got nothing left

someone just tell me
she is gonna be okay ~
of course, so will *you*

SEASON 10

Dark Dynasty

Episode 216 (Season 10, Episode 21)
Directed by Robert Singer
Written by Eugenie Ross-Leming & Brad Buckner
Original air date: May 6, 2015

---

so, now we need to
break a code to break a code?
~ quick aren't you?

on your own a lot
past couple weeks ~ I do that
~ you actually don't

screwed with financial
markets, helped Hitler, god knows
— probably disco

you'll be working with
one of the most dangerous
witches in the world

I know *all* the great
global centers of witchcraft
~ I'm not witch, I'm nerd

you studied craft where? ~
mostly at Más Java — has
excellent Wi-Fi

what are the rules? if
I'm going to referee,
should at least know them

us lying to Dean
is the choice that sucks the least
— have to make this work

I wish you trolls would
bring me good news — "Missouri
has boils" — cheerful

SEASON 10

Dark Dynasty (cont.)

I'm sure you're learning:
line between good and evil
is quite flexible

you have made them the
family you don't have ~ they
are like my brothers

I love them ~ I know:
that steadfast loyalty will
be your undoing

some dark thoughts, creepy
visions, violent urges
shrug same old, same old

just staying in touch ~
is something on your mind? ~no,
this call is pointless

I'm surrounded by
mediocrity — wonder
I stay so buoyant

she is evil ~ she
is a wicked witch, so by
definition she…

chaos breeds fear, then
panic, desperation — there's
always profit there

why not go public? ~
she wrote a book — doesn't get
more public than that

book is protected
by a spell — it's eternal
cannot be destroyed

you pulled Cas into
it, and Charlie ~ she loves you
Dean, we all love you

The Prisoner

Episode 217 (Season 10, Episode 22)
Directed by Thomas J. Wright
Written by Andrew Dabb
Original air date: May 13, 2015

I am so sorry ~
you got her killed; you don't get
to apologize

I'll never forgive
myself ~ I think it should be
you up there, not her

you've always been soft —
you're baby, it's natural
— but all that ends now

angel rejected
Heaven? like fish wants to fly,
dog thinks he's people

what are you doing? ~
I'm saving my brother ~ but
you told Dean ~ I know...

got 17 fake
IDs, trunk full of guns, knives,
freaking *ninja stars*

by the way, she said
to tell that you she should have
taken the three pigs

that's what I get for
trying to be the good guy
~ so, you're the good guy?

you have accent, suit,
snark — but at the end of it,
you are a monster

could kill you: snap my
fingers — easiest thing in
the world *hesitates*

you took something from
me — now I am gonna take
everything from you

seven nipples for
the ladies — or the fellas
shrug I do not judge

there is bad in you —
in your *blood* — you can run, but
bad will always win

took down a monster,
that's what I do — continue...
~ 'til become monster

The Prisoner (cont.)

magic like that does
not come free — comes with a price
that you pay in blood

• Cas gets real with Dean about the mark of Cain •

maybe you could fight
mark for years — centuries, like
Cain — not forever

when you finally
turn, and you will turn, Sam and
everyone you know

everyone you *love* could be long dead — everyone except me: I'm the one	who will have to watch you murder the world, so if there is even a

small chance that we can
save you, I will not let you
walk out of this room

the Dean I know would never murder that kid ~ that Dean's kind of a dick	Dean stop ~ you and Sam stay the hell away from me — next time I won't miss

SEASON 10

Brother's Keeper

Episode 218 (Season 10, Episode 23)
Directed by Phil Sgriccia
Written by Jeremy Carver
Original air date: May 20, 2015

---

consequences, but
nobody can tell what those
consequences are

you've worked some pretty
dark stuff in your day, agent
— must have left a mark

you know, I don't know
what crawled up your ass today
— frankly, I don't care

bring something I love, I'll kill it — problem is I don't love anything	this mark of Cain thing is really getting to Dean *trashes motel room*

who even summons
anymore? couldn't you call?
~ not in contacts list

tell me that's queso ~
and taquitos, tamales —
homemade, with bad fat

never thought I'd see
the day: Dean Winchester has
tipped over his king

Brother's Keeper (cont.)

• Death explains the mark of Cain's relationship to the darkness •

creatio ex
nihilo — God created
earth out of nothing

so your Sunday-school
teacher would have you believe
— before there was light

before there was God
and archangels, there wasn't
nothing, there was the

darkness: horribly
destructive, amoral force,
beaten back by God

and his archangels
in a terrible war — God
locked darkness away

where could do no harm —
created mark that would serve
as both lock and key

which he entrusted
to most valued lieutenant,
who was Lucifer

but the mark began
to assert its own will, and
revealed itself as

a curse: began to
corrupt — Lucifer became
jealous of man, so

SEASON 10

Brother's Keeper (cont.)

Lucifer banished
to Hell by God — Lucifer
passed the mark to Cain

Cain, who passed the mark
to you — the proverbial
finger in the dike

could remove the mark,
but only if you will share
it with another

ensure that the lock
remains unbroken, and the
darkness remains banned

I am not doing
that, not to anyone ~ what
if I told you that

I could relocate
you somewhere far away, not
even on this earth

still be alive, but
no longer a danger to
yourself or others?

brother I am done ~
no, no you're not ~ grab a pen;
time to say goodbye

*Crowley describes Seth's
past* how do you know all this?
~ a hamster told me

not incapable
of love — you're incapable
just of loving *me*

SEASON 10

Brother's Keeper (cont.)

• *That line between good and evil that seems so clear upon first glance is actually quite blurry, but fighting to protect your loved ones is still a good idea (most of the time)* •

whatever you are thinking of doing, don't — there is another way

you don't need to go with him, you don't need to die ~ funny you say that

I thought the only way out was my death — well, I was wrong, Sam, it's *yours*

what? he's gonna send you into outer space? ~ not… ~ this is *madness*, Dean

far from, I'm afraid ~ no one asked you ~ hear him out ~ our conundrum is

simple, Sam — brother cannot be killed, and the mark cannot be destroyed

without inciting greater evil than any of us ever known

the darkness ~ what's that? ~ what does it sound like? does it *sound* like a good thing?

even if remove Dean from the playing field, we are still left with you

loyal, dogged Sam who will never rest until he sets brother free

never rest until brother is free of the mark, which simply cannot

happen, lest darkness be set free — and there was that time you stood me up

you traded my life ~ I am willing to live with this thing forever

as long as I know that I, and it, will never hurt a living thing

Brother's Keeper (cont.)

this isn't you — this
doesn't make any sense ~ oh,
it makes perfect sense

we were in that church
making Crowley human, 'bout
to close gates of Hell

stop thinking about
yourself for one damn minute
~ for the greater good

you were ready to
die for the greater good then
~ and *you* pulled me back

once you consider
that, this makes all the sense in
the world ~ remember

I was wrong, you were
right: this world would be better
without us in it

you're twisting my words
here, Dean ~ why? because we track
evil and kill it?

the family business
is that it? look at the tapes
Sam, evil tracks us

it nukes everything
in our vicinity: our
family, our friends

your arm's evil — not
you, me ~ I let Rudy die
how's that not evil?

time we put proper
name to what we really are,
and we deal with it

I know what I am —
who were *you* when you drove that
man to sell his soul?

we are not evil
we're far from perfect, but we
are good — that thing on

you bullied Charlie
into getting herself killed
— a good end? *just* end?

SEASON 10

Brother's Keeper (cont.)

remove the mark, no
matter the consequences
— how's that *not* evil?

I have thing on arm,
and you're willing to let the
darkness into world

also summoned death
to make sure you could never
do any more harm

you summoned me 'cause
you knew I would protect you
— not an evil man

that is a good man
crying to be heard, searching
for some other way

you will never hear
me say that you the real you is
anything but good

but, before you hurt
anyone else, have to be
stopped at any cost

I understand, do
it ~ please do me the honor
~ Sammy, close your eyes

take these, and one day
when you *do* find your way back,
let these be your guide

help you remember
what it was like to be good;
what it was to love

it's for family
you must proceed, Dean — to be
what you are, become

what you've become is
a stain on their memory
— do it, or I will

---

helps Sam up okay? ~
I'll live, you? ~ fantastic — I
think I just killed death

SEASON ELEVEN

SEASON 11

Out of the Darkness, Into the Fire

Episode 219 (Season 11, Episode 1)
Directed by Robert Singer
Written by Jeremy Carver
Original air date: October 7, 2015

---

had this energy
about her — this focus — but
yeah, not a talker

just hours ago,
I killed death — I'm pretty much
up for anything

you saying I should
not kill you right now? ~ am I
saying that, or you?

how long since attacked? ~
real question is: how long 'til
I become like *them*

• *Castiel's prayer to the angels* •

brothers and sisters,
I know I have no right; I
have no standing to

ask you anything —
but, these are desperate times,
so ask you I must

I will confess my
transgressions and I accept
whatever doled-out

punishment — now, I
ask you to help me — please save
me from doing worse

I'll go find somewhere
quiet to lay low, and you
save my baby girl

didn't call for help
until after the orgy?
~ won't apologize

SEASON 11

Out of the Darkness, Into the Fire (cont.)

---

the same plan as it's
always been: in order to
get out, we go through

have we made mistakes?
hell yes — we can analyze
them over Frosties

when old, and farting
sawdust, and out of this room
— now: save that baby

if we don't change *now*,
our crap is just gonna keep
repeating itself

hunting things: we're great
at that, but that's only half
the bumper sticker

what cure? ~ Dean, there is
always a cure — you just have
to *want* to find it

you do what you do,
but you have got to let me
do what I do, too

saving people means
saving *all* of the people
— not just each other

if you are as bad
as they say you are, then why
haven't you hurt me?

I unleashed a force
on this world that could destroy
it, just to save you

we'll always be bound:
you helped me, and I helped you
— we will always help

373

SEASON 11

Form and Void

Episode 220 (Season 11, Episode 2)
Directed by Phil Sgriccia
Written by Andrew Dabb
Original air date: October 14, 2015

grew up here: learned to
ride my bike down the road, had
my first kiss at that

blue house over there
…lost virginity up there
~ bet blue house was pissed

you're so great with her ~
what can I say? chicks dig me
— gonna be okay

what's your name? ~ bite me ~
okay, "bite me," how long have
you been infected?

seen some people change
fast, some slow — in the end we
all end up the same

if you were smart, you'd
put a bullet in me, and
then eat one yourself

I'm calling father
Wyatt ~ Grandma, no ~ then who
are we gonna call?

crap happens: I asked
for a vessel that didn't
have psoriasis

when you choose between
Heaven and Winchesters, you
choose *them* every time

Form and Void (cont.)

• *The first time we see Billie the reaper, she's singing the song that was playing as Death was introduced in season 5* •

oh death, won't you spare
me over another year
reaper Billie sings

oh, what is this that
I can't see, with ice-cold hands
taking hold on me?

when God is gone, and
devil takes hold, who'll have
mercy on your soul?

you, brother have been
good for business ~ you're reaper
~ circle gets the square

• *Billie explains the new rules, now that Death is dead* •

dying and coming
back again, and again — Death
thought it was funny

next time you or your
brother bite it, not going
to Heaven *or* Hell

now, there is one hard,
fast rule in this universe —
that is: what lives… dies

gonna make mistake,
toss you into the Empty —
nought comes back from that

SEASON 11

Form and Void (cont.)

if I have to die,
I've made my peace with that, but
Dean deserves better

you know each other? ~
oh yes, Dean was a rather
scrumptious altar boy

pathetic has-been —
did I offend delicate
sensibilities?

darkness: locked away
since the dawn of creation,
and now it is free

other angels hate
you ~ what about you? you hate
me? ~ doesn't matter

listen, Velma, this
isn't the Scooby Gang ~ I'm
more of a Daphne

the child *likes* you —
it's no surprise, really — you're
very maternal

even if you *could*
murder a baby, couldn't
murder *that* baby

adorable Dean,
I get what I want — I'm not
your bloody sidekick

The Bad Seed

Episode 221 (Season 11, Episode 3)
Directed by Jensen Ackles
Written by Brad Buckner & Eugenie Ross-Leming
Original air date: October 21, 2015

---

cut crap, Rowena —
you just want protection from
hunter Winchesters

if anyone can
protect you from rascally
deity, 'tis I

nothing involving
a crappy Continental ~
you think it's crappy?

loves waffles — try there?
~ every restaurant in the
entire country

where you are? the date? ~
earth, several billion years
from the beginning

they've been scouring
the earth for the perp — it's slang
for "perpetrator"

I am what you are
becoming; you and I are
mightier than God

you know what gets squeezed?
grunts like us ~ yeah, punch a clock:
you're expendable

that's God for you: not
thought out — the whole big bang thing?
more of a big bust

SEASON 11

The Bad Seed (cont.)

---

we can shape things to
our own worldview — virtue is
extinct; pure evil

watching a human
reject the light and embrace
their depravity

that optimism —
that's what I admire in you
— that plucky, stupid…

what new hell has Dean
unleashed upon the world? book
wasn't specific

we're not going to
take the cuffs off ~ there's no trust
— are we not a *team*?

glad conversation going — family relations: speciality	(when Rowena says that last word of the haiku it's 5 syllables)

there aren't words ~ you're right
Cas, because there's no need: you
were under a spell

SEASON 11

Baby

Episode 222 (Season 11, Episode 4)
Directed by Thomas J. Wright
Written by Robbie Thompson
Original air date: October 28, 2015

---

what's up with the shorts? ~
it's a free bunker — I've washed
every car here twice

what is that? ~ it is
a smoothie ~ where is the beer?
~ under the smoothies

Swayze wouldn't come
to this roadhouse ~ never use
Swayze's name in vain

good times, and time heals
all wounds — *especially* good
times — what do you say?

• *Night Moves* •

do not "*Night Moves*" me ~
shh... just let it wash over
you; just take it in

a little too tall,
could've used few pounds — tight pants,
points hardly renown

she was a black-haired
beauty with big dark eyes ~ this
is ridiculous

and points all her own,
sitting way up high ~ one of
greatest rock writers

SEASON 11

Baby (cont.)

all time, Samuel ~
it's Sam ~ way up firm and high,
out past the cornfields

where woods got heavy ~
in backseat of my brother's
sixty-sev Chevy

yeah, you — you started
this ~ workin' on mysteries
without any clues

here we go, come on
now ~ workin' on our night moves,
trying to make some

front page drive-in news,
workin' on our night moves ~ next
time, I choose ~ hey, hands

off the wheel ~ you're not
even looking at the road
~ in the summertime

"digging into the
lore" — is that what the kids are
calling it theses days?

tried to give number
know what she said? ~ "got tonight,
who needs tomorrow?"

you even put a
blanket down, buddy — classy
— thoughtful, as always

have you *met* us? we're
batting a whopping zero
in domestic life

Baby (cont.)

think about something?
you know, with a hunter, who
understands the life

you're not... my father
is dead ~ when has *death* ever
stopped a Winchester?

we turned out okay ~
you did — that was on you boys
— *you* did that, not me

Winchester Motel:
we don't have cable, but we
do have room service

"God helps those who help
themselves" — maybe these visions
are coming from God

not in the bible:
an old proverb that dates back
to Aesop — I read

God could've cracked this
piñata — don't see any
candy on the floor

we're looking at a
werewolf / vampire hybrid?
~ say it: were-pire

spider caught a fly ~
wheel's bouncing like trampoline,
when I get where I'm

going, gonna have
trembling — live fast, die young:
bad girls do it well

I gotta go, I
don't wanna get fired! ~ strong
work, Jessie, strong work

SEASON 11

Baby (cont.)

• *Dean fights a "were-pire" while Cas is on the phone* •

I'm mostly confused —
I am not sure how orange
correlates with black

in a way that's new ~
step away from the Netflix
— we've all had a binge

you find anything
in the lore? ~ there's a creature
that feeds on hearts, blood

it's a were-pire,
you might say? come on, I know
you wanna say it

in lore it's referred
to as a whisper ~ that's lame
~ silver will kill it

but you may want to
decapitate it, just to
be sure ~ all right, good

at crime scene — was staged
the body was dragged — there were
no signs of struggle

body was moved to
look like animal attack?
~ was pretty sloppy

what else got on them? ~
whispers have fascinating
history ~ hang on

they were once believed
to be in the bloodline of
werewolves, but in fact

they're more similar
to demons ~ deputy ~ what's
going on, agent?

they got their nickname
from how quiet their attacks
are — because of their

stealthiness, they've lived
on fringes for centuries,
although were several

Baby (cont.)

                  that were hunted and
killed during the Salem witch…
                    wait minute… okay

according to this, whispers only feed during the solar eclipse	creature of some kind — okay fine, maybe it is so-called were-pire
I don't believe what you're hunting *is* a whisper — must be another	but, to be honest, I have never heard of a creature with that name

            Dean, what is that? Dean?
Dean? Dean, are you all right? I
       hear gunshots Dean! Dean?

ah, it turns out I *did* shoot the deputy ~ wait Dean, is everything…	wait no, Dean, listen: according to the lore, the timing is off: the
the deputy was a were-pire — it's all right, silver bullets worked	next solar eclipse in North America is years away — can't be…

          hang on ~ Dean, listen,
it couldn't be — Dean? ~ scratch that:
          gotta cut off their…

          Dean it's not whisper ~
yeah I'm starting to get that
         — give me a second

SEASON 11

Baby (cont.)

growls smile, asshat —
all right, Cas you there? ~ of course,
what is going on?

whatever it is,
silver slows it down — sending
you a picture now

fangs: I've never seen
anything like it — see if
there's a match in lore

hey Cas, tell me you
got something doesn't involve
chicks in a prison

it's a nachzehrer —
a ghoul and vampire-like
creature ~ ghoul-pire!

family — you do
anything for them, don't you?
~ not if costs too much

I'm an "every part
of the buffalo" guy — you'll
be brother's first meal

j-turn, perfectly
executed by Jensen
is sexy AF

you and I: gonna
end this thing now ~ do you mind
starting tomorrow?

SEASON 11

Thin Lizzie

Episode 223 (Season 11, Episode 5)
Directed by Rashaad Ernesto Green
Written by Nancy Won
Original air date: November 4, 2015

---

something with freaky
serial killer fetish
~ it's not a fetish

whistles knowingly
working with family can
be tough ~ twenty years

I'm gonna throw up ~
we're surrounded by doilies
— they're everywhere

this one was Lizzie's
original room, and I'm
not giving it up

why don't we Sherlock
that over a beer and a
lobster roll, okay?

you can see it in
her serial killer eyes —
Lizzie def hacked them

playing part of what
used to be — fake it 'til you
make it… or feel it

SEASON 11

Thin Lizzie (cont.)

---

we don't want to kill
him, we want to save people
remember? ~ new rules

no sensitive way
tell someone: soul sucked out by
prehistoric tween

couldn't shake a guy's
hand before — God, that wetness
now, I could lick sweat

off stranger's... any
body part, I'm serious —
yeah, I feel weird, man

you're an angel ~ do
I *look* like a whiny, winged
suck-up? ~ what are you?

it is so peaceful —
it's coming for all of us
— darkness is coming

I know for sure now:
if I am not stopped, there will
be another kill

Our Little World

Episode 224 (Season 11, Episode 6)
Directed by John F. Showalter
Written by Robert Berens
Original air date: November 11, 2015

---

this is gonna hurt me *way* more than it hurts you: my dear, you're grounded	insane to leave our one and only angel friend on the bench ~ I'll call
thought were going with socially-acceptable binge-watching, you know	"Wire," "Game of Thrones" ~ yeah, well a man can't live on caviar alone
heard siren's song from idiot box — telling you: whatever you seek	you won't find it there — so, turn off the TV, go outside, get some air

I keep forgetting
all about you and Crowley's
summer of love, right

you only want me
for the power I will wield
— soon I won't need you

could have brought you back
with a snap of my fingers
— not that I *would* have

any idea
how much stuff had to steal, then
pawn to pay for that?

SEASON 11

Our Little World (cont.)

---

an unexpected
consequence of legalized
marijuana? ...sure

Crowley reads book: "Why
She Fights: Understanding Your
Rebellious Teen"

reality is
literature of era
— I'm capturing it

are you forgetting
you are human now? I could
crush you like a bug

you were always a
bit of a Nancy, but this?
you have gone full wuss

know how disturbing
it was to realize: couldn't
bring self to kill you?

learned to accept that
too much going on between
you and I — bromance

pacifism does
not pay — you're hunter, you of
all people should know

sick of my strings pulled,
which is why I won't let you
manipulate me

the sweet triumph, and
the even sweeter folly
of what he has wrought

---

to create the world,
God had to give up only
thing he'd ever known

he had to betray
and sacrifice his kin: the
darkness, his sister

---

how? ~ what part of "God's
sister" you not understand?
overpowered me

Plush

Episode 225 (Season 11, Episode 7)
Directed by Tim Andrew
Written by Eric Charmelo & Nicole Snyder
Original air date: November 18, 2015

---

you ever hear of
privacy? ~ want privacy?
then close your door, Sam

he didn't show up
for the apocalypse, why
would he give crap now?

Donna, what's shakin'? ~
fat-sucker Donna? ~ what you
mean, *killer bunny*?

ever since I've seen
what goes bump in night, I am
not taking chances

looks like somebody
might have a crush ~ I was born
at night, not *last* night

clearly have a type —
no, thank you, ma'am — I won't be
once bitten, twice Doug'd

so, what happened, pal?
what did you do? drop too much
molly? super glue

your mask to your head?
get paranoid, stab a guy?
hoo, I have *been there*

SEASON 11

Plush (cont.)

what? ~ lady cops can't
handle the heavy liftin'?
~ I didn't mean that…

next thing I know, coach
Evans is getting his ass
kicked by the mascot

I do crossfit — you
just gotta engage the core
and lift with the knees

burn bones, but he was
cremated ~ we're up poop's creek
without a paddle

Sam's phobia of
clowns is justified: this one
is creepy AF

what heck goin' on
in this doggone town? ~ told ya:
copycat killers

I don't have time for
insubordination ~ not
giving him a chance

killer clown? you are
serious ~ joking, 'cause clowns
are really funny

I spent my whole life
sticking up for my brother
— see for who he was

hoping something less
murderous brings you back, like
Prince or cheese curd fest

SEASON 11

Just My Imagination

Episode 226 (Season 11, Episode 8)
Directed by Richard Speight Jr.
Written by Jenny Klein
Original air date: December 2, 2015

Sully, you're not real ~
how did you punch me then? ~ this
can't be happening

Mork from Ork here is
your imaginary friend?
gonna get my gun

"imaginary
friend": descriptive term — how *you*
said it? *offensive*

alright, what are you
thinking? good, the Ernie and
Bert pretext... awesome

so, Sparkle is a
unicorn, also a man?
so, a manicorn

I was kind of a
lonely kid, Dean ~ you were *not*
lonely, you had *me*

blood is glittery? ~
even when Sparkle is dead,
he can't stop shining

the mermaid's boyfriend
— because imaginary
friends have boyfriends now

ever think about
running away? from here, all
this: the hunting life

Just My Imagination (cont.)

can be whatever
you want to be — you're not Dean,
not your dad — you're *Sam*

when was last time you
saw Nicky the mermaid? can't
believe just said that

manicorn? mermaid?
what is that? chick in a car —
that's terra firma

you play air guitar?
Sam plays air guitar, *I* play…
well, he's no Clapton

I'm a Winchester:
I hunt monsters — why would I
want anything else?

when you went to hunt,
I considered that one of
my biggest failures

I'm just still so mad ~
trust me revenge ain't gonna
make you feel better

ever think about
hot-wiring minivan? ~
in my *dreams* ~ let's go

I've seen real monsters —
these guys are Sesame Street
Mother Teresas

heroes aren't perfect ~
sometimes scared — thing they're facing:
super important

this lump in my throat:
no excuse anymore ~ we'll
find another way

SEASON 11

O Brother Where Art Thou?

Episode 227 (Season 11, Episode 9)
Directed by Robert Singer
Written by Eugenie Ross-Leming & Brad Buckner
Original air date: December 9, 2015

---

you're speaking of God?
truthfully, I don't think he's
that interested

it's you? ~ God you mean?
no, but let's just say he's not
only game in town

Lucifer was the
biggest monster ever hatched,
'til we hatched one worse

bush? you were in the
forest — there are bushes there,
and sometimes they burn

manipulation:
you only believe what he
wants you to believe

got bigger fish to
fry — *then* we can go back to
killing each other

unresolved issues with domineering brother, dad abandonment	summon Fergus and tell him to bring a handcart — we're going to Hell

393

SEASON 11

O Brother Where Art Thou? (cont.)

promised Dean I'd call ~
promised Lincoln a fun night
at the theater

I consumed their souls —
they're part of me, in that way
they live forever

not relationship
material — so *alpha* ~
mother, you're drooling

his universe, his
rules ~ what if no rules? no pain?
no prayer? just *bliss*

it is not easy
being a parent: knowing
when to hug or kill

you want a vessel? ~
one strong enough to hold me,
available *now*

working with Crowley:
you passed certifiable
three off-ramps ago

that would make so much
sense, if it *was* God who was
doing the talking

SEASON 11

The Devil in the Details

Episode 228 (Season 11, Episode 10)
Directed by Thomas J. Wright
Written by Andrew Dabb
Original air date: January 20, 2016

---

really, Rowena?
this is what you dream about?
~ recurring nightmare

sooner than you think,
brother's gonna walk through that
door and kick your ass

you betrayed me in
my kingdom ~ not yours: *his*, Hell
is *his*, *I* am *his*

whatever happened
to super awesome coven,
hashtag girlpower?

he is the devil ~
you say that like it's bad thing
~ I'm bad thing, he's *worse*

this is the Sam I
remember: bold, decisive,
"B" on tongue action

are we done? ~ let me
take your temperature ~ that's
not gonna happen

have I told you how
much I respect you? don't get
me wrong — don't *like* you

well, that explains it:
you're suffering from smiting
sickness ~ that's a thing?

you gonna kill me? ~
they say that I kill angels?
~ *nicest* thing they say

395

SEASON 11

The Devil in the Details (cont.)

you want to kill us? ~
make sure when you die, stay dead
— subtle difference

you'd do anything
to save him, he'd same for you
— that is the problem

instead of the world,
choose each other — no matter
how many folks die

you are strong enough? ~
snapping necks and cashing checks
that is what I do

where's Sam? ~ don't worry
about Sam ~ I'm sorry, have
you *met* me? *Dean glares*

heard stories: you *help*,
but Sam and Dean Winchester
are the real heroes

think afraid to die? ~
I know you are; you reek of
fear and self-loathing

expendable and
weak — why God took a special
interest in you, I'll

never understand…
in men, my brother always
had horrible taste

The Devil in the Details (cont.)

SEASON 11

little tip, mother:
never accept a tea from
someone who loathes you

don't know what kind of
oedipal Fifty Shades you
think you're playing at…

Gabe, Raph are dead — God
went out for a pack of smokes
and never came back

she sent this message ~
"I am coming" — is that a
threat? ~ or a promise?

you, plus archangels —
oh, and capital-G-God ~
you mean the dead weight?

okay, but let's say
you gank her, then what? ~ I move
to L.A., solve crimes

start apocalypse
again, 'cause you're an old dog
and that's your old trick

I'm ready to die,
to watch people I love die
— not to be your bitch

say the magic word
or your brother dies — both know
won't let that happen

I hate you because
when I look in your eyes, see
woman used to be

I hate you because
if I didn't, I'd love you
— but love is weakness

:: one little question ::
:: anyone else open cage? :: ~
just me ~ :: good :: *snaps neck*

397

SEASON 11

Into the Mystic

Episode 229 (Season 11, Episode 11)
Directed by John Badham
Written by Robbie Thompson
Original air date: January 27, 2016

:: the things you think you're ::
:: not gonna miss at all, you ::
:: end up missing most ::

:: I'm out of that cage ::
:: — Lucifer ex machina — ::
:: I'm here to save you ::

make reservation? ~
yeah, we should be so lucky
to live long enough

wife left me via
text, if you can believe it
— emoji series

didn't stand for that —
fought fire with fire: sent
her poop emoji

Harold was stealing
the residents' viagra ~
I know, real "dick" move

(Dean casually
tucks the stolen viagra
into his pocket)

SEASON 11

Into the Mystic (cont.)

hey, you're the one who always wanted to go out in blaze of glory	preferably while Bon Jovi song is playing ~ I'm candle in wind

like blaze of glory's
gonna happen soon — are you
okay? ~ not at all...

thanks — *Sam signs* « *fuck you* »
~ it's... « *thanks* » ~ only know little;
I took in college

apparently not
a ghost ~ ghosts do not feed on
busted-open heads

forces the vics to crack open their own eggs, then banshees feed on yolk	we're not FBI ~ you two are too cute to be FBI agents

I tried to kill her ~
:: you're connected :: ~ more than that ~
:: attraction? oh, Dean ::

« *you can have tall one;*
I'm not much of a mountain
climber anymore »

Into the Mystic (cont.)

mean she has a shot? ~
always *did* have a thing for
Blanche on Golden Girls

hey, don't judge, Sammy ~
I'm not judging — …just had a
thing for Sophia

revenge is not all
it's cracked up to be — it won't
bring your parents back

come on and sit down —
I'm not gonna bite: never
really was my thing

last time watched sunset,
without waiting for something
to go bump in night?

want to know secret
to living long, happy life?
~ yes ~ follow your heart

your hand is still on
my knee ~ I could move it *up*
~ 'kay… that's… I'm gonna

you can't call me, though ~
okay ~ I mean you can call,
but I won't answer

there's one thing I've learned:
it's when somebody's pining
for somebody else

something off with him ~
something *always* seems little
bit off about Cas

all ever mattered
is that we are together —
shut up, drink your beer

Banshees go after
the vulnerable — why did
it go after *you*?

SEASON 11

Don't You Forget About Me

Episode 230 (Season 11, Episode 12)
Directed by Stefan Pleszczynski
Written by Nancy Won
Original air date: February 3, 2016

not gonna survive
hundreds of monster attacks
to get flatlined by

some double-donut
monstrosity ~ the "Elvis"
~ calories in that?

it is just chicken~
it's *shaped* like chicken — not a
patty or nugget

Claire caught a werewolf —
turned out to be a German
Shepherd with rabies

and the vampire:
a councilwoman into
erotic cosplay

oh, we're going there…
~ if we can't talk about it,
shouldn't be doing

who is she gonna
have sex with? she doesn't *talk*
to anybody

SEASON 11

Don't You Forget About Me (cont.)

birth control pills are
useless against STDs
— suit up every time

not their mom — didn't
raise them, don't have that kind of
history with them

got nothing against
hunting… she's *hiding* in it;
she is so alone

Claire this is a crime
scene, you can't be here ~ but the
fake FBI can?

we're gonna hang out ~
hang out, huh? ~ yeah, okay then
~ he got the message

what kept me going:
I would find you one day, and
I would make you pay

the missing bodies ~
it's just a little take-out,
waiting for trash day

you were a complete
freak: angry loner creeping,
trench coat mafia

you two cooked? ~ we tried…
pancakes might be raw ~ wanted
do something for you

I know what I have —
should have seen her: she would take
a bullet for me

take a bio quiz
and pretend like you didn't
almost get slaughtered?

I solemnly swear
not to hunt like a dumbass
— teach me to vet leads

long as everyone
wears a condom, we'll be fine
~ want bumper sticker

SEASON 11

Love Hurts

Episode 231 (Season 11, Episode 13)
Directed by Phil Sgriccia
Written by Eric Charmelo & Nicole Snyder
Original air date: February 10, 2016

---

is that a hickey? ~
Valentine's Day — can't help it:
hopeless romantic

her heart was ripped out ~
on Valentine's day? like an
ironic werewolf?

first, I need bacon ~
no, first you need a shower ~
sniffs self — you're not wrong

we are back to square
zilch ~ I need a beer, regroup
— maybe get lucky

what do you say, you
with me? go scrape a few hearts
off the barroom floor?

curse transmittable? ~
magic STD, like good
old-fashioned herpes

all you need to know
is that we save people like
you from things like *that*

Love Hurts (cont.)

if she shows up here,
you punch her, stab her, drop a
freaking house on her

my deepest, darkest
desire: Daisy Duke ~ Bach
or Simpson? ~ either

Dean finally wins
rock paper scissors, for once
— bust through the plastic

only thing worse than
a cheating man, is one who
gets away with it

I can see inside
your heart, feel the love you feel
— except cloaked in shame

means you're complicit?
weak? evil? you honestly
think you had a choice?

the sister of God —
for some reason she picked you
— I won't blame or judge

we want to kill the
darkness — *need* to kill darkness
— I don't think I *can*

SEASON 11

The Vessel

Episode 232 (Season 11, Episode 14)
Directed by John Badham
Written by Robert Berens
Original air date: February 17, 2016

---

    these months pretending
      to love a Nazi *cochon*
    like you was the worst

    sir, would you like to
  hear the latest soul numbers?
  ~ :: no, 'cause I don't care ::

    we've had a coward,
  a *fool* at helm for too long
   — perhaps it's time to…

    the impudence, lack
  of humility — no way
    to talk to master

  really? it's like noon ~
you drank all the coffee, what
  should I drink, *water*?

  :: *sniffs* I can smell it: ::
  :: that delectable little ::
  :: whiff of defiance ::

:: once and future king ::
:: of Hell, what treasonous thoughts ::
:: do you have brewing? ::

    Cas, you can't even
teleport ~ :: time travel is ::
  :: a different system ::

    we get in, get the
weapon, get out: a milk run
  ~ not very good plan

expect me to sit
here and ride the pine while you
go play Jules Verne? ~ who?

  :: double-down on what ::
:: screwed us the first time — bringing ::
  :: your "A" ideas ::

  what the hell is this? ~
it's a phone ~ gonna tell us
  he's from the future

SEASON 11

The Vessel (cont.)

mission from future — not at liberty to discuss, but know this:	within the hour, German destroyer attacks and you *will* go down
odds of a German attack from a surface ship this far west hunting…	Captain? sonar's picked up surface ship on steady bearing ~ understood
Eisenhower — no Truman — this sub is going down, but allies win	was more impressive… the Ark of the Covenant ~ so, full-on "Raiders"
it's not like your war — big: biblical, end-is-nigh big — need your weapon	it is spell-bound to my blood, my heart; its power lives and dies with me

it's worth the risk, Cas —
Dean needs our help; I trust you
~ :: *laughs* I don't need you ::

:: why do I spare you? ::
:: you're like the girl at prom who ::
:: kept turning me down ::

The Vessel (cont.)

:: I'll tell him the truth ::
:: I will say "Dean"... (in Cas voice) ::
:: "Dean, he knew the risks" ::

some advice, Delphine:
if you want a Thule to stay
dead, burn the body

weapon to Nazis —
we're supposed to die, let us
die with a purpose

only Lucifer
can beat her ~ you chose this? you
have to eject him

we need him to save
Dean ~ you can not time travel?
~ only Lucifer

*Cas appears on sub,   :: insufferable ::
just in time to rescue Dean*   :: mortal enemies — working ::
~ that's not Cas ~ :: cat's out ::   :: *with* you? soul crusher ::

:: donning this Cas mask? ::   who would have thought the
:: this grim face of angelic ::   hand of God would turn out to
:: constipation? ugh ::   be a one-hitter?

what'd you do? ~ nothing...
they... I was just a witness;
tell another day

Beyond the Mat

Episode 233 (Season 11, Episode 15)
Directed by Jerry Wanek
Written by John Bring & Andrew Dabb
Original air date: February 24, 2016

---

it's a barn-burner —
off the ropes, picks him up and…
it's a back-breaker

have you seen the… uh…
Dean tosses the aspirin
yeah, thanks ~ bottoms up

if he even *wants*
to be saved ~ he *does*, even
if doesn't know yet

:: A-B-C: always ::
:: be closing — you little storm ::
:: clouds, find hand of God ::

:: look high, low, far, wide, ::
:: each warehouse, farmhouse, henhouse, ::
:: outhouse, and doghouse ::

may I return to
my task? ~ :: of course, one minor ::
:: tweak: use your tongue :: *licks*

that's Gunnar freakin'
Lawless ~ groupie much? ~ shut up
— should I go say hi?

you were my first crush ~
you didn't have my poster
above bed, did you?

got first B&E —
borrowed pay-per-view for you
and Tower of Power

Rio? you dog — did
you tell her about poster
over your bed? ~ no

Beyond the Mat (cont.)

hardly seems worth it:
town after town, putting your
ass on the line for

nothing? no money,
no glory ~ you realize you
just described *our* jobs

---

gives glove a to kid ~
maybe next time ~ it's all right,
I'm not a child

the body was marked ~
he get in tickle-fight with
Edward Scissorhands?

arena: empty —
Dean tries his best wrestling
moves out in the ring

you're not a dog — you're
Crowley, and the devil should
be afraid of *you*

been beat up, spit on,
stabbed, roughed up — but I'll be damned
if don't get back up

I've learned you gotta
keep on grinding, no matter
what is thrown your way

the cops are thinking,
and I quote, "it's some kind of
weird satanic crap"

SEASON 11

Beyond the Mat (cont.)

*Crowley dispatches
two demons like a badass*
how did…? ~ I'm Crowley

what happened? ~ mostly
tequila, cut with holy
water — I bought drinks

can I touch it? ~ all
due respect, I don't think you
can handle my rod

if you're a demon,
there's a Hell and a Heaven:
shot at paradise

:: is it just me, or ::
:: is it getting a little ::
:: bit phallic in here? ::

:: really thought you could ::
:: double-cross me? *me*? you know ::
:: I *invented* it ::

:: once were evilest ::
:: evil that ever eviled, ::
:: present excluded ::

really think you could
double-cross me? *me*? you know
I *perfected* it

trust me, I've been there
— but it is never too late
to do the right thing

gotta keep grinding,
no matter how much it hurts
or how hard it gets

we're gonna save Cas,
we're gonna ice the devil,
and shank the darkness

SEASON 11

Safe House

Episode 234 (Season 11, Episode 16)
Directed by Stefan Pleszczynski
Written by Robbie Thompson
Original air date: March 23, 2016

---

this case seems like a
layup ~ when was the last time
we had a layup?

you know, I knew you
were in the area — thought
a win would be nice

your backup? ~ yeah, you
do the heavy lifting while
I watch: it's Shabbat

were you *ever* nice?
~ 1985: it was
worst year of my life

don't religiously
persecute me ~ sorry to
disturb reading time

"ghost hunt with jackass
in Grand Rapids Michigan"
that is all he wrote?

if keep world spinning,
not everyone's gonna be
on that bus ride home

Safe House (cont.)

stepped one foot inside
that house and filled my drawers:
could *feel* the badness

if memory serves,
things about to get hairy
~ wanna hold my hand?

Dean, Bobby in soul
eater's nest… each an echo
of a different time

"Fine, you ass, you win —
for once… enjoy —R": the same
bottle Jody finds

in season seven
"Time After Time" in amongst
some of Bobby's books

nest exists outside
of space and time: Bobby and
I there at same time

messed up that seeing
a vision of dead me is
kind of comforting?

SEASON 11

Red Meat

Episode 235 (Season 11, Episode 17)
Directed by Nina Lopez-Corrado
Written by Robert Berens & Andrew Dabb
Original air date: March 30, 2016

---

running out of things
to interrogate, unless
we talk to the trees

we *saved* you, okay?
we saved *both* of you ~ it is
three lives versus one

he won't leave you, and
we won't last out there without
him *suffocates Sam*

you stay, you fight, die —
sorry, he's gone ~ gonna come
back for you, promise

it's fun, like camping ~
freezing our nuts off in the
middle of the woods?

didn't believe her   so, how exactly
then, but my mom used to say   do you talk to an evil
death is not the end   scary death machine?

took you long enough —
what is with the freeze frame? ~ I'm
just savoring this

413

SEASON 11

Red Meat (cont.)

I have to say, of
all ways I thought you'd go: heart
attack, fang, choking

on a burger while
binge-watching Charles in Charge
~ that was peak Baio†

never took you for
the suicide type — doesn't
fit whole martyr thing

pretend you're trying
to save Sam for greater good —
doing it for *you*

said I could leave, but
where am I even supposed
to go? after all

survived together,
watched man I love die — there's no
normal after that

what did you do when
you thought I was dead? ~ thought 'bout
redecorating

†An earlier version of the script shows this line a little differently; compare the resulting haiku in Appendix B.

SEASON 11

Hell's Angel

Episode 236 (Season 11, Episode 18)
Directed by Phil Sgriccia
Written by Brad Buckner & Eugenie Ross-Leming
Original air date: April 6, 2016

I've had a good life —
it seemed worth a soul at the
time ~ it always does

I'm who communes with
the natural forces, and
channels them to help

you can destroy your
enemies, remake the world
any way you choose

Castiel: one of
Heaven's wanted, possessed by
Heaven's most hated

:: lesson: you need me ::
~ you exploded Jofiel ~
:: did he explode *self*? ::

:: who do you think spread ::
:: that headline? was captain G, ::
:: the eternal one ::

:: mankind: what a mess — ::
:: the Salem witch trials… the ::
:: third reich… twin towers… ::

he said you're evil ~
incarnate… evil incarn—
~ :: it is marketing ::

want to stay around? ~
:: oh, I like the way you think ::
:: — you could call *me* God ::

SEASON 11

Hell's Angel (cont.)

it's a strong vessel ~
it's not an "it," Sam, it's Cas
~ ...wanted to do this

times I want to get
slapped during sex by a girl
wearing Zorro mask

this is how we screw
ourselves: we make the heart choice
instead of smart choice

I would rather stick
white-hot skewers in my eyes
than listen to this

:: your people on board? ::
:: or do we need to do a ::
:: little wing-twising? ::

:: don't think long — know what ::
:: they say: he who hesitates, ::
:: *snaps* disintegrates ::

the hand that giveth
can quickly taketh away
~ yes, we getteth it

yes ~ well, he may have
a more objective view of
the situation

replace me, as if
ambition and posturing:
same as majesty

SEASON 11

The Chitters

*Episode 237 (Season 11, Episode 19)
Directed by Eduardo Sánchez
Written by Nancy Won
Original air date: April 27, 2016*

---

definitely likes
me ~ know gotta be careful
~ not an idiot

sleeping is the new
smoking ~ what? no it's *sitting*
~ that cannot be right

the last legs of their
cannabis-tasting tour
~ so, a trippin' trip

was 18 ~ sinner ~
dude, it was college ~ rebel
~ you're an idiot

gran said if you got
chitters: so revved-up with lust,
eyes shine like emeralds

(Etta looks at the
green-eyed Winchester boys like
they're pieces of meat)

SEASON 11

The Chitters (cont.)

---

how long been hunting? ~
about seven years — we've heard
of the Winchesters

you guys fight just like
brothers ~ well, it's more like an
old married couple

settling down with
a hunter? ~ smelly, dirty,
twice the worrying

I have seen it: when
someone loses someone when
they're young, never heals

hunters get revenge,
they are never fixed ~ gotta
help him anyway

you'd leave me to hunt —
thought monster finally got
ya — I was just lost

we had a deal: when
we finished this hunt — if we
caught 'em, hang up spurs

yeah, two hunters who
make it to the finish line?
~ you leave that alone

SEASON 11

Don't Call Me Shurley

Episode 238 (Season 11, Episode 20)
Directed by Robert Singer
Written by Robbie Thompson
Original air date: May 4, 2016

---

yeah Toto, I got
a feeling we aren't on Earth
anymore, either

it is not just a
bar, genius — this is one of
the Big Man's constructs

I would know his work
anywhere — we were besties
~ wouldn't exactly…

limbo: where I'll spend
eternity in crappy
bar with hack writer

then you put yourself
in the story, ugh ~ okay
that's fair, constructive

of all books I've read,
"Supernatural" didn't
crack top 10… thousand

I always forget:
people can't see me unless
I want them to see

just don't use G-word
okay? just call me Chuck ~ Chuck?
I need stiffer drink

I like front-row seats —
figured I'd hide in plain sight
— plus, acting is *fun*

every writer needs
good editor — did best work
with you, Metatron

what humanity's
greatest creation has been?
music, nacho cheese

last time I saw that
look on an editor's face,
just handed in "Bugs"

SEASON 11

Don't Call Me Shurley (cont.)

"in the beginning,
there was me" — what a grabber!
— I'm hooked, I was *there*

makes you seem like a
really grounded, likable
person ~ yeah, what's wrong?

neither grounded, nor
a person ~ so you're saying
I am likable?

chapter 10: why I
never answer prayers; you
should be glad I don't

chapter 11:
divine intervention and
why I avoid it

as close as I got
to better than me ~ national
park system? ~ nature

rebuilt Castiel
more times than I remember
— look where *that* got me

nature knows sometimes
no fixing things — you just have
to wipe the slate clean

just closest angel
to the door when I walked in
— you're nothing special

nature is divine;
human nature: toxic ~ they
like blowing stuff up

I am not hiding,
I am just done watching my
experiments' fails

Don't Call Me Shurley (cont.)

• *Metatron lays it all out there for Chuck* •

you know you really
are terrific editor
Metatron ~ I was

terrible writer
a worse God — it's good I got
something going for

you know, I have to
say: I didn't see the whole
evil-turn coming

why try to be me?~
was just a sad, pathetic
cry for attention

whose attention were
you trying to get? ~ *yours* — you
are light and beauty

creation and wrath,
damnation and salvation
— and I don't care if

I *was* just angel
nearest the door — you picked *me*;
your light shined on *me*

oh, and the *warmth*! but
then you left me — you left *all*
of us — it wasn't

just the saps on earth
who were praying to you — the
angels prayed too, and

so did I, every
day ~ I know ~ do you want to
write the bestselling

auto-bio? you
explain to me — tell why you
abandoned me, us

did it because you
disappointed me — you all
disappointed me

look, I know I'm a
disappointment, but you're wrong
re: humanity

SEASON 11

Don't Call Me Shurley (cont.)

they are your greatest
creation because they are
better than you are

they're weak, they cheat, steal,
destroy, disappoint — but they
also give, create

sing and dance and love,
and above all, they never
give up — but *you* do

not gonna make it ~
there's no quitting here ~ we were
never gonna make

I can't fight this — go,
before I hurt you ~ I'm not
leaving you, ever

• *Chuck's song* •

if I had wings like
Noah's dove, fly up river
to the one I love

fare well — remember
one night in the drizzling rain,
and around my heart

fare thee well, honey,
fare thee well — I knew a man
who was long and tall

I felt aching pain —
fare thee well, honey, fare thee
well — one of these days

he moved his body
like a cannonball — oh fare
thee well, oh honey

it won't be long, you'll
call my name, and I'll be gone
fare thee well, honey

SEASON 11

All in the Family

Episode 239 (Season 11, Episode 21)
Directed by Thomas J. Wright
Written by Eugenie Ross-Leming & Brad Buckner
Original air date: May 11, 2016

---

guys, you're looking stressed —
it's cool, trust Chuck — whatever
he needs you to do

thinks you can handle it — *I* always trusted you ~ yeah, *that* ended well	you've been in the veil long enough — time you had an upgrade ~ holy crap

• *Dean calls Chuck out for ignoring humanity for centuries* •

I'm getting that not
everyone's totally on
board ~ here's the thing, Chuck

mean no disrespect —
I'm guessing you came back to
help with the darkness

that's great, that's — you know,
it's fantastic, but you've been
gone a long, long time

and there's so much crap
that has gone down on the earth,
for *thousands* of years

SEASON 11

All in the Family (cont.)

I mean plagues and wars,
slaughters — and you were — I do
not know… writing books

and going to fan
conventions — were you even
aware, or did you

just tune it out? ~ I
was aware, Dean ~ but you did
nothing, and again

I'm not trying to
piss you off, you know, I don't
want to turn into

a pillar of salt ~
actually didn't do that
~ people *pray* to you

people *build churches*
for you, *fight wars* in your name,
and you did *nothing*

you're frustrated, I
get it — believe me, I was
hands-on — real hands-on

for ages — I was
sure if I kept stepping in,
teaching, punishing

that these beautiful
creatures that I created
would grow up, but it

only stayed the same,
and I saw that I needed
to step away and

let baby find its
way — being over-involved
is not parenting

it's enabling ~
but it didn't get better ~
well, I've been mulling

it over, and from
where I sit, I think it *has*
~ well, from where I sit

it feels like you just
left us, and you are trying
to justify it

had complicated
upbringing, but don't confuse
me with your dad, Dean

All in the Family (cont.)

:: you're strong, Amara ::
:: you may defeat him, but you ::
:: will never *be* him ::

I've always had faith
in you, even if didn't
return the favor

needed solitude,
and he needed a fan club,
so he made all that

can't believe it, but
for once I actually wish
Rowena were here

does God sleep? ~ I know
he takes really long showers
~ sings crappy folk songs

had to tell him to
cool it, three times ~ told *God* to
cool it? ~ yeah, *I* sleep

Chuck walks in with box
of Voodoo Doughnuts… in the
bunker… in Kansas

Donatello ~ named
for mutant ninja turtle?
~ Renaissance sculptor

I can't be prophet —
I'm an atheist, chemist
— molecules, not God

don't have to believe,
just *act* like you do — people
do it all the time

that my computer? ~
I've never seen so much porn
— not in one sitting

was an atheist
until 10 minutes ago
— is that an issue?

All in the Family (cont.)

your skepticism
is expected — included
free will in the kit

it's in his own words
— not autobiography,
it's suicide note

we're not just some toys
you throw away — I think you
owe us more than that

why I saved you years
ago: you're the firewall
between light, darkness

I missed you, and the
sensations you arouse — I
know you feel the same

this world is flawed, but
I am not ready to say
goodbye to it yet

Chuck sighs you have changed ~
Lucifer, beaten :: you've changed ::
~ I'm pretty much same

met God, Lucifer,
darkness — you'll need a spa day,
or pair of hookers

We Happy Few

Episode 240 (Season 11, Episode 22)
Directed by John Badham
Written by Robert Berens
Original air date: May 18, 2016

:: bandaid on my knee ::
:: we're even now? let's play catch ::
:: in the yard? *screw you* ::

a little time is
not something that we have — the
end is freakin' nigh

you're God, but could you
be a little less *lordly*?
~ but I am the lord

shouldn't bother you —
you a rat — find your way off
any sinking ship

:: know what it's like to ::
:: argue with your father, when ::
:: your father is *God*? ::

the great thing about
apologies is you do
not have to mean them

I lie and tell Sam
I'm sorry all the time *Sam
glares* I'm sorry... see?

I wasn't supposed
to have favorites, but *you*
were my favorite

I saw I was wrong:
I watched my choice devour
my most cherished son

SEASON 11

We Happy Few (cont.)

I hated myself,
and so I punished you, and
I am so sorry

read his aura: he
under potent protection
— never seen before

invented free will
for a reason ~ tying our
hands on principle?

God's back: why would *I*
care? hello, pagan here — I
serve magic, not God

you offered them a
chance to stroke your ego? you
wonder why said no

for once we have God
on our side; for once we can
just do things his way

:: I apologize :: ~
you think you are the first man
to try to kill me?

been rooting against
you both, although you're one of
my guilty pleasures

world needed to be
born, and you wouldn't let me
~ *your* story, not mine

we stood only in
relation to each other,
and we were equals

you made archangels
to create lesser beings —
to make you large, lord

there's value, glory
in creation that's greater
and truer than pride

didn't come from my
hands — it was there waiting to
be born — it just is

SEASON 11

Alpha and Omega

Episode 241 (Season 11, Episode 23)
Directed by Phil Sgriccia
Written by Andrew Dabb
Original air date: May 25, 2016

---

you know when you are driving, and a bug hits your windshield? I'm the bug

hit Amara with everything, she walked it off ~ it's last call? ~ that's right

something for me to punch, shoot, or kill — how are we supposed to fix sun?

you're the best friend we've ever had; you're our brother — want you to know that

these meaningful looks between Crowley and Billie... a history there?

this is desperate and stupid ~ desperate and stupid's all we got

how do I smuggle? ~ we could always shove it up your... I mean you *could*...

so you are here to help us? ~ little tip: you want souls? call a reaper

I could go with you ~ I got to do this alone — Sam will be a mess

want big funeral: open bar, choir, Sabbath cover band, Gary

Busey reading the eulogy — for my ashes... I like it here ~ done

Alpha and Omega (cont.)

no chick-flick moments,
come on ~ yeah, you *love* chick flicks
~ yeah, you're right, I do

revenge'll get you
out of bed in the morning
— great for five minutes

no matter how bad
it got, we always made it
right; we're family

I need him, he needs
me, and when everything goes
to crap: all you've got

you might be an all-
powerful being but you're
human where it counts

put aside the rage,
put aside the hate, and tell
me: what do you want?

what you've made — it is
beautiful… it took me a
long time to see that

what about us? what
about earth? ~ earth will be fine
it's got you and Sam

Dean, you gave me what
I needed most — I want to
do the same for you

the damage you've caused:
archangels, leviathans,
the darkness: enough

just hunter playing
with things you don't understand
— do more harm than good

SEASON TWELVE

SEASON 12

Keep Calm and Carry On

Episode 242 (Season 12, Episode 1)
Directed by Phil Sgriccia
Written by Andrew Dabb
Original air date: October 13, 2016

• *Dean proves to Mary that he's really her son* •

I'm Dean — I'm your son ~
no, *my* Dean is 4 years old
~ I *was*, when you died

Mom, listen to me:
your name is Mary Campbell,
born December 5th

1954
to Samuel, Deanna
Campbell — your father

he bounced around for
work, and you bounced with him, and
you ended up in

Lawrence, Kansas ~ how
do you know that? ~ Dad told me —
on March 23rd

'72, walked
out of movie theater —
saw "Slaughterhouse Five"

you loved it, and you
bumped into a big Marine,
and you knocked him flat

Keep Calm and Carry On (cont.)

on his ass — you were
embarrassed, and he laughed it
off — he said you could

you talked, and he was
cute, and he knew the words to
every Zeppelin song

make it up to him
with cup of coffee, so you
went to Mulroney's

so, when he asked you
for your number, you gave it
to him, even though

you knew your dad would
be pissed — that was the night you
met ~ John Winchester

on August 19th,
1975, you
married in Reno

was *your* idea —
a few years later, I came
along, then Sammy…

then I burned — how long
have I been gone? ~ 33
years ~ Dean ~ hi, Mom *hug*

no way, I am a
veterinarian ~ people,
animals: all meat

whatever? ~ are you
a 14 year old girl now? ~
I possessed one once…

didn't work out: lots
of feelings and urges and
ugly snot-crying

SEASON 12

Keep Calm and Carry On (cont.)

wondering how far
I'll have to walk back to town
after I kill you

ask any question —
the answer's gonna be the
exact same: screw you

I've been tortured by
devil himself — you're just an
accent in pantsuit

he's an angel with
a capital "A": wings, harp
~ I don't have a harp

Dean opens laptop
is that a — a computer?
~ yes, I don't trust them

how did you do that? ~
hacked the traffic cams — welcome
to the future, Mom

this was John's car — oh
she's still beautiful ~ hell, yeah,
she is ~ hi, sweetheart

think you're being brave?
you're hero of this story?
just bad at your job

even powered down,
he could kick your posh spice ass
~ *stabs* who's laughing now?

she offered me a
hundred grand ~ and you took it?
~ student loans: a bitch

I *will* find you — if
he is not in one piece, I
will take you apart

:: I'm dead because of ::
:: you — this is your fault — should have ::
:: been you — you're a freak ::

spent my life running
from this: hunting — I never
wanted this for you

saving people and
hunting things: this is our life
— we make world better

434

SEASON 12

Mamma Mia

Episode 243 (Season 12, Episode 2)
Directed by Thomas J. Wright
Written by Brad Buckner & Eugenie Ross-Leming
Original air date: October 20, 2016

I mean these people
had a freaking plane, maybe
they do things legit

been kind of weird with
Mom back — don't know how to act
around each other

it's like it's all just
too much, and I do not want
to overwhelm her

just do not make things
needlessly complicated,
as humans tend to

stuff I'd forgotten
about — stuff your dad did… he
was a great father

did you look inside? ~
powerfully warded? ~ that
was your headline there

you're like a boil —
keeps coming back no matter
how many times lanced

can't believe you talked
me into this ~ I'm your mom
must do what I say

the thing is: hunters,
no matter how good, they all
end up the same way

SEASON 12

Mamma Mia (cont.)

Dad gone, the only
thing we had (aside from this
car) was each other

he is the only
Satan in the phone book ~ it's
witchcraft, not Google

I can't believe I'm
once again down some dank hole,
seeking the devil

Lucifer wearing
Vince Vincente — would have thought
Bieber: your style

anything to add? ~
no, I just came by for some
tea and a beating

using mind control
technique — turns out this ape *did*
read a book or two

I reckon he could
finish me without breaking
a sweat ~ I don't sweat

should call internet,
find out as much as we can
— did I say that right?

Dean said you got out
~ well, this is my family;
my family hunts

I wanted to snap
miserable neck again,
keep it snapped this time

Sam, teary Mom, for
me, just having you here fills
in the biggest blank

The Foundry

Episode 244 (Season 12, Episode 3)
Directed by Robert Singer
Written by Robert Berens
Original air date: October 27, 2016

---

when'd it start to feel
like you fit… you belonged here?
~ still not sure I do

hasn't been on this
planet since Jane Fonda was
wearing leg warmers

Cas healed your s'mores foot,
Baby's mint, we're road-ready,
and Mom wants to hunt

that's probably cold
by now Mom ~ it's *bacon* ~ we
are *so* related

drunk Vince, depressed Vince,
megalomaniacal
"I'm a Golden God"

why give bad guys long,
pullable hair? ~ trying to
tell Sam that for years

Agent… Beyoncé?
skeptical ~ I guess that makes
me Agent Jay Z

fate brought together —
it's been *months* since we last tried
to kill each other

we wanted to ask
you a few questions about
your bro… *slams door* …ther

you're just mad because
you are only my second
choice for a team-up

The Foundry (cont.)

kind of nice; no one
talks on the phone anymore
you know? ~ I've noticed

give your vessel strength
of mightiest tree ~ :: there's a ::
:: woody joke in there ::

struggling: try to
bury herself in hunting
to avoid dealing

sped up the decay,
and you thought Keith Richards was
bad? try Iggy Pop

how do you know that?
~ personal experience —
like mother, like sons

so you'll help us then? ~
that whole FBI pantsuit
look? not my hex bag

• *Mary leaves her (no longer baby) sons* •

I miss John, I miss
my boys ~ we are right here, Mom
~ I know… in my head

I'm still mourning them
as I knew them: my baby
Sam, little boy Dean

feels like yesterday
were together in Heaven,
and now I am here

John is gone, and they're
gone — every moment I spend
with you reminds me

every moment I
lost with them — I thought hunting
would clear my head

I have to go, I'm
sorry… just need a little
time — I love you both

SEASON 12

American Nightmare

Episode 245 (Season 12, Episode 4)
Directed by John F. Showalter
Written by Davy Perez
Original air date: November 3, 2016

Mom, just checking in —
is "Mom" still okay, or weird?
should call you Mary?

one's an angel, one's
a demon — apparently
solve crimes ~ any luck?

"the victim's skull was
filled with a goopy mush" ~ he
paints quite a picture

about yesterday ~
next time you gotta take a
leak, I'll pull over

Magda Peterson? ~
that's not my name — not Magda
— I am the devil

you know, sometimes in
order to figure things out,
a person needs space

gave me her number ~
you were gonna shoot her ~ I
know — weird, kinda hot

Dean — phone died; didn't
have a charger — things are good
— I'll always be "Mom"

The One You've Been Waiting For

Episode 246 (Season 12, Episode 5)
Directed by Nina Lopez-Corrado
Written by Meredith Glynn
Original air date: November 10, 2016

---

how about some pie? ~
in the middle of something ~
all right, something's wrong

won't talk about it?
Dean, it's called sublimation
~ that's kind of my thing

don't touch anything
'til we figure out if this
stuff wants to kill us

Nazi connection,
immolation M.O. — sound
like anyone? ~ Thule

they crashed the party,
took the watch, torched bystanders
~ Nazis — *hate* these guys

you put on those big
girl pants, and you take off his...
well... regular pants

Thule activity? ~
Deutsch-nozzles have been sticking
to the fatherland

see that? we gotta
follow that car — I've always
wanted to say that

you can't just shoot him
~ oh, I do it all the time ~
you don't want to watch

the watch: it's like a
Horcrux ~ Harry Potter thing
~ oh, you *would* know that

The One You've Been Waiting For (cont.)

they'll upload Hitler
into the body of one
of his relatives?

I'm related to
the biggest genocidal
maniac of all?

times when you run, times
when you stand and fight — now is
a time when you fight

all you wanna do:
relive Hitler glory days
~ ...you *millennials*

know what was like to
have Nazi necromancer
for father? it sucked

lifts grenade launcher ~
no ~ why? ~ we need to be stealth,
do this quietly

should have just brought the
grenade launcher — admit it
though: you're having fun

nice new meat suit — did
it come with two testicles?
~ :: of *many* upgrades ::

:: sold 10 million ::
:: of Mein Kampf — what do you think ::
:: can do with Twitter? ::

burned a pile of
dead Nazi zombie bodies:
third-worst day ever

so, *now* you want pie? ~
I just killed *Hitler* — I think
I deserve some pie

did I mention I
killed Hitler? ~ never gonna
hear the end of this

SEASON 12

Celebrating the Life of Asa Fox

Episode 247 (Season 12, Episode 6)
Directed by John Badham
Written by Steve Yockey
Original air date: November 17, 2016

I'm retired ~ if
you retire, who's gonna
save people like me?

oh, Netflix — what do
you recommend to fill my
day off? speak to me

oh, since the last time
we saw you, I killed Hitler ~
thank you? ~ you're welcome

Jody, you watching
some kind of chick flick here? ~ well,
Dean, I am a chick

badass sheriff chick,
not rom-com chick — wait, are you
rom-com chick? ~ are *you*?

the wake's tonight, and
they're gonna salt and burn the
body tomorrow

SEASON 12

Celebrating the Life of Asa Fox (cont.)

Dean Winchester ~ *the*
Dean Winchester? ~ no way — aren't
you dead like four times?

think stories about
Asa are crazy, should hear
what they say 'bout *you*

she was a good witch,
very Enya — it was the
'90s ~ with crystals

she taught me to hunt ~
what did she teach *you*? ~ mostly
how to seduce men

people tell stories
'bout us? ~ apparently a
bit legendary

he died on the job:
no better way to go ~ you
really believe that?

it's not like we're in
the "live 'til you're 90, die
in your sleep" business

son and husband back?
would give anything — would scare
the hell out of me

'cause what if I've changed?
what if *they* changed? what if it
just didn't work out?

SEASON 12

Celebrating the Life of Asa Fox (cont.)

hunting was his whole
life — he never married, had
a family, kids

between us: always
nice to see a Winchester
can't get what he wants

you like stories? this
is the story everyone's
gonna tell 'bout you

I was wrong — Asa
did have a family, kids —
I've got grandchildren

I gotta tell you,
mom to mom, they are good men
— best I've ever met

I'm big believer
in what dies, stays dead — laws of
universe and all

I didn't *ask* to
come back ~ no, and you hate it
— look in your eyes: dead

reapers don't kill: rules ~
I guess you're just gonna have
to wait ~ Winchesters

Rock Never Dies

Episode 248 (Season 12, Episode 7)
Directed by Eduardo Sánchez
Written by Robert Berens
Original air date: December 1, 2016

---

we team up to save
the world, and then bupkis — you
don't call you don't write

how you been, huh? health?
family? Hell? ~ doesn't matter
don't care, been better

a soul's a soul — but
certain prestige to owning
a Swift or a Drake

dudes in skinny jeans
wearing sunglasses inside
— I like yoga pants

:: humans desperate ::
:: to put someone above them ::
:: — God ain't cuttin' it ::

maybe a third-tier
agent ~ at least I don't look
like a lumberjack

don't listen to him —
feathers and I are all but
inseparable

:: religion, Twitter — ::
:: if not *gaining* followers, ::
:: *losing* followers ::

he's devil ~ I'm in
P.R., my job is making
saints out of devils

he'll kill you, Cas — you'll
last three minutes, tops ~ then I'll
buy you three minutes

:: I was inside you — ::
:: you are a weak, duty-bound, ::
:: pleasureless dullard ::

Lucifer was bad
enough when he had a plan
— now just having fun

it's all on us: we
let him out — we're not winning
we're just losing slow

SEASON 12

LOTUS

Episode 249 (Season 12, Episode 8)
Directed by Phil Sgriccia
Written by Eugenie Ross-Leming & Brad Buckner
Original air date: December 8, 2016

Lucifer is not
content with slutting it from
one vessel to next

he is moving on
to blue chips, celebrities,
captains industry

we will look around —
if Lucifer, we'll call the
rest of Scooby Gang

:: need to believe that ::
:: I am, in fact, President ::
:: of United States ::

someday real couple
wedding, baby — know you'd make
amazing father

get damn news without
the drama? ~ can I get *you*
without the flannel?

LOTUS (cont.)

explodes fiancé
that is the sweetest thing you've
ever done for me

nephilim has come
into being: offspring of
angel and human

not a typical
angel ~ Lucifer? didn't
know he was dating

they'll meet us — we have
a plan? ~ impeach LOTUS, find
Rosemary's Baby

Ketch: grenade launcher
everyone ducks for cover
except Castiel

you: halo — do you
sense I'm lying? ~ my name is
Castiel... and... no

you're making it up;
it's impossible ~ well, so
is teleporting

under arrest for
assassination attempt
of the president

SEASON 12

First Blood

Episode 250 (Season 12, Episode 9)
Directed by Robert Singer
Written by Andrew Dabb
Original air date: January 26, 2017

FBI started
investigating them ~ for
what? ~ assault, murder

multiple counts of
desecrating a corpse ~ same
corpse? ~ different corpses

by "probably," you
mean, "maybe," and by "maybe,"
you mean, "I don't know"

• *Camp tells Sam and Dean about the boredom torture he has planned* •

you are gonna talk
to me, son, you just *are* — now
that is not a threat

I don't believe in
torture: doesn't work — I've seen
folks waterboarded

SEASON 12

First Blood (cont.)

cut on, and they talk,
ooh, they do — but they never
tell you what you need

you know what works, though?
every time? nothing — when I
leave, that door closes

it stays closed, you stay
in the dark — maybe doesn't
sound bad, but after

a month, year… you spend
enough time staring at walls
— just you and nothing

you'll get so crazy
to talk, to see someone real,
you'll tell exactly

what I need — you'll tell
me with a smile — it'll
take some time, of course

the thing is, after
what you did, nobody's in
such a hurry to

get you that phone call —
so you and me, we got all
the time in the world

no offense: you can
take your offer and you can
shove it up your ass

I am sure it won't
be too painful, what with those
soft hands of yours, right?

SEASON 12

First Blood (cont.)

Sam, Dean: like herpes —
just when you think they are gone
hello: boys are back

in the words of the
immortal Lawrence Tureaud:
"I pity the fool"

they've only been gone ~
6 weeks, 2 days, 10 hours
~ we will find them, Cas

• *Cas explains his hunting failures to Mary* •

saw it on the news,
and I thought: that's the sort of
thing Sam and Dean would

investigate — they
would roll into town, save the
day, kill the monsters

with them gone, I tried
to work the case — I *tried* but
don't know what I did

wrong: I asked questions,
but maybe they were the wrong
people, wrong questions

and I just never
found it — I never found the
monster, I never

even got close — three
more died before I left town
…before ran away

First Blood (cont.)

the Winchesters are
out there, and this time we are
doing it my way

so you're telling me
you took on devil himself?
~ yes ~ did you *win*? ~ yes

you're a different breed:
surly, suspicious, you don't
play well with others

• <i>The Winchester boys are skilled and dangerous predators,
but if you're human they probably won't kill you when they hunt you
(and might even hand you a first-aid kit for your bullet wound)</i> •

tell you how this is
gonna go: call your boys, you're
gonna turn around

nobody's gonna
get hurt ~ no, *here's* how this is
gonna go: I take

highly trained soldiers,
track your ass down, you get hurt
…a lot — you can't run

forever: you're trapped
out here ~ well, what we have here
is a failure to

communicate — we're
not trapped out here with you — *you're*
trapped out here with *us*

SEASON 12

First Blood (cont.)

president possessed
by devil, we saved his life
— and that is the truth

do not come after
us ~ who *are* you? ~ we are the
guys who save the world

thermal imaging
satellite saw you from space
~ borrowed for a bit

you left survivors? ~
they were soldiers just doing
what they were told to

deal: die and come back ~
come midnight, a Winchester
dies permanently

we were dead: locked in
that cell with nothing — I've been
to Hell — this was worse

a pact bound in blood —
break that, there's consequences
on a cosmic scale

a Winchester dies?
I'm a Winchester ~ works for me
~ Mom ~ don't ~ I love you

First Blood (cont.)

*• Castiel unleashes potentially cosmic consequences
because he just can't bear to let a Winchester die •*

sad, doomed little world:
it needs you — it needs every
last Winchester it

can get, and I will
not let you die... I won't let
any of you die

and I will not let
you sacrifice yourselves — you
mean too much to me

to everything — you
made a stupid deal, and I
broke it — you're welcome

• Mick convinces Mary to help the British Men of Letters •

let me paint you a
picture of a world without
monsters, or demons

or any of those
little buggers that go bump
in the night — of a

world where nobody
has to die because of the
supernatural

SEASON 12

Lily Sunder Has Some Regrets

Episode 251 (Season 12, Episode 10)
Directed by Thomas J. Wright
Written by Steve Yockey
Original air date: February 2, 2017

---

we don't have a mom
who's gonna stay home and make
chicken soup dinner

Billie said there'd be
"cosmic consequences," — do
you know what that means?

neither do I, but
I am pretty sure it ain't
jellybeans, g-strings

what I like about
him: sarcastic, but thoughtful,
appreciative, too

I'm not a hero,
but sometimes doing the right
thing needs sacrifice

Benjamin: woman? ~
Benjamin is an angel;
vessel is woman

scoot over ~ I said
to come alone ~ these are my
friends who don't listen

well, if I plan to
do anything else stupid,
I will let you know

no wings, no home — just
ratty old coat and pair of
poorly-trained monkeys

is he a hero,
or is he a spanner in
the works? I don't know

humans: most of them
good, true — how could anyone
know them, *not* love them?

Lily Sunder Has Some Regrets (cont.)

can reason with her? ~
four dead angels indicates
not reasonable

my friendship with Sam
and Dean has made me stronger
~ you can't believe that

knock on her door, and
ask her nicely not to kill
any more angels

and what if she says
no? ~ well, then we burn that bridge
when we come to it

I had my daughter
long before I ever laid
eyes on an angel

before angels fell,
before they lost their wings, no
way to hunt them down

amazed what can do
with little bit of purpose,
abundance of time

she's a liar ~ why
would she lie? ~ she's human, it's
kind of what they do

cure human weakness
the same way I cured my own:
by cutting it out

didn't know we were
killing innocent — does not
excuse ignorance

revenge is all I've
had for over a hundred
years — it's what I am

what are we gonna
do? ~ let's drink and hope we can
find a better way

SEASON 12

Regarding Dean

Episode 252 (Season 12, Episode 11)
Directed by John Badham
Written by Meredith Glynn
Original air date: February 9, 2017

I'm starvin' — waffles?
dumb question, right? what psycho
doesn't love waffles?

I mean they're fluffy
little pockets for syrup,
covered in whipped cream

mom of Lucifer's
love child ~ devil baby
mama drama, right

I am not gonna
apologize for loving
that fish — not to *you*

the Rat Pack partied
'til the day they died, and I
can still kick your ass

trying to read lips
"now salsa you mittens" ~ you
can't… ~ I can't read lips

monsters are real, and
we're the guys that kill 'em — come
on, best job *ever*

greasy diner food,
crappy motel rooms, more than
one apocalypse

begun to forget
himself, everyone he has
ever known, loved… *you*

we kinda sound like
heroes to me… *and* our best
friend's an angel: *whaaaat!*

you know, I've seen my
brother die, but watching him
become *not him*: worse

Regarding Dean (cont.)

• *Dean tries to remember who he is* •

okay, my name is
Dean Winchester, Sam is my
brother, uh… Mary

Winchester is my
mom and Cast— Cas is my best
friend… my name is Dean

Win… Winchester… my
name— my name is… my… my name
is… my… I don't know

they said "not up to
snuff" ~ witches sound like dicks — you
got plenty of snuff

pain in the arse, but
everything you've done, you've done
for the greater good

why you telling me
this? ~ because I know you won't
remember *boops snoot*

you know what they say ~
hmm? ~ nothing heals old wounds like
opening fresh ones

SEASON 12

Regarding Dean (cont.)

a gun? you really
think that's gonna work on a—
witch killing bullets

can't believe you rode
Larry ~ I was awesome on
that bull: like a god

nice to drop baggage?
maybe, hell probably, but
wasn't just the crap

it was everything —
if that's what being happy
looks like? think I'll pass

• *Dean's Broomstick Cowboy memory montage* •

dream, little broomstick
cowboy, of rocket ships and
Mars, of sunny days

for all too soon you'll
awaken, toys will all be
gone, your broomstick horse

and Willie Mays and
chocolate candy bars — dream on,
li'l broomstick cowboy

will ride away to
find another home, so, dream
on, broomstick cowboy

dream while you can, of
big green frogs and puppy dogs,
castles in the sand

dream while you can, for
soon you'll be a dreadful thing:
son, you'll be a man

SEASON 12

Stuck in the Middle (With You)

Episode 253 (Season 12, Episode 12)
Directed by Richard Speight Jr.
Written by Davy Perez
Original air date: February 16, 2017

---

she is into you —
it's good: we've been looking for
teachable moments

downloaded bunker's
files to a new archive—
~ *snores* nobody cares

waitresses get hit
on all day long, so you've got
to bring your A-game

upside: they always
smell like food ~ why would you want
them to smell like food?

classic demon sign ~
virgins go missing ~ classic
horny demon sign

question: my shy but
devastatingly handsome
friend was wondering

when do you get off? ~
whenever I can ~ *hey*-O!
~ zing! ~ point 1 for *her*

459

Stuck in the Middle (With You) (cont.)

Lucifer's kid: that's
a joke right? it's not a joke
~ let's get rambling

Cas groaning ~ can you
heal yourself? ~ I tried, something's
wrong ~ how bad is it?

did you see his eyes?
yellow ~ Mom, what the hell did
you get us into?

you never really
wanted this ~ since when is life
getting what you want?

you look like hammered
crap ~ yeah, that sounds about right
~ you know, I've had worse

I think I'm dying ~
just need some time — you'll heal up
the old-fashioned way

you're him? King of Hell? ~
must be mother Winchester
~ touch me, I'll kill you

you seem ambitious,
conniving, slimy enough
— so, *you* take the crown

what the hell is a
prince of... Hell? ~ old demons, first
gen after Lilith

anyone bothers
a prince of Hell, gonna be
on your head, Crowley

I've been sent by Hell ~
and what, they do not teach you
how to knock in Hell?

demon: you go up
in a puff of smoke — angel:
you just rot away

Stuck in the Middle (With You) (cont.)

I was growing fond
of the choir boy, too ~ shut
up, we don't have time

I don't have friends; I
make deals with those I can use
— kingdom needs allies

three humans with one
good liver between them, and
busted-up angel?

not much, but every
Armageddon: Winchester
stopped it — they're assets

• *Cas is dying, and he must tell the Winchesters how he feels* •

thank you — knowing you:
it's been the best part of my
life, and the things that

the things we have shared
together, they have changed me
— you're my family

I love you — I love
all of you — just please, please don't
make my last moments

be spent watching you
die — just run — save yourselves, and
I'll hold Ramiel

off as long as I
can — you need to keep fighting
~ we're fighting for you

and like you said: you're
family, and we don't leave
family behind

SEASON 12

Stuck in the Middle (With You) (cont.)

you stabbed one of our
friends ~ your friend was trespassing
~ tell how to cure him

hang in there, all right? ~
Crowley breaks spear the magic's
in the craftsmanship

that's not good enough —
I lost a friend — I almost
lost one of my boys

(she means Castiel)
(Mary's talking about Cas)
(Cas: one of her boys)

anything like that
happens again, and I will
burn all of you down

only five things in
all creation it can't kill
~ know about the Colt

boys got you down? can't
believe you're working for the
Dukes of Haphazard

SEASON 12

Family Feud

Episode 254 (Season 12, Episode 13)
Directed by P. J. Pesce
Written by Brad Buckner & Eugenie Ross-Leming
Original air date: February 23, 2017

---

so, you brag of your
superior power — well,
genius trumps brute force

you could have had me
back in cage, but you needed
sad little revenge

a lot of action
in here, okay? I'm switching
vote from witch to ghost

whenever pops out,
you're totally gonna love
the little devil

behind whole moron
facade, you and your brother
are, in fact, morons

I love that: we're both
single fathers — could use a
little dad advice

ain't all black and white,
good, evil — "people" tryin'
to kill you: angels

SEASON 12

Family Feud (cont.)

none born good or bad —
it's all in the upbringing
— kid could save us all

grandmother? *couldn't*
be alive ~ well, technically
dude, neither can *you*

I'm sure they're fine lads,
but it might be best if you
disengage from them

go to his death? that's
your solution? ~ didn't say
it was the fun one

he's not like us, he
believes in things — let him do
what believes is right

so, I'm just gonna
say it: I have sort of been
working with the Brits

don't give me the face ~
what face? ~ you know the face ~ there's
no face ~ *that's* the face

obvious reasons —
like broken ribs and burnt feet
— we don't trust the Brits

payback? ~ I am your
mother, dear — who better to
crush your shriveled heart?

The Raid

Episode 255 (Season 12, Episode 14)
Directed by John MacCarthy
Written by Robert Berens
Original air date: March 2, 2017

---

    runnin' an errand
for the Brits — you kept it from
    us… Cas almost died

    unpack, reshelve — Sig
Sauer could use good scrubbing
    ~ I've three PhDs

    Dean I am *trying* ~
how about for once you just
    try to be a mom?

    your mother, but not
just a mom, and you're not a
    child ~ never was

    dead guy in Akron
throat ripped ear-to-ear ~ well, good
    morning to you, too

    you're always playing
the middle, Sam — for once why
    don't you pick a side?

    you know, really dig
the whole low-budget Mission
    Impossible vibe

    excellent fit: one
with our inclinations
    ~ as in *you* and *me*?

    you are a killer,
Dean Winchester, so am I
    (common fallacy)

    go too long without
something to trap, punch or gut
    — well, things get ugly

SEASON 12

The Raid (cont.)

he calls himself the
"Hunter King of Baton Rouge"
— worked together… once

tell us where your friends
are ~ hunting, they went hunting
~ hunting who? ~ hunters

not built for defense —
those doors won't hold long — who here
has killed… anything?

and that'll work? ~ if
not, start praying 'cause we will
need a miracle

I'm old, like living
quietly — you've been making
life awfully noisy

back the way things were —
hunters, vampires: cops and
robbers — a fair fight

don't know how it is	adults — you're gonna
in ivory tower — down	make your own choices, even
here in muck, folks die	if I don't like 'em

alpha vampire
is dead — you're changing the world
— I want to be part

… SEASON 12

Somewhere Between Heaven and Hell

Episode 256 (Season 12, Episode 15)
Directed by Nina Lopez-Corrado
Written by Davy Perez
Original air date: March 9, 2017

---

commune with nature?
thought we were out here to get
naked, do weird stuff

you're covered in ghoul
and wraith, and there's a piece of
siren in your hair

weird that you know how
much underwear I packed ~ *that's*
what's weird about this?

computer told me ~
computers: monsters, porn — there
anything can't do?

not just aliens —
reptilians — you know, like
the Queen of England

it is why I do
not use new tech — anything
past '96: trap

that is why you are
here — FBI: man in black
— or, well, you know… beige

hi, I'm Sam, this is
my much handsomer brother
Dean — we hunt monsters

guy you were banging?
we're pretty sure he made a
deal with a demon

I'm still gonna peel
off your skin and eat your soul
— gonna be messy

467

SEASON 12

Somewhere Between Heaven and Hell (cont.)

that was a hellhound ~
a what? ~ a hellhound — it's kind
of hard to explain

basically: giant
invisible hounds from Hell...
wasn't hard at all

wanted a Hello
Kitty backpack, or the death
of an enemy?

I thought gig couldn't
get any weirder ~ it can
always get weirder

it's Ramsey: she got
out, my lord ~ have the kennel
guards killed, painfully

take care of her ~ the
car? ~ just imagine she's a
beautiful woman

you have got more field
experience than thousand
angels combined, Cas

don't get me wrong, I
love Earth — it's quirky, smells like
hay — but it's not home

the only thing I
care about is making Hell
great again ~ mm-hmm

take me, fallen one —
my life: yours to devour
~ you just made it weird

maybe you've rubbed off
on me, maybe I've rubbed off
all over you *cringe*

Somewhere Between Heaven and Hell (cont.)

SEASON 12

• *Crowley reveals the true nature of Lucifer's vessel-prison* •

what was that you said,
re: always two steps ahead?
~ that's not what I said

I am glad you had
a little taste of freedom
— what I *said* was: I

am always *10* steps
ahead — I said you cross me,
I crush you, hit me

I hit back twice as
hard; make me your dog, I'll make
you my slave — the chain

around your neck was
nothing but a stylish
accessory... this

vessel: true prison,
warded with runes, spellwork from
the cage carved into

every molecule —
in there, I *own* you — I am
just getting started

---

didn't tell you 'cause
I know how much you hate them
~ no, *we* hate them — *us*

we work with people
we don't trust all the time — I
just worked with Crowley

# Ladies Drink Free

Episode 257 (Season 12, Episode 16)
Directed by Amyn Kaderali
Written by Meredith Glynn
Original air date: March 30, 2017

---

have you never seen
horror film? two kids, dark road,
creepy noise in woods?

world-class repression —
you *are* British ~ we prefer
a stiff upper lip

Kendricks School: where the
British Men of Letters train
it's like our— ~ Hogwarts?

put on a flannel,
pick up a gun — get good fast,
or get dead faster

limeys ruined me —
went for a swim this morning
~ you brought swimsuit? ~ no

when was your last hot
meal that didn't come from Gas-
n-Sip microwave?

who do you think kids
gonna wanna talk to? me,
or some old skeezer?

recognize this girl? ~
not really ~ I'd lie if served
underage girls, too

you like high school girls?
you get older, they stay the
same age, is that it?

what are you, her dad? ~
you ever touch her again,
I will break your face

killing monsters: what
we do, not palling around
with demons, witches

SEASON 12

Ladies Drink Free (cont.)

don't tell me how to
do my job ~ well, then do it
~ think it's that simple?

things aren't just black, white
out here — all you have is a
case in front of you

we *do* care ~ then stop
treating me like stupid kid
~ stop acting like one

if there's any chance
I could hurt Jody, Alex…
I would rather die

hey, you do not get
a vote in this ~ it's my life,
I get *all* the votes

it hurts at first, but
eventually like best drug
~ right, eat me, Teen Wolf

who says they're nice guys?
clingy, insecure bitches
with mommy issues

we're good? ~ not quite, but
we'll give you a second chance
~ there won't be a third

• *Claire leaves a message for Jody* •

I have been hunting,
alone — and I know it's not
what you want to hear

know it sounds scary —
scares me too sometimes, but this
is something I have

to do on my own,
just for a little while
— but I am ready

I never would have
been, if it wasn't for you
being my mother

I better go — tell
Alex: better not touch my
stuff — I love you guys

SEASON 12

The British Invasion

Episode 258 (Season 12, Episode 17)
Directed by John F. Showalter
Written by Eugenie Ross-Leming & Brad Buckner
Original air date: April 6, 2017

---

you said you'd give me
a second chance ~ doesn't mean
we wanna hang out

look, it's not Kelly's
fault okay — she didn't know
Lucifer: boyfriend

I'm not saying it
was gonna be easy, but
the code demands it

we don't have time to
court a handful of mangy
colonials now

not a discussion —
an order: assimilate
or eliminate

your mum and Ketch make
quite the team ~ would you want *your*
mom working with him?

for the little champ's
record, what can you tell me
about his father?

in school together ~
ah, major in murder and
minor in mayhem?

The British Invasion (cont.)

he works for Dagon,
covers her tracks ~ smart ~ dude, don't
compliment bad guys

no formal training?
I was top of my class at
Kendricks ~ no one cares

I'm Renny Rawlings,
graduated Kendricks top
of my— ~ I don't care

you only have to
do what you know is right — you
answer to own code

choice to make: work or
family ties ~ you know what?
it's not either / or

my boys: I did not
choose hunting over them — why
one or the other?

weird little pains? taste
of what's to come — birthing a
nephilim: fatal

The British Invasion (cont.)

*• Mick Davies has learned a thing or two from the Winchester boys
about doing what is right, and stands up to Dr. Hess
re: "the code" — it does not go well for him •*

at first, I was shocked
at how Sam, Dean operate
— what Lady Bevell

doesn't mention is
lives they've saved, monsters destroyed,
outcomes made better

not because of the
Code, because of Sam and Dean's
sense of what is right

and that is the crux
of the matter — the code is
not a suggestion

it's an absolute
the code is what separates
us from the monsters

it is the order
by which we all live ~ no, the
code is what makes a

young boy kill his best
friend… when I was a child
I had nothing, I

owed you everything
and I obeyed, but I'm a
man now, Dr. Hess

and I can see the
choices, and I choose to do
the right thing *Ketch shoots*

SEASON 12

The Memory Remains

Episode 259 (Season 12, Episode 18)
Directed by Phil Sgriccia
Written by John Bring
Original air date: April 13, 2017

---

goat dude with name like
pirate: even for *us* is
a little insane

this coffee is hot,
kind of like *seductively
points at the waitress*

come on, this guy is
adorable — he plays a
freakin' flute ~ that's Pan

feast on victims 'til
belly full-to-bursting with
moist, slippery meat

*raw beef carcasses
hang from hooks in meat plant* you
hungry? I'm hungry

seriously, Dean
after what we just saw, how
can you *eat*? ~ grow up

burger's beef, bacon's
pig, Soylent Green is people
— but *this* is heaven

how's Sam get hair so
shiny? how many ratty
flannels does Dean own?

475

SEASON 12

The Memory Remains (cont.)

I mean, are they like,
"croquet's all right, but know what
would be great? murder"

that sound fair to you? ~
honestly? sounds like a bad
ep. of "Dynasty"

that's what we do right?
hunting people, killing them:
the family business

how are you feeling? ~
like I just went 12 rounds with
a god, so… normal

family: messed up — remind me that we could be psycho goat people	the people we saved: *they're* our legacy, and they will remember us

we'll fade away — that's
fine, because we left the world
better than found it

Dean pulls out his knife
~ what are you doing? ~ leaving
mark *carves initials*

now we're reporting
to a low-rent Christian Bale?
that guy creeps me out

SEASON 12

The Future

Episode 260 (Season 12, Episode 19)
Directed by Amanda Tapping
Written by Robert Berens & Meredith Glynn
Original air date: April 27, 2017

I love you, but we
won't ever be together
— no happy ending

what you'll do to the
world: all that pain, all that death
— can't let that happen

where have you been? ~ let
me rephrase that for Sam: where
the hell have you been?

• *Cas returns Dean's Top 13 Zepp Traxx (it's a gift — you keep those)* •

sorry Dean, I just
wanted to return this ~ it's
a gift, you keep those

with everything that's
going on, can't just go dark
— we didn't know what

happened, and we were
worried ~ I didn't mean to
add to your distress

I just keep failing —
when you were taken, I searched
months: couldn't find you

SEASON 12

The Future (cont.)

then Kelly escaped
on my watch, and I couldn't
find her, and I just

wanted... I needed
to come back here with a win
for you, for myself

think you're the only
one rolling snake eyes here? me
and Sam — we had her

had Kelly, lost her ~	Hell-bent on finding
and if you find her again?	something won't kill her or kid
~ Sam's working on it	~ if he doesn't find?

and if you run out
of time, could either of you
kill an innocent?

we will find better
way ~ you mean "we"? ~ yes, dumbass,
we: you, me, and Sam

we are just better
together — now that you're back,
let's go: Team Free Will

so let's get it done ~
I would like that ~ great... *nods* and
I would like a beer

The Future (cont.)

you'll be Mary of
Nazareth, Part 2: Evil
Jesus Edition

I stole the Colt — I
will kill this girl, so that Sam
and Dean don't have to

Colt was in safe, right? ~
it was under my pillow;
like to keep it close

yeah, he played us both ~
I say we find him, and we
kick his feathered ass

I say we find him,
figure out what's going on,
then kick feathered ass

came to kill; didn't ~
please don't thank me... I had a
mission, and I failed

through enough to know:
everyone is just winging
it, some quite badly

there are kinks, but it's
a plan, and it beats the hell
out of certain death

you asked me who would
protect, guide him when I'm gone
I know now: it's you

thought he was gonna
save you? this sad, fluttering
aimless little moth?

thank you for coming
to fight — I've been so lost, I'm
not lost anymore

SEASON 12

Twigs & Twine & Tasha Banes

*Episode 261 (Season 12, Episode 20)
Directed by Richard Speight Jr.
Written by Steve Yockey
Original air date: May 4, 2017*

---

last night when I looked
at him, did not recognize
the guy staring back

their mom is on a
hunting trip, and hasn't been
home in a few days

can you call me back?
some stuff going down that's kind
of got me spun out

perhaps we could find
some privacy and tire
ourselves out — it's not

illicit motel
sex, but ~ we agreed that it
was a onetime thing

torture session: a
waste of time (is Mary still
talking 'bout the sex?)

Twigs & Twine & Tasha Banes (cont.)

---

anyone who says
torture isn't the answer:
never under knife

parents seem smart, strong —
it's only when you grow up,
realize: just people

leave you alone to
have girl time ~ since when are *you*
not part of girl time?

an unfortunate
werewolf mishap ~ a werewolf
shot him in the head?

Enochian brass
knuckles just work on angels
~ they're still brass knuckles

gotta burn bodies,
Max ~ like my dad: I can do
it; I *should* do it

we do terrible
things all the time to save each
other — for family

if only you had
been as ruthless as I hoped,
this could have worked out

SEASON 12

There's Something About Mary

Episode 262 (Season 12, Episode 21)
Directed by P. J. Pesce
Written by Brad Buckner & Eugenie Ross-Leming
Original air date: May 11, 2017

I'm not being terse —
I'm not being curt either
— manners 101

second hunter death
in two weeks ~ two doesn't mean
a pattern ~ *three* would

people who do what
we do know there are going
to be deaths, but this…

after you died, your
beloved John was a man
slowly going mad

the drunken rages,
the weeks of abandonment,
the child abuse

your relationship
with Winchesters: it's a bit
cozy for my taste

There's Something About Mary (cont.)

Kelly's in clutches
of the Winchesters' love slave,
Castiel, no doubt

dragging her to a
gruesome death ~ as opposed to
fun-packed death you planned?

I'm not really an
administrator ~ you are
merciless killer

all I ever had
besides family: my will
— it's going away

rule of thumb: if you
think that we killed someone, then
we probably did

your bunker is an
excellent fortress — it's an
even better tomb

easier to hurt
people I love? ~ those you don't
remember loving

Who We Are

Episode 263 (Season 12, Episode 22)
Directed by John F. Showalter
Written by Robert Berens
Original air date: May 18, 2017

I assure you, I'm
an extraordinarily
shallow breather ~ right

purification
ritual: use on our blood
~ re-virginize it?

an old sewer pipe ~
wait a sec, we're just gonna…
~ straight Shawshank this bitch

thought we had it made:
we saved the world — we got Cas
back, we had Mom back

I just followed 'cause
it was easier ~ than what?
~ *considers* leading

I always thought we'd
go out like Butch and Sundance
~ yeah: blaze of glory

you are lunatics —
this is a colossally
stupid idea

big, beautiful, dumb —
I've been waiting so long for
the perfect moment

lunatics: action
movie-loving, cheeseburger-
eating lunatics

okay, beautiful —
aims yippee ki-yay, mother—
Dean launches grenade

wanna play mother
to my son? he is all yours ~
Dean, that's not your mom

she's hiding behind
impenetrable psychic
walls — grenades won't work

Walt, Roy ~ well, damn ~ we
haven't seen you ~ since you killed
us? no hard feelings

SEASON 12

Who We Are (cont.)

• Sam's speech as he becomes a leader among hunters •

I have called you here
'cause our people are being
slaughtered, and we're next

the British Men of
Letters came here because they
thought they could do our

job better than we
could, and they hooked us with their
flashy gear, their tech

and I see most of
you had the good sense to turn
'em down — I didn't

and they've killed people —
innocent people — just 'cause
they got in the way

they said they wanted
the same thing we wanted: a
world free of monsters

they think that the ends
justify the means, but we
know better, we know

they really wanted
control — they want to live in
a world where they can

hunting's not about
killing — it's doing what's right,
even when it's hard

sit in some office
and decide who gets to live
and who gets to die

so, we go by our
gut, right? we play by our own
rules, and that scares them

SEASON 12

Who We Are (cont.)

that is why they want
us dead: because we're the one
thing they can't control

want you to follow —
take the fight to them, hit them
before they hit us

we go in fast, hard —
fight, beat them down 'til they give
up, or 'til they're dead

they're well-trained, well-armed
— some of us might not make it
back, but we *will* win

take down the bad guys,
'cause that's what we do — they're scared
of us — they should be

I'll take jacked-up Dean
over any 10 other
hunters, any day

careful, I promise ~
not what I was gonna ask:
kick it in the ass

you got this, come here
Sam and Dean bro hug you come
back ~ promise ~ bitch ~ jerk

I'd like to see son
again: not asking for pass,
asking for head start

SEASON 12

Who We Are (cont.)

• *Inside Mary's head: the I hate you / I love you scene* •

know they messed with head:
feels better in here, safer
— need you to hear me

thinking maybe we
should take Sammy to the park
before Dad gets home

Mom look at me — you're
choosing this ~ your favorite
~ yes! ~ after you eat

I only want good
things for you, Dean, I'll never
let anything bad

happen to you *smiles* ~
I hate you; you lied to me
— I was just a kid

you promised you'd keep
me safe, and then you make a
deal with Azazel

yeah, it saved Dad's life,
but I will tell you something
else that happened — on

November 2nd,
1983, yellow
eyes came to Sam's room

because of your deal,
you left us — alone, because
Dad was just a shell

his perfect wife — *gone*;
our perfect mom, the perfect
family… was *gone*

I had to be more than
a brother — I had to be
father *and* mother

and that wasn't fair —
I couldn't do it — wanna
know what that was like?

they killed girl he loved,
got possessed by Lucifer,
tortured him in Hell

and he lost his soul —
his *soul* — all because of you
— all because of *you*

487

Who We Are (cont.)

I hate you — *hate* you,
and I love you, 'cause I can't
help it: you're my mom

I understand, 'cause
I have made deals to save ones
I love, more than once

I forgive you *sighs*
I *forgive* you, for all of
it — for everything

on the other side
of this, we can start over,
okay — you, me, Sam

we can get it right
this time, but need you to fight
right now, need to *fight*

I need you to look
at me, Mom — I need you to
really look at me

see me — Mom, I need
you to *see* me, please ~ *slowly
turns, eyes meet eyes* Dean?

when you left us, *knew*
you were psycho — didn't
think you were stupid

they're unstoppable —
you can not face that alone
~ listen to her, boy ~ pass

everything happened:
made us who we are — we kick
ass, we save the world

scared: what if he can't
forgive me ~ Mom, you don't have
to be scared of me

All Along the Watchtower

Episode 264 (Season 12, Episode 23)
Directed by Robert Singer
Written by Andrew Dabb
Original air date: May 18, 2017

> I'll never teach him to ride a bike, watch him get married, or even look him in the eyes — but I can build for him a *stupid Swedish crib*

> I know how hard this is — that's a lie — I have *no idea* how hard

> I will raise him, and I will make him someone that you will be proud of

> let me get this straight: we beat Brits, kicked their psycho tea-swilling asses instead of popping champagne, headin' to Vegas we get *Lucifer*

> Crowley's a cockroach — I'll believe he's gone when I see body, burn it

SEASON 12

All Along the Watchtower (cont.)

gonna try, but you
can't kill me — you've never been
able to kill me

child-rearing books —
one thing they all agree on:
everybody poops

been focused so long
on keeping my job, never
realized I hate it

alright then — I kind
of always wanted to punch
devil in the face

place my bets on you
big, beautiful, lumbering
piles of flannel

Rowena is dead ~
funny, always thought *I'd* be
the one to kill her

it is what they called
contractions in my doula
class… took it online

tear in space and time:
doorway to another world
~ what, like Narnia?

it's an alternate
reality ~ bizarro
world? like when we got

zapped to actors on
TV ~ supernatural
fake, you were Polish

All Along the Watchtower (cont.)

scale of 1 to 10,
how bad is this? ~ a hole in
reality that

leads to a bombed-out
apocalypse world? gonna
go with 11

I have faith ~ really?
in your unborn baby-God?
well, you're a dumbass

this is a world where
you were never born; it's a
world you never saved

it ain't so bad if
you like killing angels — it's
my hobby, passion

apocalypse, take
two: that's your plan? ~ when in doubt,
go with the classics

I'm gonna enjoy
wiping smug, self-satisfied
look off of your face

whatever you try:
gonna lose ~ even when I
lose, I win†... bye boys

rift in space and time —
one side: Lucifer, Mary
— the other: Cas, dead

---

† This brilliant phrase didn't make the final cut, but it was a much better end for Crowley. Our beloved, mordant King of Hell deserved to be at least a little bit in control of his own demise, and he certainly deserved a snarky final line. The line is canon, as far as this writer is concerned.

SEASON THIRTEEN

SEASON 13

Lost and Found

Episode 265 (Season 13, Episode 1)
Directed by Phil Sgriccia
Written by Andrew Dabb
Original air date: October 12, 2017

• *Season 13 opener: The Road So Far, "Nothing Else Matters"-style* •

Lucifer is back ~
so close no matter how far
~ a nephilim has

come into being ~
couldn't be much more from heart
~ can feel it inside

forever trust who we are, nothing else matters — I never opened	nothing else matters — never cared for what they say, never cared for games
myself this way, life is ours we live it our way — these words don't just say	they play, never cared what they do, never cared what they know, and I know

*son of Lucifer
sees Lucifer's true vessel
for first time* Father?

Crowley's dead, Kelly's
dead, Cas is… Mom's gone, devil's
kid almost killed us

494

Lost and Found (cont.)

had under control ~
sorry, are you defending
the son of Satan?

Castiel: always
knew he would meet a bad end
~ he deserved better

so weird ~ there's no such
thing as "weird," everyone is
normal in own way

I remember when
the bad woman burned, and when
the universe screamed

dude, how high *are* you?
it means like wasted, lit, chonged,
blitzed, blasted, blazed, baked…

look, I'm not judging
you; I'm jealous, what are you
on? you are so stoned

in most feminist
screw-the-patriarchy way:
giant super bitch

my name is Dean, that
big fella is my brother
Sam — we kill monsters

don't think he's ever
had candy before ~ I like
it… I like nougat

are you some kind of
superhero? ~ I'm just a
guy doing a job

SEASON 13

Lost and Found (cont.)

you take things, and break
things, and piss people off, and
just do whatever

you want, no matter
who it hurts — also: you're a
giant super bitch

want golden ticket —
Lucifer 2: Electric
Boogaloo, okay?

bring him home: at least
the only people he can
hurt are you and me

maybe we can bring
him back — Chuck did — if we prayed...
~ you don't think I've tried?

• *Dean prays to Chuck to bring Cas back* •

okay Chuck, or God
whatever... I need your help
see, you — you left us

you *left us*, you went
off... you said... you said the earth
would be fine because

it had me, it had
Sam — but it's *not*, and *we're not*
— we've lost everything

SEASON 13

Lost and Found (cont.)

and now you're gonna
bring him back, okay? you are
gonna bring back Cas

gonna bring back Mom —
gonna bring 'em back — all of
them, even Crowley

after everything
that you have done, you owe us,
you son of a bitch

so, you get your ass
down here, and you make this right
— right here and right now

I… what do you say? ~
you say thank you, you're sorry,
you hope they're somewhere

without sadness, pain —
you hope they're somewhere better,
and you say goodbye

goodbye Cas, Kelly,
Crowley, Mom ~ we don't know if
Mom— ~ yeah we do, Sam

hunter's funeral
pyre for Castiel: Sam
is sad, Dean is wrecked

SEASON 13

The Rising Son

Episode 266 (Season 13, Episode 2)
Directed by Thomas J. Wright
Written by Eugenie Ross-Leming & Brad Buckner
Original air date: October 19, 2017

---

12 hours 'til home —
you want me to drive? ~ do I
ever want you to?

when we pretend that
the bad guys aren't so bad, or
that things will get fixed

people we care 'bout
get hurt — so, this time, let's start
with the obvious

in perfect world, I
kill you and your plodding sons
— but life isn't fair

he's new to this world,
but full of timeless knowledge
and unschooled power

God: he's in here, too
Jack points to bible is he
famous or something?

The Rising Son (cont.)

at moral crossroad:
"what would Mr. Rogers do?"
— I'm usually good

turn on, start buzzin' ~
we are brothers; it's kind of
like a family crest

pain: part of human
experience — accept: sign
of maturity

Dean feels like it's job
to protect —*you*, but also
protect folks *from* you

maybe I'm not worth
all this ~ your mom thought you were,
and Cas — so do I

*Dean throws angel blade
like a badass* — housekeeping's
not gonna like this

these yellow-eyed things… ~
hope fourth Prince of Hell is the
last Kardashian

if I'm right, and it
comes to killing you, *I'll* be
the one to do it

Patience

Episode 267 (Season 13, Episode 3)
Directed by Robert Singer
Written by Robert Berens
Original air date: October 26, 2017

---

don't like that at all ~
you don't have to *like* it, you
just have to *do* it

there'll be none of that ~
you know, this would be a lot
more fun if you screamed

I'm ripe, gotta hit
the showers — later (Patience
has seen this before)

woman you describe
who walked out on her family
— that's not Missouri

Mom said I could be
good, that I had the choice, that
it was up to me

know what it feels like:
don't belong, darkness inside,
scared of who you are

milk that beautiful
brain of yours ~ first: gross, second:
I am not psychic

Patience (cont.)

life: hunting, monsters —
no joy in it: nothing but
pain, horror, and death

don't have to listen
to either of them if not
what you really want

force it down to make
someone else happy: you will
be miserable

when I was drinking
demon blood ~ that's totally
different ~ was it?

you could've put a
bullet in me — Dad *told* you
to — but you didn't

use him as sort of
interdimensional can
opener — that's fine

don't act like you *care*
about him; you only care
'bout what he can do

SEASON 13

The Big Empty

Episode 268 (Season 13, Episode 4)
Directed by John Badham
Written by Meredith Glynn
Original air date: November 2, 2017

---

you wanna save her ~
I do, but if this doesn't
work, that is okay

I'm not gonna hold
his hand, not gonna be his
mother, nor are you

grief journal ~ shrinks: snake
oil for the mind ~ or, how
healthy people deal

"I see the program
works" the program? one Kool-Aid
away from Jonestown

doctor's gonna eat
our liver with some fava
beans and Chianti

at least you had a
relationship with Mom — I
never will have one

• *Cas vs. the Empty, part 1* •

I know you are there;
I can feel you — what are you?
~ :: I'm just your friendly ::

:: neighborhood cosmic ::
:: entity :: ~ you look like me?
~ :: yes, well, I show up ::

:: in my *real* form, and ::
:: you freak out, rip out your own ::
:: eyes, et cetera ::

:: be embarrassing ::
:: wouldn't it, for both of us? ::
~ so, what is this place?

:: excellent question: ::
:: before God and Amara, ::
:: create, destruction ::

The Big Empty (cont.)

:: Heaven, Hell, precious ::
:: little earth, what else was there? ::
~ nothing ~ :: yes, that's right ::

:: nothing, nothing but ::
:: empty: you're soaking in it ::
:: — angels and demons ::

:: you all come here when ::
:: you die :: ~ every angel that
ever died is *here*?

:: sleeping an endless, ::
:: peaceful sleep — you know, I was ::
:: sleeping too — hey, uh… ::

:: since we are pals, there's ::
:: something I've gotta know, I've ::
:: just gotta ask, hmm ::

:: why are you awake? ::
:: fun fact: in all of forever, ::
:: nothing ever wakes ::

I don't know ~ :: well, *think* :: ~
the Winchesters: Sam and Dean
must've made a deal

:: here — I mean *ever* ::
:: ever, and second fun fact ::
:: is when you woke up ::

:: no, no, not with me, ::
:: and I'm the only one that ::
:: has any pull here ::

:: *I* woke up, and I ::
:: don't like being awake, so ::
:: what is up, smart guy? ::

:: not Heaven, not Hell, ::
:: not g-o-d himself, so ::
:: think harder — rack that ::

:: perky little brain ::
:: of yours :: ~ stay away from me
~ :: I'll rack it for you ::

The Big Empty (cont.)

• *Cas vs. the Empty, part 2* •

what'd you do to me? ~
:: read your mind, such as it is ::
~ so, what do you want?

:: what do I want? I ::
:: want you to shut up, I want... ::
:: having you awake ::

:: it is like a gnat ::
:: flew right up here, and it's trapped, ::
:: and it is buzzing ::

having me awake
causes you pain ~ :: if *you* can't ::
:: sleep, *I* can't sleep, yeah? ::

send me back to earth ~
:: or, throw you so deep into ::
:: the Empty that you ::

:: and I *like* sleep, I ::
:: *need* sleep :: ~ then get rid of me
~ :: oh I should, should I? ::

:: cannot bother me ::
:: anymore :: ~ except you know
won't work, or would've

done it already ~
:: that's pretty smart, pretty smart, ::
:: dummy :: ~ send me back

:: that's not part of the ::
:: deal, besides you don't want to ::
:: go back :: ~ yes, I do

:: tulips: memories ::
:: your little feelings... know what ::
:: you hate, *who you love* ::

Sam and Dean need me ~
:: oh save it, I have tiptoed ::
:: through all your little ::

:: what you fear — there is ::
:: nothing for you back there, no, ::
:: here, let me show you ::

The Big Empty (cont.)

doesn't matter what
you are — matters what you do
monsters can do good

• Cas vs. the Empty, part 3 •

:: come on, Castiel, :: :: wouldn't you rather be a :: :: fond memory than ::	:: constant festering :: :: disappointment? just let's lay :: :: down, just try and sleep ::

:: just think about it — ::
:: infinite peace, no regrets, ::
:: no pain, save yourself ::

I'm already saved — you can prance, and you can preen, and scream and yell and	and I will keep you awake 'til both go insane — I will fight, and fight
remind me of my failings — somehow, I'm awake — I will *stay* awake	and fight forever — for eternity ~ :: no, no :: ~ release me, release

need you to keep faith
for both of us, 'cause I don't
believe a damn thing

SEASON 13

Advanced Thanatology

Episode 269 (Season 13, Episode 5)
Directed by John F. Showalter
Written by Steve Yockey
Original air date: November 9, 2017

---

hey, pb&j
for breakfast, strong work ~ yep ~ you
want a beer with that?

wow, how you ever
got laid I'll never know ~ yeah
tell me about it

seen monsters: I know
that when they're gone, they never
really go away

me and my brother —
we're the guys that stop monsters,
the guys that scare them

go to Clam Diver? ~
great reviews ~ you read *reviews*
for the Clam Diver?

last lap dance you spent
trying to convince girl to
go to nursing school

you *do* believe in
things, you believe in *people*
— that is who you are

fight back, same way I
always do: bullets, bacon
booze… a lotta booze

you're talking about
killing yourself ~ worked before
~ insane risk to take

funny to hear a
Winchester talk of dying
as finality

universe can be
so many things, and sometimes
it is poetic

I'm not one breaking
cosmic bargains left and right
~ not like you hold grudge

Advanced Thanatology (cont.)

whole multi-versal
quantum construct we live in
is like house of cards

don't need some big, dumb
Winchester knocking it down
~ that *does* sound like us

the man who has been
dead so many times, but it
never seems to stick

it doesn't matter;
I don't matter — I couldn't
save **Mom**, or save **Cas**

heart attack, burned by
a red-haired witch, stabbed by a
ghoul in a graveyard

unfortunately,
none of these books say you die
today ~ come again?

what I see? you and
your brother: you're important
— you have work to do

talk about later ~
but we *won't* talk about it
later, you know that

I saw Death, *the* Death ~
he's dead ~ no, she's not: Billie
— she got a new gig

always believed that
what we do was important,
no matter the cost

no matter who we
lost: making world better… I
just need a damn win

SEASON 13

Tombstone

Episode 270 (Season 13, Episode 6)
Directed by Nina Lopez-Corrado
Written by Davy Perez
Original air date: November 16, 2017

---

yeah, I annoyed an
ancient cosmic being so
much, he sent me back

don't know what to say ~
welcome home pal ~ how long was
I gone? ~ too damn long

two salty hunters,
half-angel kid, and dude back
from the dead... again

really likes cowboys... ~
Ringo, Billy the Kid, Doc
Holliday! hey-O!

I said I needed
a big win... we got Cas back:
pretty damn big win

angels tried to kill
me — I thought angels were good
~ good: relative term

Dean drinks his coffee
I told you, he's an angry
sleeper — like a bear

we're gonna have to
blend ~ which is why you're making
me wear absurd hat

Tombstone (cont.)

"Tombstone" ~ the city? ~
the *movie*, with Kurt Russell
— I made you watch it

the one with the guns
and tuberculosis… "I'm
your huckleberry"

he's an **FBI**
agent? did his parents sign
a permission slip?

getting real sick and
tired of fighting things that
look like other things

ghoul ate some old west
gunfighter and stole his face?
~ that's what it looks like

keep simple: tell her
the guy she's bangin' eats dead
people… or, we lie

will always protect
you, but we need to get the
hell out of Dodge, now

should tell you I'm not
taking him alive ~ neither
am I ~ aim for head

this was a mistake —
that doesn't mean you can't be
better, do better

hey, how did it go? ~
was the usual: killed the
bad guy, saved the girl

we've all done bad, have
blood on our hands — if you're a
monster, we all are

know that if I stay,
I'm gonna hurt you — I can't
— you are all I have

SEASON 13

War of the Worlds

Episode 271 (Season 13, Episode 7)
Directed by Richard Speight Jr.
Written by Brad Buckner & Eugenie Ross-Leming
Original air date: November 23, 2017

---

gripes with the old man:
self-righteous narcissism
"my way or highway"

when he banged out the
universe, had creative
chops, optimism

look at you: you claim
to be a god in your world
— here, you're pathetic

I've assembled all
elements annotated
in angel tablets

not done this before —
predictions are predictive,
not declarative

probabilities
being what they are, or could
be, maybe, or not

I'm a vertebrate;
I'm neither an annelid,
nor a nematode

I know you do not
like witches, but I also
know you help people

I am confused, aren't
you Satan, which would make *you*
the evil monster?

how are you not dead? ~
why should I be? ~ we *killed* you
~ apparently not

War of the Worlds (cont.)

do I look stupid
to you? ~ ...that a trick question?
~ *punches Ketch, again*

you're seriously
gonna sit there with straight face,
tell us: evil twin?

mercenary: man
with my sort of training has
limited options

there's weird and then there's
just straight up bull — thinking Ketch
is door number two

what you doing back? ~   you'll forgive me if
what are you doing *alive*?   I'm a little on-edge: the
~ complicated ~ same   last time, you killed me

shelve the "eternal   from his description:
enemies" thing a sec, we've   he's evil Colonel Sanders
a situation   — it's Asmodeus

if you'd done prescribed
cavity search, as you should
have, you'd have found it

it occur to you
I might be one of good guys?
~ no, not even once

SEASON 13

The Scorpion and the Frog

Episode 272 (Season 13, Episode 8)
Directed by Robert Singer
Written by Meredith Glynn
Original air date: November 30, 2017

---

gotta find something
in the lore, or wait for Jack
to make a mistake

you know what demon
miracles called? pretty sure
it's not "miracles"

how 'bout this: let's hear
the guy out ~ all right, and then
after that: kill him

famous Winchesters ~
some random demon ~ the name's
Barthamus; Bart's fine

you two are a real
pain in the pitchfork... and the
halo: natural

disrupters — we have
that in common, you and I
~ hmm, yeah we're twinsies

when demon tells us
to jump, we don't ask how high
— we just ice their ass

The Scorpion and the Frog (cont.)

Jack is out there in
the world, and he's alone, scared,
and he's dangerous

wait, safecracking? is
this a heist? *changes tone* hold
up, *is this a heist?*

there will be curveballs,
and you boys tend to hit those
right out of the park

glares at demon I
will kill you ~ I bet you say
that to all the girls

I mean, there could be
anything in there — there could
be spiders, there could

be the spiny blade
thing, snakes… spiders… you do not
even know, do you?

there was supposed to
be a safe, not dollar-store
Indiana Jones

SEASON 13

The Scorpion and the Frog (cont.)

Dean, he's immortal ~
Dean punches Luther good thing
he's got a glass jaw

I like you: don't mean
I will renegotiate
the terms of your deal

don't watch those movies,
but you saw "Entrapment"? ~ *shrugs*
Catherine Zeta Jones

it make you feel good
whoring yourselves out to pure
evil? 'cause he is

you two do-gooding
idiots: willing to welch
on our deal, because

I killed blackmailing
piece of garbage? ~ yeah, that, and
we just don't like you

what you did for me —
you didn't have to do that
~ hey Alice, stay weird

SEASON 13

The Bad Place

Episode 273 (Season 13, Episode 9)
Directed by Phil Sgriccia
Written by Robert Berens
Original air date: December 7, 2017

---

you talked about your
process, your inspiration
— mind moves into worlds

this isn't an "I
told you so" — I actually
like the kid, I do

dealer: businessman
just trying to make it in
Trump's America

it's the only thing
that keeps me awake, that keeps
me from the bad place

that door was triple-
locked ~ was it? ~ what are you? ~ that
is a long story

I saw your mother —
she's alive, but in danger
~ what kind of danger?

you thought, you… you both
thought… that I could do *that*, that
I could kill Derek

you mean Lucifer?
he's no one to me — you, Cas:
you're my family

a friend's in danger
…*going to be* in danger
~ you had a vision?

you raised me to do
what's right, and this is what's right
— don't go: people die

515

SEASON 13

The Bad Place (cont.)

I'm not the kind of
girl folks come for; don't even
rank a milk carton

I'm not white, rich, blonde —
no one's gonna fight for me,
I do not matter

you are insane ~ yeah
well, the whole world is insane,
you get used to it

we just saved your life ~
thanks, but they only wanted
me because of *you*

bad dreams? when I get	Heaven is running
hurt there, I don't wake sweaty,	out of angels — he can save
I wake up *bloody*	us ~ you dicks can fry
sees better visions	go out, guns blazing —
our powers can be good, can	sorry to drag into this;
do good in this world	this was not your fight

what if something goes
wrong? ~ something already *is*
going wrong: do it

answers door Patience?
~ Jody, I had a vision:
something bad's coming

SEASON 13

Wayward Sisters

Episode 274 (Season 13, Episode 10)
Directed by Phil Sgriccia
Written by Robert Berens & Andrew Dabb
Original air date: January 18, 2018

---

who the hell do you
think you are? ~ I kill monsters,
that's who hell I am

boys were on hunting
trip, and I haven't heard from
them for a few days

it's a uniform,
what is your excuse? you look
like biker barbie

if I stuck around,
would have worried all the time
~ Claire, she never stopped

pick up scent, don't stop ~
so you fight them? ~ no, I run
— sometimes they catch me

the door's still open,
find Sam and Dean ~ if they're there,
they're already dead

don't tell me it tastes
like chicken ~ it's a lizard,
it tastes like lizard

we're stuck here in this
freaking monster-land — no one
even knows to look

your mom's burying
a monster in the backyard
~ must bury somewhere

Wayward Sisters (cont.)

meet Sheriff Donna:
she's killed lot of vampires
~ I do what I do

*Claire toasts monster with
flamethrower* I called, didn't
answer: we worried

I'm gonna go out,
that's how I wanna do it
— doing something great

protecting me, but
I need to save Sam and Dean
— you have to let me

Sam, Dean saved my life,
can't sit this one out ~ if you
go, I'll go with you

ever shot a gun? ~
no ~ okey-doke, here ya go:
aim, relax, and squeeze

we'll handle it — you
guys take care of the world, we
got Sioux Falls covered

get it now: why you
are the way you are with me
because this feeling...

you don't have to do
this alone — when you're ready
we're all here for you

I killed a monster ~
Donna and Alex chuckle
welcome to family

we saved Sam and Dean:
all these amazing women
— family, my army

thing that killed Kaia:
still out there — going to find,
going to kill it

SEASON 13

Breakdown

Episode 275 (Season 13, Episode 11)
Directed by Amyn Kaderali
Written by Davy Perez
Original air date: January 25, 2018

---

why don't you smile
some — you can get whatever
you want to darlin'

sorry for calling ~
hey, never apologize
for you calling us

you are related?
family reunion:
pretty wild time

breaker 1-9, this
is 67, Midnight
Rider, looking for

the 4-1-1 on
my Alice in Wonderland:
she is family

I'm weak: made of flesh ~
oh, *that's* your excuse? ~ God knows
I am a sinner

I've done wrong, but I've
never hurt anybody
— never, believe me

takeout for… ~ monsters
— we'll talk about it later
~ what's to talk about?

Breakdown (cont.)

not related to
you, are they? ~ hunters, they kill
monsters… so do I

shouldn't have been so
rough with me, I hold a grudge
~ well, bring it, Twilight

those freaks that you and
your brother chase: those are just
the ones that can't pass

most monsters, hell, they
could be your next-door neighbor,
mow lawn Saturdays

Dougie Bear, are you
okay? ~ feel like you wanna
bite any of us?

I'm sorry I lied —
I can't give this up ~ you kill
monsters: damn hero

you're gonna be fine ~
fine? I was a *vampire*!
~ …for couple hours

when has knowing us
worked out? ~ we save people, Sam
~ we get people killed

tried to pretend, but
this ends one way for us, Dean:
ends bloody, ends bad

SEASON 13

Various & Sundry Villains

Episode 276 (Season 13, Episode 12)
Directed by Amanda Tapping
Written by Steve Yockey
Original air date: February 1, 2018

mom taught us three things:
always look your best, never
get attached to man

always make the death
look non-magical, so you
don't attract hunters

literally in
alternate reality ~
come up with plan B?

should get out of here,
in case the one with the hair
actually wins

you said it yourself:
heads down, do the work ~ *you* said
that ~ and I was right

did you know he loves
movies? movies with heroes
who crush the villains

you say you're too weak
to overcome even your
weakest creation?

moment of weakness:
I may have put a tracking
spell on the Grimoire

doesn't a kiss, like,
usually wake up true love?
~ thank you, you saved me

we've handled witches
before ~ you're familiar
with our work ~ I've changed

am I *all right*? I'm
in love: I am like full-on
twitterpated here

gasps Fergus is dead? ~
yep, he killed himself for us
~ doesn't sound like him

SEASON 13

Various & Sundry Villains (cont.)

rather living son —
even one who hated me
— than a dead hero

the book is in this
area, we will need to
speak to the yokels

they get to fifth base? ~
there's no such thing as fifth base
~ you poor, sheltered boy

useless, impotent,
unnecessary; you will
die alone, unmourned

you sure I can't just
enslave some townsfolk and make
them take us to them?

I'm sure you *can*, but
I'm also sure you *shouldn't*
~ just described my life

I don't talk 'bout it —
he'd listen, but not something
I know how to share

Sammy, they're really
weirdly strong ~ I think it is
probably a spell

gonna be really
mean? because it is about
damn time *someone* was

you double-crossed us
~ triple-crossed, actually
— ended up: your side

something wrong with soul?
maybe he was a really
bad guy or something

getting beat up by
girl: story to tell ~ girls beat
us up all the time

*Cas stabs Lucifer
with angel blade* — this is me
learning from mistakes

we'll figure it out ~
no plan, so how? ~ don't know, but
we will, you and me

Devil's Bargain

Episode 277 (Season 13, Episode 13)
Directed by Eduardo Sánchez
Written by Eugenie Ross-Leming & Brad Buckner
Original air date: February 8, 2018

---

without your grace, you're
only human — be careful
accidents happen

oh Cas, I told you
specifically not to do
anything stupid

what are you gawking
at? you've never seen the prince
of darkness before?

kill… the devil? ~ nice
angel blade to the heart, he'll
go down… probably

I promised Kelly
that I would protect her son
— I intend to keep

Lucifer trying
to restore power — if does
~ we're boned ~ epically

what, no "eek"? "spare me
dark master"? no quaking fear?
~ should I quake? ~ most do

I was a so-so
angel, but turns out I'm a
great businesswoman

find out what he knows,
put bullet in him, burn his
bones, flush his ashes

last time, I saved your
lives and you shot me — doesn't
that make us even?

almost human: I
feel emotions, sensations
— the things *they* must feel

SEASON 13

Devil's Bargain (cont.)

when I'm in that place,
I can see how there'd be pain
— but there's also hope

love, even... angels
only imagine — sometimes
I envy humans

Lucifer, Prince of
Darkness, King of Lies, I am
back baby ~ then what?

your hair, Sam, it is
magnificent — is that leave-
in conditioner?

in Heaven, she was
low-level functionary
~ now Satan's gal pal

this may once again
fall on deaf ears, but I shall
have another go

if you think about
it, I'm the lesser of, well,
at least three evils

all I ask: wait to
murder me until after
I've proven useful

Good Intentions

Episode 278 (Season 13, Episode 14)
Directed by P. J. Pesce
Written by Meredith Glynn
Original air date: March 1, 2018

---

take it easy on
nitrates ~ dude, if bacon's what
kills me, then I win

stealth in, get Mom, Jack
— boom: family reunion
— just gonna take time

so much for "kill with
kindness," — we tried it your way,
now we do it mine

these men are very
dangerous ~ then I'll do it
~ I will go with you

I was there when you
were born... you should be six months
old ~ I am... sort of

not gonna hurt you,
he's gonna hurt *me* — why do
you think he brought you?

but Dean, I was dead
~ temporarily ~ I was
brought back for reason

war is what Michael
does ~ then we do what we do,
whatever it takes

Gog, Magog: only
be killed by a weapon touched
by God: angel blade

Enochian's tough —
maybe you got a word wrong
~ I don't get words wrong

this is serious ~
yeah, no, I know, but *giggles*
they're wearing *loincloths*

must face in combat
he ~ or she ~ why interrupt?
always contradict

which shall we kill first?
~ I will kill the pretty one
~ equally pretty

Good Intentions (cont.)

I hate doing this;
you are very beautiful ~
forged, touched by God: same

find him, bring him back ~
woman? ~ kill her in front of
boy, make her feel it

thought you were a ghost —
just from a whole other world,
which is… well, weirder

he attacked ~ muppet
professor attacked you? why?
~ better just show you

no soul left alive —
this ain't a war, it is an
extermination

Mary Campbell: a
complicated woman — brave,
sad, full of regret

demon deal? ~ didn't
make one, lost the love of her
life, never moved on

well, all work and no
play makes Donatello a
homicidal boy

something I promised
would never do to human
without permission

I won't let you — or
anyone — hurt the people
I love, not again

I had to come back;
Sam and Dean — they wouldn't run,
they would stay and fight

some just can't be saved ~
who gets to make that choice? you?
what gives you the right?

this is the only
way we win, survive ~ you said:
whatever it takes

SEASON 13

A Most Holy Man

Episode 279 (Season 13, Episode 15)
Directed by Amanda Tapping
Written by Robert Singer & Andrew Dabb
Original air date: March 8, 2018

---

where is this market?
ah, the internet: not just
for porn anymore

Montgomery Ward
suits and cheap ties, I'm guessing
don't have small fortune

I assume you won't
be above a little bit
of chicanery

not a perfect world —
if I'm not perfect trying
to save, so be it

you're like a boy scout:
always prepared ~ yeah, you're like…
don't know what you're like

why would he whack the
guy before he finds the skull? ~
"whack"? ~ it's mob talk ~ mob…

officially you
guys both died six years ago
~ well, funny story

I'm just saying: you
are taking a lot of shots
to the head lately

…and the sisters: they
have faith in me ~ how is that
working out for them?

SEASON 13

A Most Holy Man (cont.)

imagine thing you
loved: just gone, what would you do?
~ try to get it back

world will never be
perfect — if good men do good
things, can be better

If someone stole the
Impala, what would— ~ murder
— I'd murder 'em all

there'll be torture first —
a lot of torture — and then
it would end with death

all right here's the play:
we head in there, and we kick
the fake cop's real ass

what your brother is
doing is a good thing ~ yeah,
or a stupid thing

Pope, he called me "un
uomo santissimo" —
"a most holy man"

what are you doing? ~
creating a distraction
— lying: it's a sin

monsters: there's always
gonna be another one
around the corner

SEASON 13

Scoobynatural

Episode 280 (Season 13, Episode 16)
Directed by Robert Singer
Written by Jim Krieg & Jeremy Adams
Original air date: March 29, 2018

---

you boys just took down
an evil plushie that was
trying to kill me

when did you have time
to do all this? ~ when it is
important: *make* time

didn't think we'd end
up ~ killing Barney? ~ pretty
satisfying, though

animated? weird? ~
it's *beyond* weird ~ "beyond weird"
is kind of our thing

cartoon with talking
dog ~ not just any talking
dog, *the* talking dog

this: like a dream come
true ~ your dream is to hang out
with the Scooby Gang?

these guys: they're friggin'
role models, man — except Fred
he's a wad ~ he's… what?

we do not have a
talking dog ~ Cas is kind of
like a talking dog

you know what that means:
road food! ~ oh, heck yes! Sam, look
how big my mouth is!

he thinks he's so cool:
good hair, can-do attitude,
that stupid ascot

so, bunk together? ~
oh Dean, boys and girls don't sleep
in same room, silly

SEASON 13

Scoobynatural (cont.)

---

called a sleeping robe —
it's freakin' comfortable:
like I'm wrapped in hugs

he's actually
dead ~ jinkies ~ jeepers ~ ruh-roh
~ zoinks ~ son of a *bitch*

Scooby-Doo could die —
won't happen on my watch; take
bullet for that dog

wouldn't expect a
big, broad-shouldered fella like
you to be chicken

bargained with the djinn —
I think I'm technically
married to their queen

once led armies, now
paired with scruffy philistine
and a talking dog

ghosts: real, we hunt them
~ simple fact is: monsters are
nothing more than crooks

in masks — usually
unscrupulous real estate
developers, Sam

if we can count on
you, Scooby-Doo, I know we
will catch that villain

almost: Dean had him
by the thigh ~ he *what*? ~ almost
caught him, that's the point

Scoobynatural (cont.)

that isn't a guy
in a mask and a costume
— that's vengeful spirit

it is… a child ~
yeah, it's a creepy ghost kid;
you get used to 'em

can't fight: we don't have
the proper tools or weapons
~ that's okay, we do

I was right, ya big
lug, there's no such thing as the
supernatural

you are amazing,
but we can help, we *have* to
~ [bleep]ing right you can

should have known Velma
was good to go — gah, it is
always quiet ones

coolest thing ever,
that includes the Cartwright Twins
~ what'd you do with them?

you think anyone's
gonna believe that? ~ no, but
we hacked financials

not big on taxes? ~
if good enough for Capone,
good enough for you

I would have gotten
away with it, if wasn't
for meddling kids

no but, come on, I
look cool with the ascot right?
red is my color

SEASON 13

The Thing

Episode 281 (Season 13, Episode 17)
Directed by John F. Showalter
Written by Davy Perez
Original air date: April 5, 2018

---

jinkies ~ you're gonna
stop saying that, right? ~ I don't
know, probably not

this is what a car
looks like now, or, well, they should
— welcome to future

that's exciting, it
comes with a lemon… you sure
you can handle that?

how are you so calm
I'm alive? ~ this kind of weird
— it's sort of our thing

I am watching my
cholesterol ~ I'm watching
…watching it go up

souls are messy, all
conflict, confusion ~ I know
who I am ~ *do* you?

I see your chewy
middle: you want redemption
— we can't be redeemed

if she fed on him,
he would be here ~ if she's not
feeding, she's breeding

my god, that's tragic —
it's like a Hallmark movie,
but with tentacles

don't know what kinky
Gatekeeper-Keymaster thing,
but I think I'll pass

seal take us somewhere
besides tentacle-porn land
— nothing wrong with that

sure all right? ~ almost
an interdimensional
booty call: all right

Asmodeus will
be hunting me — it's better
if I'm not on earth

you want Ketch to go? ~
don't care if he dies… hell, kind
of rootin' for it

SEASON 13

Bring 'em Back Alive

Episode 282 (Season 13, Episode 18)
Directed by Amyn Kaderali
Written by Brad Buckner & Eugenie Ross-Leming
Original air date: April 12, 2018

---

what is this "we" crap?
you came here to save yourself,
so go save yourself

I know you, you're not
the usual human scum ~
slick line, Captain Charm

he's with Ketch, so he's not alone ~ because that makes it *so* much better	my old man: if he said, "scour the earth," they'd say "S.O.S.? Brillo?"
should be doing king things: commanding the angels, inspiring mankind	Gabriel was gone, and suddenly I was free: no obligations

did what anyone
would: moved to Monte Carlo,
shacked up with porn stars

Lucifer: beast, scourge
of mankind ~ hand it to God:
perfect marketing

Dean winces ~ you don't
look good ~ yeah, well you're not my
type either, I'm fine

Bring 'em Back Alive (cont.)

• Sam convinces Gabriel to emerge from his catatonia •

Gabriel, you have
to dig yourself out of this
hole... look, I know you

think: safer inside —
no more torture, no more pain,
no expectations

I've been there — you were
nothing like your family
— sure as hell weren't like

your dad — me either, and just like you, I got out — or *thought* I got out	many times I tried to fight it, this is what I was put here to do
then my family needed me, and this is my life — no matter how	this is where I make the world a better place... and sure, yeah, hookers in

Monte Carlo sounds
great, but your family needs you
— Jack: nephew needs you

the world needs you, *we*
need you, Gabriel — *I* need
you, so please help us

Bring 'em Back Alive (cont.)

Charlie: family —
she was a sister to me
— more than I can say

friends, colleagues died on
my watch, didn't try to save
them ~ well, you *do* suck

impossible and
stupid, huh? you say that like
it is a bad thing

you are too weak ~ not
anymore — I have always
hated dumbass suit

bite me ~ you're trying
my patience ~ sorry, I will
try harder: *bite me*!

thank you for rescue,
and for the redemption arc,
but I'm gonna bounce

dude, this is my home;
my friends are here, in trouble
— if you really do

have a way to take
down Michael, do it — until
then, this is *my* fight

son of a bitch — when
we get close, it falls apart
every freakin' time

SEASON 13

Funeralia

Episode 283 (Season 13, Episode 19)
Directed by Nina Lopez-Corrado
Written by Steve Yockey
Original air date: April 19, 2018

---

very sure I've done
nothing (that you know of) to
make you want to call

the handsome angel
is there, isn't he? hello
tweetie-pie ~ …hello

surprised recognize
sounds of a party, since you're
all work and no play

won't be easy, but…
all right, *come on* ideas,
come on, here we go

this would be a Hail
Mary: sports term, like slam dunk,
or ball-handler

Cas, you wanna try
this angel thing, go for it
— don't get dead again

are you drunk? ~ not yet
but if keep at a pace, starts
to take the edge off

we can say we fought —
just angel-blade me right now,
that'll be okay

you want to murder
me; you have good reason to
want to murder me

I want fun, flirty
Rowena who mostly helps…
gotta be ready

hovering around
like babysitter? ~ more like
baby monitor

ever heard of the
butterfly effect? ~ Ashton's
second-best movie

536

Funeralia (cont.)

Death keeps notebooks: all
the ways a person might die;
Dean's got a whole shelf

but in Rowena's
notebook, death: always the same
— she's killed by you, Sam

message from your boss? ~
Death doesn't negotiate
with witches ~ we'll see

what's over / under
this: a trap? ~ it's Rowena,
of *course* it's a trap

stole my memories,
threatened to tear me apart
— you also made me

repeatedly act
out Dean Winchester's murder
~ those: simpler times

there's nine angels in
Heaven, present company
included… that's all

we're talking about
Fergus: man abandoned and
loveless, tricked by a

demon, died in a
gutter — he deserved better
from the world, from me

SEASON 13

Funeralia (cont.)

powerful, gorgeous,
paying fortune — she didn't
have to cast a spell

flawed, petty, evil —
Samuel, I don't know if
I can be redeemed

you have to stop ~ I
can not stop Samuel, you
will have to shoot me

you don't have to ~ what
haven't you done for family?
what *wouldn't* you do?

sometimes life unfair,
and sometimes we lose things, and
sometimes make mistakes

some things can never
be repaired, no matter how
powerful become

how are you feeling? ~
like got punched in face, a lot
~ yes, Bernard's very…

every one of us
done something we have to live
with, to make up for

without extra juice,
you're still the deadliest witch
around ~ flatterer

Unfinished Business

Episode 284 (Season 13, Episode 20)
Directed by Richard Speight Jr.
Written by Meredith Glynn
Original air date: April 26, 2018

I vowed to do this
honorably — no tricks, just
mano a mano

felt witch's tracking
spell the second she cast it:
tasted like haggis

not a big joiner ~
so, you have *better* things to
do than save the world?

broke into junkyard,
stuffed demigod into car
crusher — need answers

selling me to that
Kentucky-fried b-hole? for
them? that was profit

don't let anyone
ever tell you that you are
just a pretty face

disagree, Dean-o —
we all have our demons, mine
are here in this town

everyone knows you
don't take on the big bad from
the jump — you work up

what am I looking
at? ~ never seen a kill list?
~ this is so stupid

thinking you can win,
running blind into each fight:
how you make mistakes

can't help if you're dead —
I can't lose another boy~
you won't, I'll come back

he wants to break you —
said to tell you: even if
you win, you still lose

SEASON 13

Unfinished Business (cont.)

:: he was my father ::
:: you understand — what would you ::
:: do for *your* father? ::

Rich Speight fights Rich Speight
while directed by Rich Speight
Gabe vs. Loki

:: poor Gabriel, with ::
:: his deadbeat daddy and his ::
:: mean older brothers ::

what, no tricks? ~ a deal
is a deal — if I'm being
honest: tricks for kids

:: a joke, a failure ::
:: you stand for nothing; that's what ::
:: you'll die for :: ~ you first

you are treating me
like I deserve to be back
at the kids' table

remember last time
we saw Lucifer / Michael
show? because I do:

you died, went to Hell —
apocalypse not looking
for us, we seek it

don't care what happens
to me, but I *do* care what
happens to brother

if something happens
we'll deal with it together
— die? together, too

SEASON 13

Beat the Devil

Episode 285 (Season 13, Episode 21)
Directed by Phil Sgriccia
Written by Robert Berens
Original air date: May 3, 2018

---

that's your seventh piece ~
Castiel's right, I counted
~ first, don't be a narc

he said he wanted
to extract his grace himself,
in private: Dean's room

yeah, well we don't have
any better ideas ~
…inspirational

never stopped being
our responsibility —
we let out of cage

Gabriel defends
his virility, holds book
titled "Laying Pipe"

a drunk six-year-old
could execute that magic
— 'twas ingredient

the Three Amigos,
with all their bro hugs, pep talks,
and melodrama

we were just… ~ reading…
books… here in the library…
the room we're in now…

had Heaven and Hell
in palm of my hand — what I
learned: they don't matter

all the people I
love to torture in same room
— what's the occasion?

what is this about?
humiliation? revenge?
~ no, just bonuses

tumbling through rift,
Dean keeps his feet, Gabe lands in
Castiel's nethers

541

SEASON 13

Beat the Devil (cont.)

far as they're concerned
I'm a screw-up — as far as
I'm concerned: screw-up

Heaven run into
ground by upstanding angels
— screw-up: change we need

thanks to you: Sam, Dean
will be trapped in some sort of
nightmare universe

with Devil himself —
au revoir, bon voyage, not
my problem… *bollocks*

vamps drag Sam away
Dean, he's gone, we don't have time
— Dean, we *can't* save him

Mary asks after
Sam — Dean failed to protect him;
can't even tell her

what do you want? ~ a
relationship with my son:
I want what you have

SEASON 13

Exodus

Episode 286 (Season 13, Episode 22)
Directed by Thomas J. Wright
Written by Eugenie Ross-Leming & Brad Buckner
Original air date: May 10, 2018

---

trying to keep me
from my son? ~ Kelly Kline's son
— he's nothing like you

I am powerful
dangerous, ruthless — only
in the best sense, though

hey mama, miss me?
*Mary punches Lucifer
in the face* ~ nice shot

do you have questions?
don't let my status as a
legend hold you back

humans: not perfect —
hardwired to fall, and then
they need a fall guy

you've no idea
who Lucifer is ~ and won't
'less I talk to him

you let Charlie go
with *Ketch*? ~ she let Ketch come, it's
her operation

so, thing about Gabe:
class clown ~ and you're an assclown
~ ha! such a cut-up

Exodus (cont.)

he is not like you:
mother's bloodline, influence
of the Winchesters

humans: innocent
and beautiful — the old man
loved them more than you

you temped them, and
you corrupted them, just to
prove how flawed they were

:: you align yourself ::
:: with the humans? :: ~ I vastly
prefer to angels

:: do not think that you ::
:: are better than me... we are ::
:: the same :: ~ yes, we are

I can buy some time —
all I did on earth was run,
won't run anymore

you did it: got us
all here, we owe you one ~ don't
think I won't collect

let's not forget our
absent brothers and sisters
— we'll do right by them

SEASON 13

Let the Good Times Roll

Episode 287 (Season 13, Episode 23)
Directed by Robert Singer
Written by Andrew Dabb
Original air date: May 17, 2018

---

let me get this right:
idjit from "The Apprentice"
is the *president*?

they're talking about
whether Kylie Jenner would
make a good mother

Rowena, Charlie
road tripping — oh, that's ginger
trouble: the worst kind

• *Dean imagines life in a safe world* •

the kid did great ~ yeah
no kidding, I mean he keeps
this up and… ~ and what?

I don't know — hey, do
you remember when you asked
if we could stop it?

could stop all of the
evil in the world? if we
could really change things?

545

SEASON 13

Let the Good Times Roll (cont.)

maybe with Jack, we
can ~ maybe you're right, but then
what will we do? ~ yeah

this... a whole lot of
this, but on a beach somewhere
— can you imagine?

you, me and Cas... our toes in the sand, a couple of umbrella drinks	matching Hawaiian shirts — obviously — hula girls... ~ talking about

retiring? you? ~
if I knew the world was safe?
hell yeah, and you know

why? 'cause we freaking
earned it man ~ I'll drink to that
~ *tips bottle* hell, yeah

just having bad dream — me too, mostly about the folks I couldn't save	I don't like to speak ill of people, but Sam is a big fat liar
nobody's perfect, but we get better — each day we can get better	humans: limited and fragile — I'll admit they bring out worst in me

Let the Good Times Roll (cont.)

does it matter? it
kinda seems you have bigger,
Satan-y problems

you'll be the first life,
the first soul I save — some would
consider: honor

enjoy it: moment
when the soul leaves the body
— it is beautiful

you're not my father,
you're a *monster* — everything
you told me: a lie

this is the end of
everything ~ no, what if... what
if you had your sword?

you can stop him, Jack,
you can get your power back
~ no, I can't beat him

it turns out we have
something in common: we both
wanna gut your ass

you did it ~ no, we
did it *grunts* we had a deal
:: thank you for the suit ::

SEASON FOURTEEN

SEASON 14

Stranger in a Strange Land

Episode 288 (Season 14, Episode 1)
Directed by Thomas J. Wright
Written by Andrew Dabb
Original air date: October 11, 2018

---

you're… God? ~ :: close, not quite ::
~ Gabriel? ~ :: the better one ::
~ Michael? ~ :: *there* we go ::

:: you're not worth saving :: ~
what do you want? ~ :: what always ::
:: wanted: better world ::

doesn't come easy:	ain't how hard you hit —
had my ass handed to me	how hard you can *get* hit and
more times than can count	keep moving forward

did you just say that
you lost a Winchester? one:
that's… interesting, two

lost Dean? I thought the
two of you were joined at the
you know… everything

you're the archangel	why would he say yes
Michael from another world,	to you? ~ :: love :: ~ really? that is
and possessing Dean	so Hallmark channel

550

Stranger in a Strange Land (cont.)

you're the rebel: the
angel who doesn't like to
play by Heaven's rules

(hmm, rebel angels...
does Dean have a thing for them?
...or is it Jensen?)

I'm the boy who's got
your angel — if want to see
alive, we should chat

it's like saltwater
taffy, or infants — you know,
I just like the taste

why are you using
me as bait? ~ it's kind of what
you're *for*, isn't it?

have to think about
the good, because if I don't,
I'll drown in the bad

you're a damn legend,
icon: the shoulders, the hair
— you're my Beyoncé

all right, you've got some
good lines, I'll give you that much
— but you're no Crowley

take this — do you know
how to use it? ~ uh, stab them
with the pointy end?

no new King of Hell —
not today, not ever — and
you can come through me

all I did was get
punched in the face ~ to be fair
all got punched in face

SEASON 14

Gods and Monsters

Episode 289 (Season 14, Episode 2)
Directed by Richard Speight Jr.
Written by Brad Buckner & Eugenie Ross-Leming
Original air date: October 18, 2018

:: a little of this, ::
:: a little of that… too much ::
:: that: disappointing ::

angels ain't known for
their veracity ~ I tend
to agree with you

not babysitting ~
they're not infants, but both have
to be supervised

you were in a lot of pain, and Lucifer saw and exploited it	I had myself — just the basic me — without all the bells and whistles
mourning what you've lost wasteful — smarter to focus on what you still have	where you came from is important, but not as much as where you're going

:: you think I didn't ::
:: know what you are? you think *you* ::
:: picked *me*? I picked *you* ::

Castiel, you're just
a stone-cold body snatcher,
same as Lucifer

Gods and Monsters (cont.)

what befell Jimmy
Novak and his family is
my greatest regret

:: cognac: strong notes of ::
:: vanilla and apricot, ::
:: zero of silver ::

she would sing, and talk
to him before he was born
— he felt safe, wanted

I hope that some day
I have a little of her
courage and purpose

you *let* me escape? ~
:: rule number one: you can't have ::
:: a trap without bait ::

:: rule number two: once ::
:: the trap has been sprung, you don't ::
:: need bait anymore ::

it was a kindness;
there are worse ways to be a
human than be kind

if stopping Michael
means that Dean has to die, he
would want it that way

The Scar

Episode 290 (Season 14, Episode 3)
Directed by Robert Singer
Written by Robert Berens
Original air date: October 25, 2018

I can't eat, can't sleep —
it's always just there, watching
~ Dean, it's just a beard

wanted to be there —
Michael would sense my presence
~ Sam said, ain't no thing

Cas I need you to
get in my head, do the whole
Vulcan mind-meld thing

don't know why he let
you go, what he wants ~ who his
favorite spice girl is

what, me vs. some
assbag archangel, who'd you
take? ~ you, every time

they were John Does, hard
to tell: three heads, three headless
bodies — the math works

re: Kaia, she's a
powder keg — first love strikes quick
…to lose it like that?

The Scar (cont.)

you're Kaia's double
like bad Cas, or new Bobby
~ :: I to her: she, me ::

:: no different than him — ::
:: threats, violence, anything ::
:: to get what you want ::

Lora's life force, it's
in here ~ Jack are you sure? ~ no
smashes amulet

:: I saw what you did ::
:: when you got angry: you shoved ::
:: your gun in her face ::

:: I know where it comes ::
:: from — your anger, impatience ::
:: — it's fear: you're scared, weak ::

raising three hunters,
fearing every day that I
might lose one of them

don't want a ride to
hospital? ~ I've driven with
broken arm before

today you proved that
you have mind of a hunter,
heart of a hunter

---

don't remember most:
was underwater, drowning
— felt every second

clawing, fighting for
air — thought I could make it out;
wasn't strong enough

SEASON 14

Mint Condition

Episode 291 (Season 14, Episode 4)
Directed by Amyn Kaderali
Written by Davy Perez
Original air date: November 1, 2018

Superman's not real,
and I've seen you get winded
eating a taco

with kryptonite gloves
I could beat up Superman:
that is science, Sam!

horror marathon
on Shocker: just made my way
through the Halloweens

oh wow ~ yes, I shaved ~
I mean it's so *smooth*, it's like
a dolphin's belly

you don't even like
scary movies ~ our *life* is
a scary movie

M-I-R-L: it
means "meet in real life" ~ why do
you know what that means?

---

killed in prank gone wrong,
mechanic David Yaeger
comes back every year

on the day *after*
Halloween — on All Saints' Day,
he takes his revenge!

Mint Condition (cont.)

you are not from an
insurance company, are
you? ~ not exactly

pretty sure this will
work ~ where'd you learn to do this?
~ messed-up childhood

just went toe-to-toe
with David freakin' Yaeger
— do not ruin this

I don't blame you, no
one blames you... you gotta stop
blaming yourself, please

• *Dean suggests possible matching Halloween costumes for next year* •

next year, we're doing
Halloween right — I'm thinking
matching outfits, like

Batman and Robin,
Bert and Ernie ~ no ~ that's weird...
Rocky, Bullwinkle

Shaggy and Scooby ~
why would we... ~ Turner and Hooch
~ *scoffs* ~ Ren and Stimpy

Thelma and Louise:
we just put it in drive and
go ~ *Sam shakes his head*

SEASON 14

Nightmare Logic

Episode 292 (Season 14, Episode 4)
Directed by Darren Grant
Written by Meredith Glynn
Original air date: November 8, 2018

---

it's good, got very
camp counselor vibe — need to
get you a whistle

we just wish you had
checked in with the main office
before coming here

case obviously
ain't a milk run ~ is something
on your mind, Bobby?

ready, or you ain't —
real leader would've seen that
a mile away

walls for a reason:
whatever's behind Bobby's,
I doubt it's pretty

that's not possible ~
pal, you have no idea
what is possible

nothing you can do
about the past now: it's just
baggage, let it go

you'll feel lot lighter ~
is that what you do? ~ I try
every single day

save Michael's monkey
suit, but I am curious:
what are *your* nightmares?

dozens waiting for
you, your family ~ you don't
know my family

thought war'd kill me —
looking for other options
— hunting ends the same

SEASON 14

Optimism

Episode 293 (Season 14, Episode 6)
Directed by Richard Speight Jr.
Written by Steve Yockey
Original air date: November 15, 2018

Dean, what happened with
Michael, no one blames you ~ cool,
well, *I* blame me, so…

I'm allergic to
sitting, doing nothing ~ what
you want to do? ~ hunt

sighs listen, "deep state"—
flashing a badge might work on
people who don't have

a working knowledge
of the constitution, but
that ain't me *rolls eyes*

it's a fact about
society: it all falls
apart ~ not here ~ yet

that was chivalrous —
I'm fine, thank you for stepping
in — didn't have to

I hate hunting, who
wants to hunt? this job, it's just
lots of tears and death

okay, great — our perp
might just be a giant fly
with low self-esteem

Optimism (cont.)

99%
sure she is in love with me
~ that's not how it works

okay, but if she
is, I need to know every
thing about sex: go

people need people ~
why? 'cause they're the luckiest
people in the world?

don't want to tackle
some guy just 'cause he's into
weird fashion ~ don't we?

liked you, but: hunter,
and I come from a long line
of necromancers

apparently my
dead high school boyfriend attacked
me, and I forgot

but I tried to kill
you ~ every relationship
has got its stuff, right?

not saying that all
people are good people, or
even that most are

if we help people,
then maybe *they'll* help people
— and that is worth it

silver stake through the
heart… actually love can get
crazier than that

SEASON 14

Unhuman Nature

Episode 294 (Season 14, Episode 7)
Directed by John F. Showalter
Written by Eugenie Ross-Leming & Brad Buckner
Original air date: November 29, 2018

---

perhaps the peace I'm
looking for *does* lie in the
power of prayer

yeah, weird stuff happens
to kids all the time: they get
coughs, bloody noses

father: cause of death? ~
he was stabbed through the heart, and
then he exploded

don't have time for this —
he's sick, father exploded…
you've got the basics

soon as I figure
out what happened that night, these
demons will vanish

let's get him out of
here, bring him home, do what we
do: let's find a way

hell, I was even
thinking maybe Rowena…
~ already called her

brought book of the damned ~
which you stole ~ which I *borrowed*
amidst the ruckus

Unhuman Nature (cont.)

folks have strong feelings
about my father — trying
not to be like him

what do you think? ~ it
is like I am you ~ no, it's
not — eyes on the road

want to get a tan,
see hockey game, get parking
ticket, or get bored

we've lost people ~ this
feels different; losing a
son feels different

• *Dean and Jack go fishing* •

well, bait and beer: you
are a cheap date… certainly
isn't Tahiti

I could tell — I guess
my point is that if I don't
make it, the stuff I'd

once told me: you and
your father did the exact
same thing — it was your

miss — it wouldn't be
things like Tahiti or the
Taj Mahal — I'd miss

happy memory
of him ~ I didn't say that
~ was *how* you said it

more time with you — I'm
getting that life isn't all
these big, amazing

moments, it is time
together that matters: like
this ~ well who'd have thought

hanging out with me
would make you sentimental?
~ I've had a good life

Unhuman Nature (cont.)

---

this is the hand that
murdered family — even
if not you: still you

• *Nick calls Lucifer back from the Empty* •

I say that I do the terrible things I do because I couldn't	I don't want to stop — I'm bonded to you, and what you are — I mean it's…
find who killed Sarah and Teddy, and that once I did, I would be free	it's how you first found me — I don't know who I am if I am not you
of this darkness, this rage — but I lied, truth is: I *like* doing these things	no consequences, pain, sorrow: I want that back — I don't want to feel

now what I didn't
feel then — where are you? where are
you? help me, help me…

so, what can we do? ~
sighs watch over him, stay by
his side as he dies

SEASON 14

Byzantium

Episode 295 (Season 14, Episode 8)
Directed by Eduardo Sánchez
Written by Meredith Glynn
Original air date: December 6, 2018

---

do not give me that
"meant to be" crap, this isn't
part of some damn plan

what happens next for
someone like me? it's gonna
be an adventure

next steps ~ wake and a
bonfire, hunter-style —
Jack would have wanted

tried to build pyre —
couldn't even do *that* for
him... should've done more

everything: spells, lore
— what good is any of it
if we can't save him?

so what do we do? ~
we say goodbye, tomorrow...
tonight: get loaded

• *The boys drink to celebrate Jack* •

one last look before
you leave, 'cause oh, somehow it
means so much to me

if you need me, you
know where I'll be — please call home
if you change your mind

oh, I don't mind, so
go on, I won't say no more;
my heart ain't in it

Byzantium (cont.)

SEASON 14

but I'll hold the door,
and just remember what I
said before: please call

home if change your mind
~ we did everything we could
right? here's to you, Jack…

you got old ~ did I?
unfortunate side-effect:
giving up magic

then your boy can use
my magic to stay alive:
resurrection, cure

weighing of the heart
not Anubis: Osiris —
met him ~major dick

Heaven hired a
temp to make sure the soul trains
kept running on time?

Cas: supposed to take
care of you ~ he and Sam, Dean
did… they tried their best

I don't like rolling
the dice on the word of an
ex angel-killer

taking risks, making
crappy deals: that's what we do
~ usually bites us

SEASON 14

Byzantium (cont.)

---

           50 billion   an abacus? ~ you
human souls will be cast in   were expecting a scale and
the wind — what's one boy?   a feather? may I?

     Death, subordinates   we have nothing to
get all the face time; I get   offer you, nothing to say
    stuck with paperwork   but: he is our kid

how could you ever
ever let *anyone* go
through what you went through?

take me in his stead —
I'm the one you want, I'm the
one who woke you up

:: when finally give ::
:: yourself permission to be ::
:: happy, and let the ::

:: sun shine on your face — ::
:: that's when I'll come, that's when I'll ::
:: drag you to nothing ::

---

why did you do that? ~   I am curious:
because I made a promise;   did you know, then, what doing
   because I love you   the spell would cost you?

SEASON 14

The Spear

Episode 296 (Season 14, Episode 9)
Directed by Amyn Kaderali
Written by Robert Berens
Original air date: December 13, 2018

---

there's a war coming:
for my family, gotta
be on winning side

can't sleep 'cause recent
events ~ you mean dying and
coming back to life?

we've all been through it;
it's something of a rite of
passage around here

Empty won't come 'til
finally given myself
permission: happy

not anytime soon —
this life may be lot of things,
but rarely happy

you take decoder
ring? ~ the secret password is
"cookie-tacular"

I'll just pull the old
"fake swallow and then spit it
out" cough syrup-trick

immune to silver —
only thing can take him now:
the full Ichabod

SEASON 14

The Spear (cont.)

nobody's guard's up —
nogged-up, waiting for Santa
on freakin' Christmas

there are people that
I care about: family,
and they're in danger

we have a broken
tape deck, and we drove this whole
way without music

your loyalty to
Castiel, the Winchesters,
humans: it will fade

Jack's back — when was last
time we had a big no-strings-
attached win like that?

Sam, he's in my head ~
you do not have to do this,
you can fight this one

zero element
of surprise ~ walking into
a trap ~ which was set

by a full-power
archangel ~ impossible
odds: it feels like home

why'd you come alone?
advance scout? strongest player
first? you're not that strong

:: Dean was resisting ::
:: me; he was too attached to ::
:: you, to all of you ::

:: whole army out there, ::
:: waiting, ready for command ::
:: — ready for this: *snaps* ::

SEASON 14

Nihilism

Episode 297 (Season 14, Episode 10)
Directed by Amanda Tapping
Written by Steve Yockey
Original air date: January 17, 2019

---

sorry you wasted
your trip out here, but Rocky's
still isn't for sale

why you always have
a boyfriend? ~ why you only
want what you can't have?

you don't want me, you
just like to flirt — I'm psychic
so I kinda know

worst part of working
here is having to clean up
the blood after some

pissed-off monster busts
in to kill you ~ well, what can
I say? I'm famous

it's my shift — we have
shifts now because you mess up
so, so many things

if those cuffs won't hold
him, neither will the dungeon
~ :: I can still hear you ::

Jack, let's lock it down ~
:: yes, go put a chair against ::
:: the door, that'll help ::

Nihilism (cont.)

:: either my monsters ::
:: come, or I break these chains — but ::
:: everybody dies ::

:: the last thing you'll see ::
:: is this pretty smile as ::
:: I rip you apart ::

still working that ghoul
thing in Wichita with Cas;
should be back tonight

:: I've got Dean under ::
:: control :: ~ no, Dean: he is strong
~ :: he's gnat, I'm a god ::

:: you think that they care ::
:: 'bout you? love you? you're a job ::
:: none of them wanted ::

you are confusing
loyalty and compassion
with weakness, Michael

why do you hate this
world enough to burn it to
ground? ~ :: because I *can* ::

Nihilism (cont.)

:: Chuck: writer, churns out ::
:: draft after draft — my world? this? ::
:: nothing but failed drafts ::

there's so much trauma
in Dean's mind, so many scars
~ Dean's been through a lot

to distract Dean, give
him something he's never had
before: contentment

you're just a complex
manifestation of Dean's
memories designed

to distract him ~ you
really know how to talk to
a lady, don't ya?

you're blind? ~ I've been blind
for a while, you can thank
feathers for that one

people in your life,
in your *real* life, need you to
come back: Poughkeepsie

Nihilism (cont.)

:: tolerate angel ::
:: because you think you *owe* him, ::
:: because he "gripped you ::

:: tight and raised you from ::
:: perdition," or whatever… ::
:: since then, what's he done? ::

:: you don't *need* them, they're ::
:: your responsibilities — ::
:: weight around your neck ::

we keep him in — it
will hold: my mind, my rules — I
got him, *I'm* the cage

it's not just about
you staying alive, it is
about staying *you*

I warned you about
dangers of jumping between
worlds — you ignored me

all end the same way:
Michael escapes your mind and
burns down this world — all

except *one* ~ what am
I supposed to do with this?
~ that is up to you

SEASON 14

Damaged Goods

Episode 298 (Season 14, Episode 11)
Directed by Phil Sgriccia
Written by Davy Perez
Original air date: January 24, 2019

---

actually, I was
kinda hoping for some one-
on-one time with Mom

we hug, but only
if it is *literally*
the end of the world

oh my god ~ the best
burger in Minnesota
— glad it satisfied

just wondering if
you've run out of ways to ask
me how I'm doing

I'll give you a hand:
two terrible cooks, what could
possibly go wrong?

everybody keeps
asking how I am — don't want
to talk about it

you feel like screaming,
you can go ahead, because
we're pretty remote

how far's Grand Rapids?
~ 30, 40 minutes? ~ I'll
be there in 20

it's called compassion —
look, what happened to Nick could
have happened to me

since when do we give
up on people? since when do
we cut people loose?

when past the point of
saving, maybe you need to
learn to walk away

I'll answer when you
kill her — she locked me in a
box; I hold a grudge

no particular
reason… you were chosen, but
you are not *special*

Damaged Goods (cont.)

    I needed revenge / for my family, you would / have done the same thing

    you couldn't fix me, / 'cause I don't want to be fixed / — was never broken

• *Dean explains to Sam what he's been building in Donna's shed* •

it's a Ma'lak box: / secured, warded — once inside / nothing can get out

    even archangel — / especially archangel ~ / I've read about these

    that's your plan? want to / be buried alive? ~ buried / is not safe enough

    but no one's ever — / they're impossible to build / ~ yeah, well, not so much

    plan: pay a little / hush money, charter a boat / to take me out to

the Pacific: splash ~ / you, Michael, trapped together / for eternity?

    you do realize how / insane this is, right? ~ only / sane play I have got

    you know that for sure? / ~ because I do, because I / can feel in my head

    Michael gets out, that's / it for this world, and he *will* / get out ~ well, how do

    that door is giving — / I can *feel* it giving ~ has / to be another

Damaged Goods (cont.)

way ~ there's not, okay?
Sam, you've tried, Cas has tried, Jack…
love you for trying

none of it's gonna
work ~ we don't know that ~ yeah, we
do… Billie ~ Billie?

paid me a little
visit, she said there's only
one way this ends right

and this is it: this
right here, this box — she gave up
special recipe

all I had to do
was the work, it's fate ~ since when
we believe in fate?

now, Sam, since now ~ so
you came out to see Donna
to see Mom on some —

what? some sick, secret
farewell tour? were gonna
leave, you weren't even

I could be around,
'cause you're the *only* one that
could've talked me out

gonna tell me — *me* —
do you realize how messed up
that is, how unfair?

of it — and I won't
be talked out of it, I *won't*
— I'm doing this, now

didn't have a choice!
Sam, you're the *last* person I
could tell, *last* person

you can either let
me do it alone, or help,
but I'm doing this

SEASON 14

Prophet and Loss

Episode 299 (Season 14, Episode 12)
Directed by Thomas J. Wright
Written by Brad Buckner & Eugenie Ross-Leming
Original air date: January 31, 2019

don't have to act like
what you're planning to do is
business: usual

I know you are scared ~
never said I wasn't scared,
but, doesn't matter

Cas, Jack: haven't told ~
that's because I'm not good with
the whole big goodbyes

I don't need to get
shaky on this thing ~ well it
wouldn't be worst thing

well, the woman has
a remarkable command
of profanity

I have never seen
him like this — if we don't find
some way, Dean is gone

Prophet and Loss (cont.)

• *These late-night Impala broments are getting real deep
(just like the intended final resting place of the Ma'lak box)* •

do you ever think
'bout when we were kids? ~ maybe,
yeah, sure, sometimes... why?

I know I wasn't
always the greatest brother
to you ~ Dean, you were

one who was *always*
there for me — the *only* one
— you practically

raised me ~ I know things
got dicey, you know, with Dad...
the way he was, and

I just, I didn't
always look out for you the
way that I should've

I had my own stuff,
you know — in order to keep
the peace, probably

looked like I took his
side quite a bit — sometimes when
I was... was away

you know, it wasn't
'cause I just ran out, right? Dad
would... send me away

when I really pissed
him off, I think you knew that
~ I left that behind

a long time ago —
I had to — and if we are
gonna get through this

I have to do like
you said, and try and keep my
mind off where we are

going — so, if we
could not have conversations
that sound like deathbed

apologies, I
would really appreciate
it ~ right, yeah, okay

SEASON 14

Prophet and Loss (cont.)

on the way — one last
case for the Winchester boys
~ you had to go there

losing him was like
losing a part of myself
— never knew: this bad

I have to say, Dean
this plan of yours: it was born
of desperation

anyone can be
a prophet, right? it's not like
there's a background check

people you killed were
innocent — you're not chosen,
you're just a psycho

unfinished business
isn't just about how I
died, Nick — it is *you*

didn't come for peace,
came here to find him: where you
became one with him

where are you going?
~ wherever it is darkest,
wherever *he* is

I know them: Mr.
Winchester, and the other
Mr. Winchester

I know the feeling ~
please don't compare this with your
suicidal plan

if you are a friend,
you will understand, and you
won't try to stop me

Prophet and Loss (cont.)

Dean if there is a
spark, a hope, then I have to
try — you taught me that

the regular him,
but he doesn't have a soul
~ nobody's perfect

tomorrow morning,
we're back on track: no rest for
the self-destructive

I believe in us —
I believe in us, why don't
you believe in us?

• *Dean agrees to delay the Ma'lak box plan, at least for now* •

maybe Billie's wrong — I *do* believe in us; I believe all of us	I'll keep believing until I can't, until there's absolutely no

other way, but when
that day comes — *if* that day comes
— you have to take it

for what it is: the end, and you have to promise me that you'll do then	what you can't do now: and that is let me go, and put me in that box

# Lebanon

Episode 300 (Season 14, Episode 13)
Directed by Robert Singer
Written by Andrew Dabb & Meredith Glynn
Original air date: February 7, 2019

people say that they're
brothers — all I know is I
was standing right here

when I heard this... *bam!*
from the trunk of their car, then
this shallow breathing

so we're talking, like,
31 flavors of weird,
huh? ~ pretty much, yeah

where do they even
come from? those two, or their weird
sidekick with trench coat

what about that kid
with the dumb Bambi look on
his face all the time?

Lebanon (cont.)

just tell us what you
saw ~ I don't want to narc ~ you
do not have a choice

want me to give you
an underage girl's address?
~ no, it's not like that

serial killer
clown: it's like the best-worst thing
that's ever happened

to you — you know, 'cause
you love serial killers,
also: you hate clowns

you want some sort of   aren't you supposed
rational explanation,   to be in Palo Alto?
but… there isn't one   what happened to you?

saved the world, now you
live in bunker with angel
and Lucifer's kid

can we just have one
family dinner? just one?
us, all together

SEASON 14

Lebanon (cont.)

• *Sam is way too forgiving of John Winchester,
but Sam needed this moment anyway* •

I screwed up with you
a lot, didn't I? ~ no, that's
okay ~ no, it's not

Sammy, tell me the
truth ~ don't want to talk about
that ~ you didn't have

a problem talking
about it before you left ~
Dad, for me? that fight…

a lifetime ago —
I don't even remember
what I said, I mean

you did some messed up
things, but when I think about
you — and I *do* think

about you *a lot* —
I don't think about our fights
— I think about you

on the floor of that
hospital, I think about
how I never got

to say goodbye ~ Sam
son, I am so sorry ~ I
am sorry too, but

you did your best, Dad —
you fought for us, you loved us
— and that is enough

Lebanon (cont.)

there's wanted poster ~
yeah, I Googled me as well
— lotta beheadings

come on, Constantine ~
I do not understand that
reference ~ you *wouldn't*

I'm going to ask
one more time: who's been playing
"Back to the Future"?

okay, me versus
your mom? that is not even
a choice… does she know?

hoped you would get a
peaceful life, a family
~ I have family

I don't know who *that*
Dean Winchester is, and I'm
good with who I am

I'm good with who you
are — our lives: they're *ours*
— I'm too old to change

you two take care of
each other ~ we always do
~ so proud of you boys

SEASON 14

Ouroboros

Episode 301 (Season 14, Episode 14)
Directed by Amyn Kaderali
Written by Steve Yockey
Original air date: March 7, 2019

---

why don't any of
them fight back? ~ who would just *let*
themselves be eaten

you, always blaming
witches ~ yeah, 'cause a lot of
the time, it's witches

doesn't exactly scream "snake guy" ~ no Pantera posters, for one thing	anyone who could do this: a monster, I mean, even if human
sitting here, having a cup of coffee is a Herculean feat	what's an A.V. club? ~ a special group for people who do not play sports
that is what I am supposed to say, right? "I'm fine" — it's what we all say	excuse me, this is a bit more pressing than your comedic banter
no point complaining about it: it is on me ~ no, it is on *us*	not standing alone — why doesn't he mention me? ~ maybe not his type
we'll find solution ~ if not, we still have plan B: coffin, ocean, done	it's not pretending to be the FBI, but there are *other* ways

Ouroboros (cont.)

    don't tell — but using   of the cost — that is
    dangerous, mysterious   a very on-brand, *me* thing
       magic regardless   to do ~ well, thank you

            of course, Samuel
         — until very recently,
           I was the villain

           lonely way to live:
       there's only so many ways
         you can cook human

     women have become   up from centuries
  so cautious lately — must be   of that misogynistic
        finally waking   oppression — right on

• *Cas explains to Jack the "point" of losing people you love* •

    hate seeing him like   it was a fight, it…
that — gonna be okay, right?   it was just a fight ~ every
   I mean, it's *Dean*, he…   time we go out there's

Ouroboros (cont.)

always risk ~ I can't
think about losing him, or
Sam, or you… I just

I hate thinking 'bout
it ~ yeah, so do I, but Jack,
you know, Sam and Dean

they're human, and they're
very extraordinary,
brave, special humans

but they're still humans,
and humans burn bright, but for
a very brief time

compared to, you know,
things like us… eventually,
they're gone, even the

very best ones, and
we have to carry on — it's
part of growing up

losing people? ~ yes ~
what's the point? ~ the point? ~ what's the
point of being a

cosmic being if
everyone I care about
is just gonna… leave?

the point is that they
were here at all, and you got
to know them — when they're

gone, it will hurt, but
that hurt will remind you of
how much you loved them

that sounds… awful ~ it
is, but it's also living —
so, when Dean wakes up

and he *will* wake up,
we just have to remember
to appreciate

the time that we all
have together now ~ what if
he doesn't wake up?

what about Michael?
what if— ~ I do not know, Jack
~ okay, but I could

use my powers ~ no
Jack — I know that you want to
help, but you cannot

Ouroboros (cont.)

SEASON 14

what is the good of having these powers if I can't help the people	that I love, if I can't help them when they need it? it's selfish of me
it is a story about greed, mostly — also it's about being	willing to give up thing you love in order to kill the thing you hate

:: she's much sturdier ::
:: than she looks — must be hundreds ::
:: of years of magic ::

fate: Sam Winchester's
going to off me, which makes
dinners bit awkward

:: you care about them,::
:: no matter what you tell them, ::
:: what you tell yourself ::

:: burning off your soul — :: :: you will run out soon enough :: ~ it is worth the cost	I am the son of Lucifer, I'm a hunter, I'm a Winchester

SEASON 14

Peace of Mind

Episode 302 (Season 14, Episode 15)
Directed by Phil Sgriccia
Story by Meghan Fitzmartin & Steve Yockey, Teleplay by Meghan Fitzmartin
Original air date: March 14, 2019

I thought you would sleep
until the cows dragged you home
~ that's not... never mind

just talk to him, and
then sleep until the cows come
home ~ *that's* the saying

he was probably
from Charming Acres, 'bout 5
miles up the road

must be the flatfoots
I keep hearing about ~ *keep?*
~ it is a small town

aneurism? ~ no,
head exploded like a ripe
melon on the sun

have you tried bacon? ~
do snakes like bacon? ~ I don't
know... *I* like bacon

she spends quite a bit
of time talking about the
shape and heft of his...

hands Jack some snack cakes
~ I don't think you have a firm
grasp on what snakes eat

Jack chooses angel
food cake over devil's food
cake... Dean is relieved

I'm looking for my
partner: the tall man, hair... he
has beautiful hair

588

Peace of Mind (cont.)

:: would you like one? :: ~ your
name is *Sam Winchester* ~ :: that's ::
:: a no on the hooch? ::

that wasn't my best day, but oddly, it wasn't my *worst* day either	when I need to blend in, I ask myself, "what would Mr. Rogers do?"
no soul: an absence of pity, of empathy, of humanity	Sam and Dean are the best men I know — just think: "what would Winchesters do?"

my tricks never worked
on her, she's too much like me
~ I'm *nothing* like you

I know what it is
like to lose your army... to
fail as a leader

you can't lose yourself —
if you do, you fail us, you
fail Jack, you fail Dean

in this town, I'm God ~
you're not, believe me, we've met
God ~ God has a beard

I heard you wore a
cardigan ~ I told him 'bout
cardigan ~ and wife

SEASON 14

Don't Go in the Woods

Episode 303 (Season 14, Episode 16)
Directed by John Fitzpatrick
Written by Davy Perez & Nick Vaught
Original air date: March 21, 2019

---

porn? sex tapes? nip slips?
~ the internet is more than
just naked people

you live with Sam and
Dean — are they fighting ghosts? ~ what's
a ghost? I should go

lie: makes my stomach
hurt — it's like when you have to
burp, but you can't burp

vampires, werewolves
shapeshifters, djinn, rugaru
wraiths, sirens, demons

ghouls, all sorts of things ~
you know about *all* of them?
you be my best friend?

movie nights: Tuesdays —
Dean chooses; I've seen Lost Boys
like 36 times

SEASON 14

Don't Go in the Woods (cont.)

when some animals
get a taste of people, that's
all they'll want to hunt

don't care: FBI —
nobody goes in those woods
without my say-so

Dean says that music
made after '79
"sucks ass" ~ Dean is old

we hunt things, fight things,
and kill things people do not
understand, so... talk

doesn't work like that:
even when they know how to
fight, people still die

*monster melts into
a steamy green puddle* ~ that's
like full-on "Raiders"

doesn't make his life better — do what we always do: when in doubt, lie	how many times did we tell Dad we were fine, just to make him happy?

except the beer, I
didn't have ID ~ you have
IDs ~ they are fake

591

SEASON 14

Game Night

Episode 304 (Season 14, Episode 17)
Directed by John F. Showalter
Written by Meredith Glynn
Original air date: April 4, 2019

---

you feeling better? ~
everyone asks ~ it's our job
~ well, it's annoying

Winchester game night
is a go, soon as Sammy
gets back here with the

two pepperoni
meat blasters, and *pineapple*?
— yeah, it's like a crime

they are lightly cursed,
but it is nothing that would
affect an angel

just a general
reek of ill-conceived, lone-wolf
desperation, Cas

I know how I am —
I can be closed off, hard ~ that's
where I get it from

a funny story,
and by "funny," I mean a
lot of people died

you can save him if
you can find him ~ where is he?
~ ooh, the angry voice

Game Night (cont.)

I didn't shelter
him, we were roommates; he made
a mean lasagne

you're a good man — you
are… it's one of the reasons
I'm so proud of you

just 'cause God's not here,
doesn't mean we're alone ~ why?
we have each other?

then I got to earth,
and I saw it wasn't the
paradise promised

Lucifer, I'm here:
perfect vessel — make me strong
again, make me you

we are all lonely
because we are all alone,
each last one of us

Nick: he was a bad
person, killer — I had to
stop him ~ not like that

we both know what it's
like to be hog-tied to a
nuclear warhead

it's not your fault, but
Jack *I* know would've never
done that: something's wrong

if Sam and Dean saw
what you did, they would be as
worried as I am

you need help — we'll help
you, we're your family — we
care about you, Jack

leave me alone, leave
me alone ~ listen, Jack ~ leave
me alone …Mary?

SEASON 14

Absence

Episode 305 (Season 14, Episode 18)
Directed by Nina Lopez-Corrado
Written by Robert Berens
Original air date: April 11, 2019

---

  lately it feels like   he said Jack went all
we'd be up the creek without   Kevorkian on his snake ~
 that kid: Michael, Nick   who cares, it's a snake

I'm your subconscious,
or whatever — you whipped me
up to help you out

try to understand
Jack without soul ~ we don't know
he doesn't have one

I think most humans
would bandage an open wound
before stop to eat

angels are real, friends;
angels can heal you with wave
of a glowy hand

finally they don't
have to be so alone ~ they
were never alone

I swear, if he did
something to her, if she is…
then you're *dead* to me

Absence (cont.)

• Cas tries to explain his actions regarding what was going on with Jack leading up to Mary's demise •

I was scared; believed in Jack for so long, believed that he... he was good

my faith in him — it never wavered — and then I saw what he had done

I knew that he would be good for the world, and that he was good for us

it wasn't malice, wasn't evil — it was like Jack saw a problem

and in his mind, he just solved it with that snake, what he did wasn't *bad*

it was the absence of good, and I *saw* that in him — but we were a

family, and I didn't want to lose that — I thought I could fix it

on my own, felt like *my* responsibility — left, didn't tell you

if I could go back, talk to him right then and there, I would, but I can't

I failed you, failed Jack and I failed— ~ don't say it, don't even say her name

SEASON 14

Absence (cont.)

---

tell with certainty:
Mary Winchester is no
longer on this earth

so what do we do?~
what we always do: we fight
— fight to bring them back

you've been stalling me,
tricking me ~ just talk to them,
Jack, they are your kin

parental guilt: how
much did you go through when I
wasn't there for you?

literally the
bravest, kindest, heroic
men on the planet

fell for him because
had a good heart and good soul,
and then he didn't

necromancy is
a delicate art, it is
unpredictable

under ideal
circumstances — he'll bring back
something terrible

I saw your mother's
Heaven, and she is happy
— no sorrow, no guilt

what are we supposed
to do? ~ what we always do
hunter's funeral

SEASON 14

Jack in the Box

Episode 306 (Season 14, Episode 19)
Directed by Robert Singer
Written by Eugenie Ross-Leming & Brad Bucker
Original air date: April 18, 2019

---

you know, we lost our
mom once before, but we got
second chance with her

tough and strong, stubborn
as hell, had opinions — was
not shy to use them

handle machete,
vampire, our old man, could
not cook worth a damn

Mom, you weren't here long
enough, but we're so glad for
the time that we had

memorial for
hunter, complete with monster
— Mary would have liked

I liked the kid — we
fought together — but only
one way that this ends

Bobby's right, we have
to find Jack and help him ~ what?
that kid killed Mary!

SEASON 14

Jack in the Box (cont.)

an unstoppable
monster who doesn't know right
from wrong gets put down

Dean says "need a drink"
— code for sitting by himself
in woods and sobbing

saying don't believe? ~
it's not that I don't believe
just don't believe *you*

burned through soul ~ lost his
capacity for good through
an act of goodness

so we just force him
inside? ~ no, he goes in, it's
gotta be *his* choice

God writes paperback
books while in his underwear,
and angels are dicks

Castiel, Heaven
never really had any
mercy, you know that

Heaven, your mother
knew that you have glorious
destiny ~ I do?

he is strong, yes, but
he's still a child, without
a soul to guide him

was promised every
effort made ~ Heaven promised?
take *that* to the bank

how long will it be
before I can come out? ~ not
too long, we got this

we knew it was a
long shot with him ~ but long shots
are kind of our thing

you want to forget
about him? ~ I wish I *could*
forget about him

SEASON 14

Moriah

Episode 307 (Season 14, Episode 20)
Directed by Phil Sgriccia
Written by Andrew Dabb
Original air date: April 25, 2019

---

the Ma'lak box can
hold an archangel ~ Jack is
not an archangel

because he is just
another monster ~ don't mean
that ~ the hell I don't

won't be easy, but
have to do the hard thing, to
do the ugly thing

he meant a lot to
us — he was family — but
not Jack anymore

is she in? ~ she thinks
it's dangerous and insane
but yeah, she is in

• *Sam details (just a few of the) ways Dean is actually a nerd* •

nerds ~ takes one to know
one ~ what? ~ you: come on man, you're
always calling me

a geek when you know
every word to every Led
Zeppelin song backwards

and forwards, you can
discuss in detail every
major rock drummer

from '67
to '84, and you watch
"Jeopardy!" each night

SEASON 14

Moriah (cont.)

I'm Dean Winchester,
I'm looking for the devil's
son; this badge is fake

every time I try
to say "Elvis," it comes out
~ sad, horrible truth?

must go to Hell ~ like,
metaphorically? or…
~ no, *literally*

lying keeps the peace ~
seems like an odd stance for… *you*
~ I'm writer, we lie

I know what you are
thinking: I look good ~ that's not
what we were thinking

everywhere, nowhere,
the edge of the universe,
Springsteen on Broadway

…and it's been confirmed
that the Queen of England is,
in fact, a lizard

balance: dark and light,
good and evil, chocolate
and peanut butter

I liked the old Death
better: he's all about fried
pickles, tickle porn

SEASON 14

Moriah (cont.)

---

we do not have a
choice, Sam ~ of course we do, I
mean, don't we *always*?

you want me to say
I'm cool with losing him, and
losing you at once?

how many other
universes? ~ I don't know,
most of them: boring

one's in reverse, in
one there's no yellow, one of
them's just all squirrels

of all Sams and Deans,
you're my favorite — you're just
so interesting

used to hate myself —
don't feel that way anymore…
don't feel anything

when you are not here,
are you watching us? ~ yeah, you're
my favorite show

SEASON 14

Moriah (cont.)

when world fails, why's it
always have to be on *us*?
~ 'cause you are my guys

and all I ever
wanted was to be good, but
now I'm just empty

I know what I've done,
and you were right all along:
I *am* a monster

the gathering storm,
the gun, the father killing
his own son: epic!

been playing us this
whole time — our entire lives
— Mom, Dad, everything

no offense, but your
brother is stupid, crazy
— kid still dangerous

Mom was my hero —
I will miss her every day
— she would not want this

it's not a story,
it's our *lives* — God or no
God: you go to Hell

fine, that is the way
you want it? story's over:
welcome to the end

Chuck said gun was the
only thing that could… ~ he's a
writer, writers lie

• *All the souls from Hell are released, because "God Was Never on Your Side"* •

if the stars fall down
on me, and the sun refused
to shine, then may the

shackles be undone,
may all the old words cease to
rhyme — if the sky turned

into stone, it will
matter not at all, for there
is no Heaven in

the sky, Hell does not
wait for our downfall — let the
voice of reason shine

Moriah (cont.)

let pious vanish
for all time — God's face: hidden,
all unseen, you can't

ask him what it all
means — he was never on your
side, God was never

side — see ten thousand
ministries, see the holy
righteous dogs; they claim

on your side, let right
or wrong alone decide, God
was never on your

to heal, but all they
do is steal, abuse your faith,
cheat, and rob — if God

is wise, why is he
still; when these false prophets call
him friend, why is he

silent? is he blind?
are we abandoned in the
end? — let the sword of

God was never on
your side, so let right or wrong
alone decide, God

reason shine, let us
be free of prayer and shrine
— God's face is hidden

was never on your
side, no, no, he was never
on your side, God was

turned away, never
has a word to say — he was
never on your side

never on your side
no, never, never, never,
never on your side

never on your side,
God was never on your side,
never on your side

SEASON FIFTEEN

SEASON 15

Back and to the Future

Episode 308 (Season 15, Episode 1)
Directed by John F. Showalter
Written by Andrew Dabb
Original air date: October 10, 2019

---

go outside: get ripped
apart, stay here: starve to death?
~ well, *I* wouldn't starve

the robe and the beard;
smile that's like half nice, half
will-rip-your-throat-out

abomination! ~
:: *you're* abomination, with ::
:: stupid dumb trench coat ::

:: I read the papers :: ~
you have newspapers in Hell?
~ :: yeah, the wi-fi sucks ::

look familiar
to you? ~ looks like a woman
in white ~ exactly

if *she* is back, then
they're *all* back: every last one
that we ever killed

grab Crowley Jr.
what he needs ~ no, Dean, I can't
even *look* at him

Back and to the Future (cont.)

• *Belphegor somehow manages to mention "hump" and "penis" on his way to sort of hitting on Dean all in the space of less than a minute* •

:: so people are like ::
:: crazy good-looking now, eh? ::
:: I mean the last time ::

:: I was on earth, I ::
:: was human — ah, it was a ::
:: while ago, but ::

:: and anyway, folks ::
:: back then, they were, uh, ugly ::
:: you know? had a lot ::

:: you know, we were all ::
:: worshipping this giant rock ::
:: — looked like huge penis ::

:: of humps, I mean a ::
:: lot, look at 'em now — look at ::
:: *you*! you're uh, gorgeous ::

:: difficult to blend — ::
:: so, who was he anyway? ::
~ was our kid, kind of

we need your help, so
move your ass — I'm not... move your
exquisite ass, *please*

:: there we were, minding ::
:: own business, flaying people ::
:: for eternity ::

SEASON 15

Back and to the Future (cont.)

don't tell them about
whole ghost thing ~ or angel thing
~ that might freak them out

remember when were
kids, would distract with joke? knock
knock ~ who's… ~ still got it

• *God has released every soul in Hell, just to mess with the Winchesters,
and then bounced (like he does) (maybe)… but when has a little thing
like insurmountable obstacles ever slowed these boys down?* •

screw him — he has been
playing us this entire
time, just when we thought

we had a choice, you
know, whenever we thought we
had free will, we were

just rats in a maze —
sure, we could go left, go right;
still in the damn maze

just makes you think — all
of it, you know — everything
that we've done, what did

Back and to the Future (cont.)

it even mean? ~ it
meant a lot: still saved people
~ but what for? you know?

just so he could throw
another end-of-the-world
at us, chug popcorn?

now he's gone ~ you think? ~
that's what he does: he gets bored
and pulls the ripcord

I mean, that's what he
did with apocalypse world
— probably all them

just us, for the first
time, it's just us ~ (and about
three billion ghosts)

he moves on and starts
another story — know what?
good, 'cause if he bailed

yeah, well, what is one
more apocalypse, right? but
seriously, if—

when we win, God's gone —
there's no one to screw with us,
there is no more maze

it's just us, and we're
free ~ so, you and me versus
every soul in Hell?

I like those odds ~ yeah
me too… ~ you know what that means:
we got work to do

SEASON 15

Raising Hell

Episode 309 (Season 15, Episode 2)
Directed by Robert Singer
Written by Brad Buckner & Eugenie Ross-Leming
Original air date: October 17, 2019

---

d-i-s-e-m-
b-o-w-e-l
spells disembowel

what about warding? ~
warding: a door, doors have locks,
or they can be forced

and what, a town full
of ghosts? messy even by
Winchester standards

hoping you can help ~
can you boys do *nothing* on
your own? very well

scotch, 18-year-old
single malt if you have it
~ a witch with fine taste

how about the Game
of Thrones ending? pretty great
right? ~ small talk? really?

Dean, I recognize
that I dropped the puck ~ ball, it's
"dropped the ball" ~ ball… right

maybe Chuck designed
the obstacles, but we ran
own race, made *own* moves

pretend we had choice ~
you asked, "what about all of
this is real?" *we* are

Kevin Tran: former
prophet ~ Arthur Ketch: former
assassin, mostly

since God cast me down,
got kind of a bad-boy rep
~ means you can mingle

Raising Hell (cont.)

something happened: you're
not complete, not at full strength,
and you are afraid

welcome coupling
of both: the dominating,
analytical

enforcer — you — and
the pulsating and throbbing
firebrand — that's me

you know, I always
thought of you as special: I
gutted other dates

here is our offer:
you go to Hell ~ it's not what
it's cracked up to be

oh admit it: you've
killed me once, you've been itching
to do it again

don't test me, I front
the group, you sing backup ~ oh
really? 'cause you're *God*?

even on your best
day, you couldn't force my hand
— this: not your best day

SEASON 15

The Rupture

Episode 310 (Season 15, Episode 3)
Directed by Charles Beeson
Written by Robert Berens
Original air date: October 24, 2019

I'll patch those crumbling
walls right up, we'll all be home
in time for high tea

would be like tossing
mouse traps at the great plague! I'm
telling you: over

not gonna give up;
that's now who we are — go out
there, take care of it

oh, I am not freaked
— I am angry, okay, I
am *pissed* ~ at God? ~ yes

I mean whole mess, this
sloppy-ass ghostpocalypse?
that is *Chuck's* ending

| I'll be damned if I'm gonna let some glorified fanboy get last word | :: that's the longest you've ::
 :: ever looked me in the eyes ::
 ~ you don't have eyes ~ :: true :: |

yeah, Cas'll go: you've
been to Hell before ~ sounds like
I don't have a choice

The Rupture (cont.)

such valor, for what?
you are protecting others
— you won't give them up?

what are you planning
in here? another long-shot
magic hail Mary?

it's quiet down here ~
:: *too* quiet… sorry, I thought ::
:: were doing a bit ::

Sam, Dean: just using
you; they don't care about you
~ :: learn that the hard way? ::

:: how did you find me? ::
~ got hot tip — a very hot,
very British tip

death is infinite
vessel — spell so simple, draws
power from caster

first ingredient:
my own still-coursing blood, last
is my final breath

to perform this spell,
I have to die — it has to
be *you* that kills me

The Rupture (cont.)

well, I do not care
about anything enough
to take my own life

but I believe in
prophecy, I believe in
magic, and we're here

fond of each other,
but will you let the world die
just so *I* can live?

the plan changed: something
went wrong — you know this: something
always goes wrong, Dean

why does that something
always seem to be you? ~ well,
you *used to* trust me

I've tried to talk to
you — you don't want to hear it;
I am dead to you

Jack's dead, Chuck's gone, you
and Sam have each other — time
for me to move on

SEASON 15

Atomic Monsters

Episode 311 (Season 15, Episode 4)
Directed by Jensen Ackles
Written by Davy Perez
Original air date: November 7, 2019

---

bathed in red light, dream-
sequence Dean duly defends
the bunker from... *Sam?*

Sam, listen to me:
this is just the demon blood,
you have to fight it

it's veggie bacon ~
every time I ask for it,
you say — I'm quoting:

"don't want any of
that hippie grass-eater crap
in Meat Man's kitchen"

gotta stop calling
yourself "the Meat Man" — it does
not mean what you think

that's real bacon, Dean ~
you're damn right it is... Meat Man
departs cockily

Atomic Monsters (cont.)

they have anything
in common? ~ both cheerleaders
~ *someone's* got fetish

Supernatural
merchandise: most successful
Etsy site in world

instead of reading
your stories, I wrote my own:
where the guys didn't

have to hunt monsters
all the time — just sit around,
do laundry, and talk

see if you can help
make me feel big again ~ you
want me to... *fluff* you?

I like myself, Chuck —
for the first time in a long
time, I like myself

I'm a writer too ~
fanfic: it's not really the
same... ~ writing's *writing*!

SEASON 15

Atomic Monsters (cont.)

*• Becky's notes for Chuck about the finale
(...I mean... about the story he wrote in this particular episode...), part 1 •*

the jeopardy, Chuck:
it's feeling a little... thin?
low-stakes? it's fun to

hear the boys' voices,
but a story is only
good as its villain

villains are just not
feeling very... dangerous?
not to mention: there's

no classic rock, no
one even *mentions* Cas, the
climax is little

stale — the boys tied up
again while we get villain's
monologue — frankly

isn't one of your
best — originality
wouldn't... *pauses* ...hurt

you don't have children,
because if you *did*, you would
know that to see your

child in pain rips
heart out — you'd do *anything*
— you'd die for them, kill

I killed someone that
I loved — I can't control this;
I am a monster

617

SEASON 15

Atomic Monsters (cont.)

• *Becky's notes for Chuck about the finale
(...I mean... about the story he wrote in this particular episode...), part 2* •

no, you can't ~ I did ~
this is just an ending ~ yeah,
I don't know how I'm

gonna get there, but
I know where I am going
~ but it is so... dark

but great, right? can see
it now: "Supernatural:
The End" — the cover

is just a gravestone
that says "Winchester" — the fans
are gonna love it...

well? ~ it is awful,
horrible, hopeless — you can't
do this to the fans

what you did to Dean?
what you did to Sam? ~ there, see?
making feel something...

it's a crap job — we
do the ugly thing, so that
folks can live happy

• *I mean, why are the Winchesters even still doing this crap?* •

we still do the job,
but we don't do it for us
— we do it for Jack

for Mom, Rowena —
we owe it to anyone
who's ever given

a damn about us
to keep putting one foot in
front of the other

Proverbs 17:3

Episode 312 (Season 15, Episode 5)
Directed by Richard Speight Jr.
Written by Steve Yockey
Original air date: November 14, 2019

---

ghost pepper jerky! ~
uh, you're not gonna like it:
ghost peppers are hot

Hamill and Ford, that's
a deep cut ~ look at you: you
look like a baby

the Colt is aimed, cocked —
but Lucifer, wearing Sam,
can't be killed this way

you the sheriff? ~ that's
what the mug says *gestures with
"I'm the Sheriff" mug*

had to tell papers
something ~ a person did this?
~ if so, he's monster

monsters, werewolves: they
are all real, and me and my
brother, we hunt them

"we go in the woods
at night?" "maybe we can help?"
~ don't know what to say

do you like your job? ~
I mean, there's bad — still, it feels
good to help people

want to be something
else? ~ no, not really — I'm where
I'm supposed to be

Proverbs 17:3 (cont.)

have no idea
what to do with my life ~ you
got plenty of time

wouldn't be great if
everything was just planned out
for you? ~ not really

he was my brother —
he turned into a monster
— I'm a monster, too

here for the gun he
gave you ~ the equalizer?
~ not calling it that

oh, you would promise
a girl the moon, wouldn't you
just, Dean Winchester?

demon Dean with the
Mark of Cain and the First Blade
takes out dreaming Sam

wouldn't it be great
if everything was just planned
out for you? ~ Chuck's line?

word for word, God: he
is not exactly Shakespeare —
more low-rent Dean Koontz

Proverbs 17:3 (cont.)

always ends the same:
one brother killing other
— he likes that ending

why you had to see
werewolf bros die way they did:
'cause… foreshadowing

now *Lilith* is back?
what's he gonna do, throw our
greatest hits at us?

why not just kill us? ~
because what he wants: you kill
me, or I kill you

do we keep running
in this freaking hamster wheel
until he ends us?

or we fight ~ fight God?
without the gun? it's *God*, Sam
— he's coming for us

Golden Time

Episode 313 (Season 15, Episode 6)
Directed by John F. Showalter
Written by Meredith Glynn
Original air date: November 21, 2019

---

still jokes on these things:
what is round and bad tempered?
a vicious circle

Chuck gets his end game:
the Winchester Bowl, Cain and
Abel 2.0

friend praised fishing for
meditative qualities —
wish more relaxing

Rowena's journals,
her spellwork, all of it ~ you
miss her? ~ I killed her

whole ghost thing doesn't
really come with a handbook:
don't know how this works

you ever feel like
the punchline of some cosmic
joke? ~ are you kidding?

you're like Rowena's
protégé: a regular
Ginger Junior

working on a spell —
I think I can finish it —
we can bring you back

spell you can only
use once: show Death a loophole
and she closes it

you could say we had
falling out with management
— well… and each other

the thing is, taking
yourself out of game doesn't
really change the game

Golden Time (cont.)

always you selfish
little men in positions
of authority

you take what you want,
think power protects — it won't
protect you from *me*

well, it looks like we
have got ourselves a little
stand-off, two on two

that's a miracle —
were you sent by God? ~ I can't
explain it to you

even if I *could*,
I think you're better off not
knowing ~ what's that mean?

if I stay, nothing
changes — it's time for me to
get back in the game

a ghost Eileen steps
into the bath; a solid,
live Eileen steps out

hex bags, new body —
so, you're some kind of witch now?
~ nah, I got lucky

I don't know what's God
and what isn't, and it is
driving me crazy

we break the rules, but
I can't do it without you
— I need my brother

SEASON 15

Last Call

Episode 314 (Season 15, Episode 7)
Directed by Amyn Kaderali
Written by Jeremy Adams
Original air date: December 5, 2019

---

crop circles, body
without a heart, anything…
come on, internet

you two hung over? ~
had margaritas last night
~ I *knew* I liked you

Eileen and I have
stuff to do ~ yeah, I'll bet you
do ~ it's not like that

Hollywood: could give
show biz a shot for yourself
— you have got the look

hand it over ~ my
gun? ~ this is Texas, sweetheart
— you can keep your gun

you and I need break —
why don't we do something fun?
~ ideas? ~ a few…

Cas, this is Eileen
Leahy ~ I thought you were ~ dead?
yeah, I got better

shot God, fired a
piece of your soul — there's some of
you inside Chuck ~ ew

let me ask something —
walking away: you ever
regret it? ~ not once

Last Call (cont.)

one: three bottles of
Jäger is nobody's friend,
and b: they were *twins*

they were not twins, they
were *triplets*, and we split 'em
up fair and square ~ right

let me rephrase that:
if you don't help me tonight,
I will find you and

burn you alive ~ my
how your negotiation
skills have improved, Cas

ghost sickness: all was
scary — cat jumped out at me,
had me checking pants!

who's gonna look out
after little guy? God won't
~ damn, brother, that's dark

Dean, how many lives
do you think you've saved? hundreds?
thousands? deserve break

SEASON 15

Last Call (cont.)

• Lee and Dean are a couple of good ol' boys •

can't sit around lip-synching "Eye of the Tiger" while no one's watching

just the good ol' boys, never meanin' no harm, beats all you ever saw

been in trouble with the law since the day they's born ~ straightenin' the curves

flattenin' the hills, someday mountain might get 'em but law never will

oh, making their way the only way they know how, yeah, well, that's just a

way they know how, that's just a little bit more than the law will allow

little bit more than the law will allow — making their way the only

I'm a good ol' boy ~ you know my mama loves me — she don't understand

why they keep showin' my hands and not my face on TV ~ making their

way the only way they know how, well, that's just a little bit more than

the law will allow ~ standing ovation? ~ yeah, feels pretty good, don't it?

Last Call (cont.)

she was a good girl,
you know, she loved Jesus ~ and
America, too

car got raptured, too,   black key — handle in
I guess ~ can't rapture a car   shape of skeleton — for door
it was a good car!   to death's library

just costs innocent
lives? ~ Dean, you and I both know:
no one's innocent

good or bad, the world   I should have known: Dean
doesn't care — nobody cares,   Winchester, the righter of
Dean ~ yeah, well, *I* do   wrongs, would keep digging

don't pretend like we're
still friends, I don't know you ~ you
don't, Dean? I *am* you

saw world was broken ~
then you *fix* it — you don't walk
away — *fight* for it

do you really want   why do you care so
to do this? ~ no, I do not,   much? ~ because *someone* has to
but I kill monsters   ~ I'm glad it was you

saw his memories —
Chuck: weak — think we can beat him;
think we can beat God

SEASON 15

Our Father, Who Aren't in Heaven

Episode 315 (Season 15, Episode 8)
Directed by Richard Speight Jr.
Written by Eugenie Ross-Leming & Brad Buckner
Original air date: December 12, 2019

---

were you tailing me? ~
you could've left a note ~ you're
worried about me

he has Achilles
heel ~ no, I'm saying he has
a weak spot ~ yeah, that's…

"the almighty guards
his secret fear, but it is
always there" ~ what fear?

:: prophets speak God's word ::
:: — sometimes indirectly, and ::
:: sometimes: my bluetooth ::

cool: you have spell stuff
under bed; most guys have porn ~
Dean mouths: "he has porn"†

Rowena, we thought
you were dead ~ oh, I *am*, dear
— everyone here is

• *Rowena lists the benefits of being queen of Hell* •

yes, there are things I
miss about being alive
— like flesh-on-flesh sex

Amazon doesn't
deliver here… yet — but lads,
I'm *queen*, my subjects

revere me — well, fear
me, which is better… should have
died long time ago

what am I picking
up from you two? a wee tiff?
~ it's fine ~ boys? *fix* it

:: you have your brothers, ::
:: the Winchesters :: ~ met them once
— let me rot in Hell

† This is from a deleted scene not found in the final episode, but finding and watching the clip is highly recommended.

Our Father, Who Aren't in Heaven (cont.)

we have agreement ~
oh, you have an *agreement*?
that's adorable

you could do worse, she
could certainly do better
— like, *so* much better

we bailed, there's nothing
we can say to fix that ~ how
about "I'm sorry"?

Heaven is not what
it was, and your… your father
is not who you knew

:: so you forgive them? :: ~
oh hell no… no, but that's not
what this is about

you remember me? ~
:: you called me ass-butt, and then ::
:: set me on fire ::

thought you were haughty
— you had an entire oak
tree shoved up your ass

you were never God's
favorite — weren't even star
— at least Lucifer

knew that God can't be
trusted, but I guess he was
always the smart one

a leviathan
blossom? ~ :: only grows in one ::
:: place: purgatory ::

you're good man, didn't
deserve that ~ since when do we
get what we deserve?

SEASON 15

The Trap

Episode 316 (Season 15, Episode 9)
Directed by Robert Singer
Written by Robert Berens
Original air date: January 16, 2020

I needed eyes and
ears on the inside, well, eyes
anyway ~ screw you

when it's time to get
hands dirty, you can't do it
— you just like to watch

I don't even know
what to call that ~ *I* do: I
call that *pathetic*

still this… defiant ~
not my first time on the rack
~ this is more, it's… hope

you still think you're the
hero of this story; you
still think you can *win*

blossom: grows when we
die ~ oh, okay, cool *cocks gun*
~ but body must rot

couldn't forgive me,
move on — too angry: I left,
you didn't stop me

The Trap (cont.)

the Mark made Cas go
crazy — I had to bury
him in Ma'lak box

every friend ever
had is either dead, or they
got wise: packed it in

what happened to Butch
and Sundance? what happened to
going out swinging?

Dean *I* know: never
give up, no matter how bad
~ well, he does; he will

• *In purgatory, Dean apologizes to and forgives Castiel through prayer* •

time is running out
Cas? Cas, I hope you can hear
me, that wherever

you are, it is not
too late — I should have stopped you
you're my best friend, but

I just let you go
'cause it was easier than
admitting was wrong

I love you — I don't
know why I get so angry;
just always been there

SEASON 15

The Trap (cont.)

---

and when things go bad,
it just comes out — can't stop it,
no matter how bad

I want to, I just
can't stop, and I forgive you
— *of course* forgive you

sorry it took me
so long; sorry it took me
'til now to say it

Cas, I'm so sorry —
man, I hope you can hear me,
I hope you hear me

it's stuck ~ guess that is
as far as it goes, Sammy
the end of the line

Cas, I need to say
something ~ don't have to say it,
I heard your prayer

at least we go down
together ~ Butch and Sundance
~ we'll go out swinging

I am sorry kid —
that is a crappy ending
— you deserve better

The Trap (cont.)

• *Chuck sorta admires this particular version of the Winchesters, despite his inability to control them* •

you, Sam Winchester,
have been playing fast and loose
with laws of nature

and magic for a
long time — you *and* your brother:
always breaking rules

and that's what I love
about you: so heroic,
so... *Promethean*

Sams, Deans in other
worlds: didn't think they'd do it
either, but they did

not *this* Sam, not *this*
Dean, we will *never* give you
ending that you want

I wish you would stay ~
don't know what's real anymore
~ I know *that* was real

what would happen if
we trapped him: I believed him
~ good enough for me

SEASON 15

The Heroes' Journey

Episode 317 (Season 15, Episode 10)
Directed by John F. Showalter
Written by Andrew Dabb
Original air date: January 23, 2020

---

was that a trip? ~ weird ~
there's lot of that going on:
got parking ticket

we are not cursed, we
are just having a bad day
~ this is more than that

still a hugger huh? ~
you know it, you smell so good!
~ okay, and we're done

this is Sam, I named
him after you ~ that means this
must be… ~ Castiel

yeah, for werewolves, fang
maintenance is a B: got
to floss all the time

better than I thought —
figured dead before 40
— go out young, pretty

see some cavities ~
how many? ~ 17… don't
worry, I've got you

• *After a lifetime of horrific nightmares that reflect*
his actual lived experiences, "normal" Dean's
nitrous-oxide-induced hallucinations are pleasantly wholesome •

Dean is on nitrous,
tap dancing with Garth and a
lamp, dapper AF

we're all alone, no
chaperone can get number
— the world's in slumber

let's misbehave — there's
something wild about you, child
that's so contagious

SEASON 15

The Heroes' Journey (cont.)

let's be outrageous,
let's misbehave — when Adam
won Eve's hand, wouldn't

stand for teasin' — he
didn't care about apples
out of season — they

say the spring means just
one thing to little lovebirds
— we're not above birds

let's misbehave, let's
misbehave, let's misbehave
poses in spotlight

Dean's got cavities,
you're sick, car's down — who did you
guys piss off? ~ *shrugs* God

• *Garth explains how not being the hero of the story
might actually be a good thing, with examples from such heroes
as Batman, Superman, and... Anastasia Steele* •

you're heroes; what am
I? supporting character?
a special guest star?

Garth, it's not like that ~
I *want* to be the guest star
— being hero sucks

you'll probably win,
eventually — but 'til
you do, your life blows

parents get gunned down
in an alleyway, your home
planet gets blown up

interview this good
looking rich guy, it doesn't
go well, so he shows

up at the hardware
store where you work, and man, it
starts to get, you know…

635

SEASON 15

The Heroes' Journey (cont.)

cursed ~ no, you're normal:
normal problems — you should get
colonoscopy

wow, the furrowed brow
and the puppy eyes? does that
actually work?

you? ~ yeah, I needed
the cash: I got three baby
mamas, I got bills

just 'cause God yanked the
magic horseshoe out of our
ass or whatever

doesn't mean that we're
gonna give up — this is our
job, it's what we do

need be ready for
anything ~ I guess we'd need
a grenade launcher

so, what're you? a
monster? ~ a shifter ~ shifter?
so you chose that face?

The Heroes' Journey (cont.)

so, could we ever
actually pick locks, or
was it Chuck whole time?

blood, sweat, tears: was us —
been doing this our whole lives
— we're best in the world

I tried to call — when
you didn't pick up, figured
you were super boned

Monster Squad were the
good guys, *we're* the Monster Squad
— C-4: hunter's friend

did you believe me
when I thought we could win this?
~ nope ~ yeah, me neither

this Cas keeps looking
at me weird ~ so, he is kind
of like the real Cas

saved us: not nothing
~ that is being a hero ~
I learned from the best

you know, I always
thought I could be good dancer
if I wanted to

SEASON 15

The Gamblers

Episode 318 (Season 15, Episode 11)
Directed by Charles Beeson
Story by Meredith Glynn & Davy Perez, Teleplay by Meredith Glynn
Original air date: January 30, 2020

---

between credit cards,
car trouble, constant heartburn
~ if you changed diet…

a pool hall that makes
you lucky, or might kill you?
demon or witch or…

could be awesome: pool —
the game of champions, kings
— *my* game, hell: *our* game

slinging pool cues since
before you were born ~ at 4?
between nap time, snack?

you're better than me
at pretty much everything
okay? that's okay

I'm not mad, I'm proud —
but I can wipe floor with you
when it comes to pool

SEASON 15

The Gamblers (cont.)

double or nothing
says you miss that shot ~ trying
to hustle me, Six?

think there's enough luck
in that coin to make up for
what Chuck took from us?

I'll go for a drive —
if Baby treats me right, then
we're out of the woods

when I ask why you're
killing my kind, should answer
so I won't hurt you

I'll kill him ~ you could...
— I'm sorry baby, I can
always make more sons

you're just a beach read:
sexy, skimmable ~ beach read?
lady, I'm *Tolstoy*

God cursed us ~ you've met?
~ yeah, little guy, squirrelly
as hell ~ yeah, that's him

The Gamblers (cont.)

when you apes first climbed
down from the trees, you prayed to
sun, womb, rain, and stars

now he hides behind
which religion has the best
syndication deal

we're gonna fight him ~
are you now? and when you lose?
~ we will lose swinging

they're nothing, they don't
matter ~ they matter to *me*
~ they matter to *us*

she said she thought your
kind had gone extinct ~ our kind?
~ heroes, like old days

and she gave me a
message: she said, "don't play *his*
game, make him play *yours*"

if follow her plan,
I'll get stronger, and I'll be
able to kill God

SEASON 15

Galaxy Brain

Episode 319 (Season 15, Episode 12)
Directed by Richard Speight Jr.
Story by Meredith Glynn & Robert Berens, Teleplay by Robert Berens
Original air date: March 16, 2020

Earth 2 has 2 moons,
and Hillary Clinton is
the president there

• *Chuck's villain monologue re: motivation for destroying
whole worlds (sir, this is a Radio Shed)* •

oh, then, what are you
looking for? ~ an audience;
it's monologue time

in the beginning,
it was just me and sis, and
it was fine, but I

wasn't satisfied —
I made more, I created
the world — but didn't

stop there, no, I got
the bug! I kept creating:
I made other worlds

diff combinations,
scenarios, characters
— different versions

of same characters —
you know: my other toys — is
that where I screwed up?

um, sir, this is a
Radio Shed ~ Dean says I'm
not gonna get the

ending I want — I
don't know, maybe that shouldn't
matter, right? I have

gotten what I want
from hundreds of Sams and Deans,
could get what I want

from a hundred more —
I don't care, those other toys
they don't… don't spark joy

641

SEASON 15

Galaxy Brain (cont.)

but the real Sam and
Dean: they do — they challenge me,
they disappoint me

they surprise me — they're…
the *ones* — I don't need more: more
things, more distractions

I need less — time to clear the board — all other worlds, the alternate	realities, the subplots, failed spin-offs… time to start canceling shows
we have made deals with cosmic players before — "cards up" ain't their style	left her there for dead ~ :: I left her tools she needed :: :: to survive; she has ::
I knew the story not over; Jack wasn't done ~ here's to being right	an extinct monster ~ Dad wrote about in journal — hunt: killed the last one

:: this place is cold — I ::
:: don't understand it, I don't ::
:: know how to move through ::

:: it, so I just find ::
:: empty spaces and hide — this ::
:: world doesn't want me ::

642

Galaxy Brain (cont.)

one life: ready to
risk it all? that's not just dumb,
that's *Winchester* dumb

we're taking a big,
probably stupid risk — feels
good, disobeying

cosmic entities —
doing the dumb, right thing? feels
like we're back *cocks gun*

if something goes wrong,
Claire will be devastated
— but if loses both…

:: this is home, never ::
:: should have left it — I do not ::
:: belong in your world ::

in Death's library,
everyone has book — even
God: everything dies

what do I do now? ~
you can come back to Sioux Falls
~ will Claire be there? ~ soon

no choice but to build
himself into the framework:
his only weakness

told you, Dean, you and
your brother have work to do
— it's your destiny

SEASON 15

Destiny's Child

Episode 320 (Season 15, Episode 13)
Directed by Amyn Kaderali
Written by Brad Buckner & Eugenie Ross-Leming
Original air date: March 23, 2020

• *Dean and Sam (from an alternate universe)*
arrive in a stupid little car, blasting Savage Garden •

anytime I need
to see your face, I just close
my eyes and I am

taken to a place
where your crystal mind, and your
magenta feelings

take up shelter in
the base of my spine, sweet like
a chic-a-cherry

cola — I don't need
to try to explain; I just
hold on tight and if

it happens again,
I may move so slightly to
the arms and the lips

and the face of the
human cannonball that I
need to, I want to

come stand a little
bit closer ~ :: bro, we did it ::
~ breathe in, get a bit

higher, you'll never
know what hit you when I get
to you — I want you

I don't know if I
need you, but ~ the *hell*? ~ :: the *heck*? ::
~ I'd die to find out

I want you, I don't
know if I need you, but ooh
I'd die to find out

Destiny's Child (cont.)

Occultum, Latin
for "hidden" — where to find it?
~ don't know, it's *hidden*

Death is Obi-Wan,
and we are the "messengers
of God's destruction"

then who takes over?
Jack? ~ *Jack blows bubble* I just
learned how to do that

• *Dean tries to guess the fate of the Occultum,
to an increasingly frustrated Cas* •

the Occultum is
divine in origin, it
was housed for hundreds

of years in ancient
temple ~ before was plundered
by pirates ~ no ~ it

was dug up by tomb
raiders ~ no ~ it was siezed by
King of the Dead and

his warlords, am I
close? ~ looted by invading
Mongol hordes for trade

on the ~ black market —
I was gonna say that next,
that was the next one

Destiny's Child (cont.)

gazillionaire
trumps a hundred sad sacks in
Kiwanis hall, right?

so you want me to
be on *your* side, against God?
~ we're better-looking

nice vessel: suits you
better than the blonde ~ wait, you
were *friends*? ~ oh, god no

what's good about death?
~ I recall: very little ~
when you come back, you

really get into
all life is: hot, cold, spicy,
sweet, funny, scary

will he forgive me? ~
Dean feels things more acutely
than any human

sure you can swing this? ~
well, we have Rowena's notes
~ Samwitch, let's do this

hosting reception
for newly-condemned souls, 'cause
that's a thing we do

Destiny's Child (cont.)

---

may not have a soul,
but I know killing you: wrong
— what if I screw up?

Sam, how's the big lug?
I liked him: we had good thing,
until he killed me

why do they call this
place the Empty? it is full
of sorrow, despair

full of angels and
demons dreaming about their
regrets, forever

:: you can't just traipse in ::
:: and out of here — it upsets ::
:: the order of things ::

want them to be you? ~
it's not that hard; me and Sam
do it every day

you have your own plane? ~
:: you *don't*? how do you manage? ::
~ how do you afford?

SEASON 15

Destiny's Child (cont.)

first off, I'm sorry:
you're gonna have to lose the
man-bun ~ :: I will *not* ::

loosely translated:
to be *in* the Occultum
it must be in *you*

:: hillbilly clothes are ::
:: bad enough, have to draw the ::
:: line — my hair: sacred ::

:: sure they're simple, but ::
:: there's no quarterly reports, ::
:: no investor calls ::

:: there's nothing to do ::
:: but hunt monsters, drink beer, and ::
:: watch porn — got it made ::

trust me: Brazil — far
away, nothing but beaches,
babes, and carnival

been to the garden:
crossroads of divinity
and humanity

why'd I not get it?
why didn't I understand?
my mother died too

… SEASON 15

Last Holiday

Episode 321 (Season 15, Episode 14)
Directed by Eduardo Sánchez
Written by Jeremy Adams
Original air date: October 8, 2020

I thought this place was supposed to be state of art ~ it was, in 50s

we fought the devil, I've killed Hitler — I think we can handle old pipes

lady, who the hell are you? ~ *gasps* *language!* ~ that's it, I'm getting my gun

I am a wood nymph ~ well, shouldn't you be in the woods somewhere, *nymphing*?

lads left — was told to stay behind, guard the bunker — they never returned

and so, to keep the bunker safe, I placed it and self in standby mode

even if she is what she says she is, some kind of ~ magic Roomba?

I'm picture of health ~ ignoring your trauma does not make you healthy

649

SEASON 15

Last Holiday (cont.)

any bloodsuckers
in here? ~ *vampires hiss* ~ *Sam
and Dean lop heads off*

gotta be record:
no investigation, no
dead ends… radar rules

---

don't be so dour —
take a breath, smile, enjoy
world you're fighting for

what are you? ~ he's a
millennial, don't let that
throw you: he's good kid

what are you wearing? ~
it's like I am wrapped in hugs
— gotta feel this thing

we all do things that
we're not proud of, but life gives
us second chances

---

*• Hunting is easier with a functioning monster radar and
a live-in wood nymph who cuts the crusts off your PB&J every day
and makes you slow down enough to enjoy a holiday or two •*

gonna tell you a
story about a little
town I know: they had

a real big problem
with some big mean local ghost
— those spooks were making

the whole city lose
control — well, the mayor was
frantic, the town was

SEASON 15

Last Holiday (cont.)

panicked — but they had
no sense of fear, 'cause they knew
that they were missin'

those boys with mission,
so they called them up right here
— they were boxing and

trapping and shooting
through the joint, stepped right in and
got down to the point

those ghostbusters came
in cleaning up the town, oh
yeah ~ happy birthday

oh, dear, at your age
I wouldn't think you'd *want* to
celebrate birthday

you should be nicer
to your brother ~ now why would
I do that? ~ *sighs* boys

both downstairs right now, ready to be killed by us? ~ always the smart one	why didn't you call? ~ figured you were, "practicing your sign language," Sam

Last Holiday (cont.)

• *Dean explains to Jack that even though Dean might still be angry, he won't stop fighting for his family* •

Jack, I am trying,
okay? I really am, but
what you did, that's not

easy to forget —
now, I *was* angry with you
for a while, and

maybe I still am...
a little bit, okay? but
I'm not gonna let

some evil Mary
Poppins take you out, okay?
do you understand?

Jack's a kid who's gone
from one tragedy in his
life to another

eat your vegetables
Dean — and Sam, cut your hair — and
Jack, go save the world

ta-da! I made it
myself, obviously... not
like Mrs. Butters

SEASON 15

Gimme Shelter

Episode 322 (Season 15, Episode 15)
Directed by Matt Cohen
Written by Davy Perez
Original air date: October 15, 2020

---

we have rules, but we
also have spirit; lead with
compassion on this

Chuck said Amara
loves keno ~ thought was kidding
~ he's not that funny

Atlantic City?
all-you-can-eat prime rib, and
one cosmic being

"Highway to Heaven" ~
can we wear matching ties? ~ blue's
good color on you

you look greener than
Baby Yoda ~ he's a smart,
very pale young man

social media:
so many cat photos… there
were too many cats

it says that I need
a parent or guardian's
permission to join

"Highway to Heaven,"
but with murder or something?
I would watch that show

admire their work:
it's not us — just some wacko
humans, am I right?

what even *am* I? ~
you are a deviant soul,
corrupted by Hell

it's not a monster ~
sometimes humans can be the
worst kind of monsters

knew there was gonna
be a catch — at least this time
it's not you or me

hello, where can I
find the Kool-Aid? sorry, I
mean I want to join

have more dads than most
— I always just feel like I'm
letting them all down

SEASON 15

Gimme Shelter (cont.)

    it doesn't matter:
a saint is a sinner who
    just keeps on trying

how'd you find us? ~ smelled
you from two states over — you've
    a distinctive musk

• *Castiel gives testimony at the
Patchwork faith-based community prayer meeting* •

know what blind faith is —
used to just follow orders
without question, and

I did some pretty
terrible things — would never
look beyond the plan

and then, of course, when
all of it came crashing down,
I found myself lost

I didn't know what
my purpose was anymore —
one day something changed

something amazing:
guess I found a family,
became a father

I rediscovered
my faith; I rediscovered
who I am in that

Gimme Shelter (cont.)

*• Dean asks Amara why she brought his mother back;
what was the point? •*

I wanted two things
for you: I wanted you to
see that your mother

was just a person,
that the myth you'd held onto
for so long of a

better life, a life
where she'd lived, was just that: a
myth — I wanted you

to see that the real,
complicated Mary — she
was better than your

childhood dream 'cause
she was real — now is *always*
better than then — that

you could finally
start to just accept your life
~ and the second thing?

thought having her back
would release you, put out that
fire: your anger

SEASON 15

Gimme Shelter (cont.)

but I guess we both
know I failed at that ~ you're damn
right… look at you, just

another cosmic
dick rigging the game — you are
just like your brother

it was a gift, not
a trial ~ I'm not angry,
I am *furious*

to know all my life:
I've been hamster in a wheel,
stuck in a story

can I trust you? ~ I
would never hurt you ~ then I
will think about it

Cas heals the victim ~
you are an angel? ~ well, not
a very good one

I watched you die once
— I will not do it again
~ it is not your choice

Drag Me Away (From You)

Episode 323 (Season 15, Episode 16)
Directed by Amyn Kaderali
Written by Meghan Fitzmartin
Original air date: October 22, 2020

---

we've missed funerals
for much closer friends... hunters
~ this is different

babysitting *you*
when I was your age ~ pretty
sure that's illegal

think you're gonna go
to college? ~ yes, 'cause that's what
normal people do

we saw your car when
you checked in — who's your dad? Knight
Rider? ~ my dad drives

Impala: badass —
KITT's a crappy ~ Pontiac
Firebird Trans Am

we don't even know
what this is yet ~ got a gun
got a knife, I'm good

Drag Me Away (From You) (cont.)

this ain't the friggin'
Goonies — none of you has been
on a hunt before

this is really gross ~
hunting usually means
go to gross places

shoved it down the old
memory hole; had nightmares
for the longest time

used to keep a lot
of secrets from each other
— you were just a kid

not to make light of
Death Star-level galactic
genocide ~ last one

source of her power:
this ring ~ track her down, junk her
precious: game over

*room 214's door
opens by itself* — I've seen
this movie before

that thing, where you scared?
~ always am ~ *old* you never
would have admitted

Jack is gonna die —
he's ready to sacrifice
himself to kill God

couldn't handle it —
you started second-guessing;
"ethical questions"

Unity

Episode 324 (Season 15, Episode 17)
Directed by Catriona McKenzie
Written by Meredith Glynn
Original air date: October 29, 2020

"only way," "one shot,"
"last chance" — you get tired of
saying stuff like that?

like I told you when
first met: you and I always
will help each other

last I checked, we do
not give up on family
~ Jack's not family

you, Dean had whole weird
thing ~ that wasn't you? writing?
~ ugh, not *that* part... *gross*

you'll evaporate
existence 'cause Winchesters
won't do what you say

humans are the worst:
disappointing, they ruin
everything they touch

only your story —
that makes you villain ~ villains
get all the best lines

his *aura*! ~ I know,
it's like skittles ~ she's angel
~ she's my old lady

all of them: just rocks —
existence makes them divine
— God's in everything

what I said to Sam:
you didn't need to hear that
with weight you carry

Unity (cont.)

internal compass
is functioning perfectly —
don't think you're crazy

:: your busted-ass friend ::
:: in the trench coat came along, ::
:: gave me trust issues ::

:: you are saying a ::
:: lot of dumb stuff for, you know, ::
:: Death's emissary ::

Dean: brought to the edge
of doubt — sense of duty, rage
winning in the end

poor Sam: always has
to *know* everything, can't leave
well enough alone

you orchestrated? ~
what part of omniscient do
you not understand?

wanted him to care
'bout you, but humans: they'll break
your heart every time

Sam, we don't have a
choice, Jack's about to blow ~ we
always have a choice

I'd trade 'em all for
Chuck in a heartbeat ~ what 'bout
me? would you trade *me*?

Unity (cont.)

• *Sam talks Dean down from the executing the only solution Dean can see, to save their family and their integrity once again* •

my entire life
you've protected me — from Dad,
and from Lucifer

from *everything* — I
didn't always like it, but
it is the one thing

in the whole world I
could always count on — only
thing I've ever known

that was true, so please
put the gun away, just put
it away, and we'll

figure it out, we'll
find another way: you and
me, we always do

• *Chuck tries to insult Castiel, but at this point, Cas wears "crack in his chassis" like a Team Free Will badge of honor* •

spare me your contempt,
Castiel, the self-hating
angel of Thursday

you know what every
other version of you did
after *gripping him*

*tight and raising him
from perdition*? they did what
they were told — but not

you, not the one off
the line with a crack in his
chassis: all of you

SEASON 15

Despair

Episode 325 (Season 15, Episode 18)
Directed by Richard Speight Jr.
Written by Robert Berens
Original air date: November 5, 2020

I'm coming apart —
I do not want to hurt you
— don't let me hurt you

I can not stop it,
but there is something I *can*
do ~ what did you do?

you said this was a
suicide mission ~ I said
it would be fatal

that's the order you
want restored: always been your
endgame ~ you got me

I'm sorry about
everything — I pulled a gun
on you, couldn't stop

I just couldn't snap
out of it ~ well, you did; you've
snapped *me* out of worse

how are they like this?
I've been eating rubbery
trash eggs my whole life

I saw nothing, I
heard nothing, felt nothing: no
chills, no sulfur smell

one second Stevie
was making breakfast, and the
next she just vanished

SEASON 15

Despair (cont.)

I wanted to make
things right, and now I don't know
why I'm even here

don't care about you
'cause you're useful — care about
you because you're *you*

don't have my powers — I can not protect us — I am scared, Cas ~ me too	what, is she just some collateral damage to you? what I'll be too?

texting tell me what's
going on? ~ just wait, we are
almost there ~ (• • •) ~Eileen???

we couldn't make Chuck
pay, but Billie? she left her
blade: *her* I can kill

we don't have a choice ~
I'll go with you, Dean ~ alright
let's reap a reaper

we'll wreck her place, we'll
burn her books — whatever it
takes to smoke her out

it's over, call it
off — stop killing my people
~ didn't hurt your friends

SEASON 15

Despair (cont.)

• *Billie is coming for Dean, as she has wanted to for so long* •

you, Dean: it's always
been you — death-defying, rule-
breaking, everything

I lived to set right,
to put down, to tame — you are
human disorder

incarnate — you can't
escape me... it's time for the
sweet release of death

• *First words Anna heard on angel radio, clear as a bell:
"Dean Winchester is saved." One opportunity remains for Castiel
to save Dean Winchester, with a final declaration of love* •

just led us into	*Death pounds* ~ it was Chuck
another trap, all because	all along; we never should
I couldn't hurt Chuck	have left Sam and Jack

'cause I was angry,
needed something to kill: all
I know how to do

we should be with them —
everybody's gonna die,
Cas, I can't stop it

SEASON 15

Despair (cont.)

she's gonna get through —
she's gonna kill you, and then
she's gonna kill me

Dean: his face drawn, drained
of hope — but still beautiful,
still Dean Winchester[†]

wait, there is *one* thing
she's afraid of — *one* thing strong
enough to stop her

when Jack was dying,
I made a deal to save him
— the price was my life

when experienced
moment of true happiness,
the Empty: summoned

take me forever —
always wondered, since I took
that burden, that curse

wondered what it could
be, what my true happiness
could even look like

never found answer —
the *one* thing I want: something
I know I can't have

happiness isn't
in the having, it's in just
being; just saying

I know how you see
yourself, Dean: the same way our
enemies see you

destructive, angry —
you're Daddy's blunt instrument
— that's not who you are

[†] Script stage directions: "And we see Cass's POV of Dean again-- his face drawn, drained of hope. But still beautiful. Still Dean Winchester."

SEASON 15

Despair (cont.)

    all who know you see: the most caring man,
everything you've *ever* done,   most selfless, loving human
    you have done for love   I will ever know

   raised brother for love,   ever since we met —
fought for this whole world for love   since I pulled you out of Hell
    — *that* is who you are   — knowing you changed me

'cause you cared, I cared:
about you, Sam, Jack, whole world
— because of *you*, Dean

you — you changed me, Dean ~
why does this sound like goodbye?
~ that's because it is

heart full I love you ~
hard swallow don't do this, Cas
~ goodbye, Dean… ~ *Empty*

---

this is Dean's other
other cell *beeps* ~ Sam? was it
just them? ~ I don't know…

cellphone vibrating —
incoming call; screen shows, "Sam"
— Dean can only weep

SEASON 15

Inherit the Earth

Episode 326 (Season 15, Episode 19)
Directed by John F. Showalter
Written by Eugenie Ross-Leming & Brad Buckner
Original air date: November 12, 2020

Kyoto, New York,
Vancouver SPN set:
everybody's gone

where's Cas? ~ he saved me:
Billie was coming, and Cas
summoned the Empty

his grand finale:
I resisted, pulled the thread
— thought we could beat him

can what? there's nothing
left Dean, no one left to save
— everybody's gone

enjoying little
alone time? ~ alright, you win
~ sure, I always do

I'll kill Sam, Sam will
kill me, we'll kill each other
— but put everything

back the way it was:
the people, the birds, Cas — you
gotta bring him back

on lifeless planet,
knowing it's this way because:
wouldn't take a knee

shame and loneliness —
that's deep, sophisticated
— that's a page-turner

Inherit the Earth (cont.)

laughs whoever thought that finding a dog would feel like a miracle?

gonna let a dog in Impala? ~ relax, not giving him shotgun…

believe it or not: you're the best thing that's happened in the last few days

as far as we know, only Death can open it — hoping you can too

:: Dean, I'm here; I'm hurt, :: :: can you let me in? :: ~ *runs to… …effing *Lucifer**

we're a team again, guys ~ that is *not* happening (it's gotta hurt when

you're the last person on earth and the Winchesters *still* won't work with you)

it's the first reaper to check out since Billie, right? and… meet the new Death

you sure about this? ~ of course I'm sure — I'm Death ~ been Death for an *hour*

Inherit the Earth (cont.)

decision: dump the
losers and join Gramps and me
on the winning team

Sam had recognized
some of the symbols — thought might
be Enochian

at particular
place, exact angle from sun:
unstoppable force

it's late in the game —
you sided with Winchesters:
I can't forgive that

sounds good on paper —
as viewing experience?
canceling your show

well, one for the road ~
cute — eh, what the heck: I can
get my hands dirty

why you smiling? ~
because… you lose ~ *snaps fingers*
~ *Jack sucks Chuck's power*

we won ~ this is how
it ends: my book? ~ see for self
~ there is nothing there

Inherit the Earth (cont.)

after everything:
to die at the hands of Sam,
of Dean Winchester

ultimate killer... ~
sorry, that's not who I am;
that's not who *we* are

his power, you sure
it won't come back? ~ it's not his
power anymore

this is the ending
where you grow old, you get sick,
die, and no one cares

• *Jack brings back the world* •

love is but a song
to sing, fear's the way we die
— can make mountains ring

or make angels cry —
though the bird is on the wing,
you may not know why

come on, people now:
just smile on your brother,
everybody get

together, try to
love one another right now,
right now, right now, right...

Inherit the Earth (cont.)

so, does this mean you're
the new... what do we call you?
~ who cares what call him?

what if we want to
see you? ~ I'll be in every
drop of falling rain

every speck of dust
that the wind blows, in the sand,
the rocks, and the sea

people won't need to
pray to me, or sacrifice
— they just need to know

that I'm already
part of them, to trust in that
— I won't be hands-on

when people have to
be their best, they can be: that's
what to believe in

we get to write our
own story, just you and me;
us ~ finally free

Inherit the Earth (cont.)

• *Sam and Dean are finally free* •

looking out at the
road rushing under my wheels,
looking back at years

gone by, like many
summer fields — in '69
I was 21

I called road my own —
I don't know when that road turned
into road I'm on

running on empty,	running on, empty;
running blind, into the sun,	running on, blind; running on,
I'm running behind	on into the sun
looking out at the	I'm running behind —
road rushing under my wheels,	honey you really tempt me,
don't know how to tell	way you look so kind
just how crazy this	love to stick around —
life feels — look around for friends	running behind, don't even
I used to turn to	know what I'm hoping
pull me through, looking	to find, running blind,
into their eyes, I see them	running into the sun, but
running too — running	I'm running behind

SEASON 15

Carry On

Episode 327 (Season 15, Episode 20)
Directed by Robert Singer
Written by Andrew Dabb
Original air date: November 19, 2020

    Sam: makes bed neatly —
    Dean: sorta roughly tosses
      blankets into place

        social media
looks clean, you got anything?
   Dean? ~ I got something

you sure you're ready
for this? ~ I don't have a choice:
it's my destiny

I think about 'em
too, you know what? that pain's not
gonna go away

but if we don't keep
living, then that sacrifice
will be for nothing

  Singer and Kripke ~
feds do home invasions now?
 ~ yeah, we're full-service

know what this is? mimes —
evil mimes… or vampires —
vamp-mimes, son of *bitch*

what'd you hit me with? ~
oh, it speaks, so *not* a mime
— it's still evil though

dark, creepy, something
from Wes Craven's erotic
fantasy? ~ yeah, here

SEASON 15

Carry On (cont.)

you know we tried to
kill each other back in the
day? this is so weird

like running into
somebody from high school — you
look good… little dead

are you like the big
boss or something? ~ no, I just
called dibs *fangs out* ~ *slice*

• *Dean deserved better* •

alright, let's go find
those kids ~ Sam… I don't think I'm
going anywhere

there's something in my
back: feels like it's right through me
— no, no… don't move me

it feels like this thing
is holding me together
— give me a minute

I'll call for help, I'll
get the first-aid kit ~ Sam, can
you stay with me, please?

Carry On (cont.)

get those boys someplace
safe, alright? ~ *we* are gonna
get them somewhere safe

I mean, look at us:
saving people, hunting things
— it is what we do

was always gonna
end like this for me — supposed
to end like this, right?

it's okay, it's good —
we had one hell of a ride
~ I'll find another—

I'll find a way ~ don't
bring me back, okay? you know
that always ends bad

I'm fading pretty
quick, so… there's a few things that
I need you to hear

I'm so proud of you,
Sam, you know that? I've always
looked up to you, man

when we were kids, you
were so damn smart: never took
any of Dad's crap

never knew how you
did that — you're stronger than me,
you always have been

hey, did I ever…
I ever tell you: that night
that I came for you

when you were at school?
know when Dad hadn't come back
from his hunting trip?

Carry On (cont.)

right, I must have stood
outside your dorm for hours…
because I didn't

know what you would say —
I thought you'd tell me to… to
get lost, or get dead

I didn't know what
I would've done if didn't
have you… I was scared

don't leave me, I can't
do this alone ~ yes, you can
~ well, I don't want to

when it came down to
it: was always you and me
— it's always been you…

I'm not leaving you —
I am gonna be with you,
right here, every day

you're out there living,
and you're fighting, 'cause you — you
always keep fighting

you hear me? I'll be
there every step — I love you,
my baby brother

need you to promise —
I need you to tell me… look
at me, look at me

I did not think this
would be the day — but it is,
and that's… that's okay

I need, need you to
tell me that it's okay, I
need you to tell me

tell me it's okay ~
it's okay, you can go now ~
goodbye, Sam — goodbye

Carry On (cont.)

• *Sam has a hard time living in the bunker, haunted by memories of Dean, and so he... moves on* •

mist-covered mountains
are a home now for me, but
my home: the lowlands

and always will be —
someday you'll return to your
valleys and your farms

and you'll no longer
burn to be brothers in arms
— fields of destruction

baptisms fire,
I've witnessed your suffering
as battle raged high

though they did hurt me
so bad in fear and alarm,
did not desert me

my brothers in arms —
now the sun's gone to Hell and
the moon's riding high

let me bid farewell;
every man has to die — it's
written in starlight

and every line in
your palm: we're fools to make war
on brothers in arms

he set some things right:
tore down all the walls — not just
your golden oldies

it's what it always
should have been: everybody
happy, together

SEASON 15

Carry On (cont.)

it ain't just Heaven,
it's the Heaven you deserve
— been waiting for you

so, Jack did all that? ~
well, Cas helped... it's a big new
world out there, you'll see

this tastes like the first
drink I ever shared with my
dad ~ quality stuff?

no, it's crap, but it
was fantastic — just like this:
it's almost perfect

the question is: what
are you gonna do now, Dean?
~ I'll go for a drive

• *Sam lives his life, while Dean goes for a drive
(extended dance mix / multi-version Carry On medley)* •

carry on, wayward
son, there'll be peace when you're done
~ ah, I love this song

lay your weary head
to rest, don't you cry no more
— once I rose above

noise and confusion,
just to get a glimpse beyond
this illusion — I

Carry On (cont.)

was soaring ever
higher, but I flew too high
— though my eyes could see

I still was a blind
man, though my mind could think, I
still was a mad man

I hear the voices
when I'm dreaming, I can hear
them say: carry on

my wayward son, there'll
be peace when you are done, lay
weary head to rest

don't you cry no more ~
on stormy sea of moving
emotion, tossed 'bout

I'm like a ship on
the ocean — I set a course
for winds of fortune

I hear the voices
say: carry on my wayward
son, there'll be peace when

you are done, lay your
weary head to rest, don't cry,
don't you cry no more

Dad, it's okay, you
can go now ~ carry on, my
wayward son, there'll be

peace when you are done,
lay your weary head to rest,
don't you cry no more

on a stormy sea
of moving emotion, tossed
about, I'm like a

ship on the ocean —
I set a course for winds of
fortune, but I hear

SEASON 15

Carry On (cont.)

voices say: carry
on my wayward son, there'll be
peace when you are done

lay your weary head
to rest, don't you cry no more,
don't you cry no more

now life's no longer
empty, surely Heaven waits
for you — carry on

wayward son, peace when
you're done, lay your weary head,
don't you cry no more

• *Jared, Jensen and the crew bid farewell to the fans* •

thank you, fans — through blood,
sweat, laughter, tears — you've kept us
on for 15 years

there's no way we would
have ever been here without
you, and your support

opportunity
and the honor to play these
characters for so

your love, so thank you
— we will remain forever
so grateful for the

long, and we felt you
guys here with us all the time
— so, thank you ~ and cut

Appendix A
All Occurrences of Possessions, Vessel Changes, Shape shiftings, Talking to Another Version of Oneself, or Any Other Reason One Might Be Fooled By a Face or Voice

01x04: Pilot possessed by phantom
01x06: Shapeshifter in the shape of Dean
01x22: John possessed by Azazel
02x14: Sam possessed by Meg
03x10: Dream Dean taunting Dean
04x21: Young Sam confronts Sam
05x04: Endverse Dean, endverse Cas, Sam possessed by Lucifer
05x12: Sam body-swapped with Gary
06x16: Bobby controlled by Khan worm
06x22: Sam talking to different versions of himself
07x06: Leviathan Sam, Leviathan Dean, Leviathan Bobby
08x06: Dean possessed by specter
09x02: Sam possessed by Gadreel
09x09: Sam possessed by Gadreel
09x10: Sam possessed by Gadreel
10x01: Demon Dean
10x02: Demon Dean
10x03: Demon Dean
10x16: Sister Mathias possessed by Isabella's ghost
11x10: Castiel possessed by Lucifer
11x11: Castiel possessed by Lucifer
11x14: Castiel possessed by Lucifer
11x15: Castiel possessed by Lucifer
11x18: Castiel possessed by Lucifer

11x21:	Castiel possessed by Lucifer
11x22:	Castiel possessed by Lucifer
12x01:	Dean as hallucinated by Sam
12x03:	Vince Vincente possessed by Lucifer
12x05:	Hitler uploaded into Nauhaus
12x07:	Vince Vincente possessed by Lucifer
12x08:	President Jefferson Rooney possessed by Lucifer
13x04:	The Empty shaped like Castiel
13x30:	Loki as himself, but it's the face Gabriel borrowed a long time ago
13x22:	Apocalypse world Castiel
13x23:	Dean possessed by Michael
14x01:	Dean possessed by Michael
14x02:	Dean possessed by Michael
14x03:	Dark Kaia (to distinguish from regular Kaia)
14x08:	The Empty shaped like Duma
14x09:	Dean possessed by Michael
14x10:	Dean possessed by Michael
14x14:	Rowena possessed by Michael, Dean possessed by Michael
14x15:	Sam brainwashed to believe he is "Justin"
15x01:	Jack possessed by Belphegor
15x02:	Jack possessed by Belphegor
15x08:	Chuck speaking through Donatello, Adam possessed by Michael
15x12:	Dark Kaia (to distinguish from regular Kaia)
15x13:	Alternate Universe Sam and Alternate Universe Dean, The Empty shaped like Meg
15x17:	The Empty shaped like Meg
15x19:	Lucifer using Castiel's voice to fool Dean

Appendix B
Script Comparison from Episode 11x17

A version of the script for episode 17 of season 11 featured this conversation between Billie and Dean. The version that made it into the final cut of the episode that aired (and the version featured earlier in this book) is on the left. The version from the script is on the right. Both lend themselves well to a double haiku, and both versions of the exchange highlight aspects of Billie's and Dean's personalities.

I have to say, of all ways I thought you'd go: heart attack, fang, choking	of all the ways I thought you'd go: heart attack, fang, autoerotic
on a burger while binge-watching Charles in Charge ~ that was peak Baio	asphyxiation while bingeing Charles in Charge ~ that was peak Baio

```
              BILLIE
   Just-- savoring this.
      (then, changing tones)
   Though I have to say, of all the
   ways I thought you'd go... heart
   attack, some fang, autoerotic
   asphyxiation while bingewatching
   Charles in Charge...

               DEAN
       (shrug)
   That was peak Baio.
```

www.ingramcontent.com/pod-product-compliance
Lightning Source LLC
Chambersburg PA
CBHW071956150426
43194CB00008B/889